A PASSION FOR PRIESTS

A PASSION FOR PRIESTS

Women talk of their love for
Roman Catholic priests

Clare Jenkins

HEADLINE

First published in 1995
by HEADLINE BOOK PUBLISHING

10 9 8 7 6 5 4 3 2 1

ISBN 0 7472 7832 6

Typeset by CBS, Felixstowe, Suffolk

Printed and bound in Great Britain by
Mackays of Chatham PLC, Chatham, Kent

HEADLINE BOOK PUBLISHING
A division of Hodder Headline PLC
338 Euston Road
London NW1 3BH

Contents

For my parents

Acknowledgements

Obviously, I could never have written this book without the help of all the women who have spoken or written to me over the past three and a half years. My first and greatest debt is to those who agreed to share their stories publicly, often at no little cost to themselves. I hope that their courage will inspire other women in relationships with priests to speak out, either publicly or within support groups, and to lobby for change.

I'm also grateful to those women who, for one reason or another, did not wish their stories included in this book, but who nonetheless shared them with me. They helped clarify an initially indistinct impression. So, too, did many other people within the Church whose opinions have proved invaluable. Among these are Keith Barltrop of Allen Hall Seminary, Jack Dominian, Victoria Gillick, Professor Adrian Hastings, Mary Kenny, Eileen McCabe of the Catholic Marriage Advisory Council, Dr Dorothea McEwan, Fr Louis Marteau of the Dympna Centre, Joanna Moorehead, Monika and Chris O'Neill, Angela Perkins of the National Board of Catholic Women, Wendy Perriam, David Rice, Philip Sheldrake, SJ, and others who would rather remain nameless.

My German contact has proved an enormous help in establishing contact with the German women's network; 'Lorraine' in providing similar contacts in France, and Cathy Grenier of Good Tidings in giving me an American overview.

Thanks to my editor, Roger Houghton, for his patience, sympathy and good humour. Also to Elizabeth Holloway, together with Judy Bottrill and Sarah Broughton, for excellent transcribing, and to Reini Schühle and Judith Ainslie for much-needed translating.

My family and friends have been very forbearing over the last few years, none more so than Stephen McClarence, who has – with varying degrees of patience – put up with lengthy late-night phone calls, frequent absences from home, and occasional outbursts.

Introduction

Three years ago, a dozen women met in a house in the west Midlands. They came from different walks of life – teaching, social work, personnel. One was a housewife, one an unemployed graduate, one a clergywoman. Their ages ranged from late twenties to early fifties. Some were married, some divorced, others single. The one thing they had in common was that all of them were having, or had had, relationships with Roman Catholic priests.

None of them had met before. Previously they had just been hesitant voices on the phone. They were more than hesitant as they arrived at the house. They were petrified. For most, it was the first time they had acknowledged publicly that they loved a priest. They gave only their first names and initially divulged the barest details of their lives and their relationships. Yet all seemed strong, independent and professional. As one woman wrote afterwards, 'I came expecting either mother figures in thick lisle stockings or juvenile vamps in fishnet tights. What I found was people like me.'

The event was the first meeting of Seven-Eleven (the date was 7 November), a support group for women involved with priests. It was the first time in Great Britain such women had sat down and shared their experiences of a love which is normally hidden from view, and which the Church pretends does not exist.

For six hours, they talked and listened. Some were angry, some calm, some distressed. Gradually, other differences emerged. Some had known their priests for twenty or more years, longer than many marriages last. Others had had briefer affairs. One had married the man concerned. By no means all the relationships were sexual.

Similarities emerged, too. Private fears were discovered to be common – 'What happens if he's in an accident? How will I know?' 'Who will tell me when he dies?' 'Who can I turn to when no one knows about me and him?' Many, having been active Catholics, now felt excluded from the Church to which they belong. All wanted to be open about their relationships, but couldn't, because of what they and the priest stood to lose: in his case, job, salary, pension rights, home, together with the loss of identity, status and purpose; in hers, maybe her job, if she worked within the Catholic education, social services or pastoral system, her good name (many Catholics would still see her as a Jezebel), perhaps friends and family. Worst of all, of course, she might lose him.

So these relationships are characterised by secrecy and invisibility, as well as by confusion – 'I never know where I am with him. One minute he's very loving, the next he doesn't want to talk to me,' was a familiar cry.

As the women talked, there was a lot of pain, hurt and bewilderment, but also, for some, a sense of celebration, not just of sisterhood, but also of individual relationships and the support, love and strength gained. 'Our love is a true gift from God,' said one. 'He's given me love, intimacy, sharing,' said another. 'I veer from thinking it's the best thing in my life to thinking I just can't bear it.'

Since that day, many more women have emerged from the shadows. Some of their stories are in this book, the result of nearly four years of research into a subject which remains taboo within official Church circles, yet which is gathering momentum as more and more women worldwide speak out about the injustice – for both sexes – of enforced clerical celibacy.

My own interest in the subject really began after I had written an MA thesis on women and Catholicism. Although none of the women I interviewed – my old convent schoolfriends – had had a relationship with a priest, we reminisced about teenage crushes, notably on a pair of Dominicans at Spode Abbey in Staffordshire who dressed in leather and jeans, and discussed love, sex and marriage with us.

Then there was the curate in my very Irish parish, a young and dynamic man, as active in social as in Church affairs, and not averse to delivering his sermons as he walked among the congregation. Few were surprised when, some years later, he left the priesthood and married.

Such recollections made me reflect on the idea of 'the lure of the forbidden fruit'. Was it true that women who became involved with priests were scarlet women setting their caps at unattainable men? Or was it a much more complex issue than that?

Around this time, I came across a Catholic Truth Society booklet called *A Road to the Priesthood*, by 'A Seminarian'. In it, the priest talks about his earlier life as a fashion consultant, and about his three-year relationship with Sarah, which ended the day he told her he was entering the priesthood. 'Smiling through her tears,' as the booklet puts it, she tells him he's made the right decision, and walks quietly out of the story. But what happened to her? Where was *her* story?

This book, then, is the story of many Sarahs; of women who have chosen to let the priest go, who have been rejected by him, or who have negotiated ways of remaining in the relationship, despite all the complications, compromises and constraints.

Early on in the research, I discovered that there is more than a veil of secrecy over the whole subject; there's an almost impenetrable curtain. The official Church hierarchy is reluctant to comment publicly, as are the various counselling centres for priests and members of religious orders. Organisations working outside the official Church, like the Advent Group for married priests and their families, proved much more fruitful. So did letters and advertisements placed in local and national newspapers, plus the Catholic press.

There were some interesting replies. Some newspapers refused to print anything on the subject. One Scottish paper, for instance, said it was 'too controversial for our readers'. Yet they kindly sent cuttings from the newspaper which sensationally covered cases of priests having affairs.

Very slowly, women began to respond, usually anonymously until assured of confidentiality. I grew used to late-night, hour-long phone calls or conversations which ended abruptly when a husband or child returned home. Many of these women had never spoken about their relationship to anyone. There were also a few anonymous letters along the lines of 'Anti-Christ', 'Priests don't do what you are suggesting, you dirty creature', 'Shame on you!'.

Altogether, over fifty women have come forward over the past few years. Some are in close, chaste friendship with priests, others are still dealing with the psychological effects of a long over-abusive affair, yet others are in 'pseudo-marriages' lasting for a lifetime. Half a dozen married the men after they left the active ministry. Four women have had children by priests: only one of these married the man concerned; the others are bringing the children up on their own. Two women have had abortions. Others have seen their child-bearing years disappear while they remain in a relationship which promises nothing and delivers little.

Women who do not marry priests are in a much more vulnerable position than those who do, because there is less organised support for them. Up to two and a half years ago, there were no separate support groups. They don't usually tell their family or friends. Neither does he. They certainly couldn't confess it to another priest – if they did, they would be told to disentangle themselves immediately. Their actions may be seen as shameful, something to be hidden rather than broadcast. So, up to now, they haven't had a voice.

For the purposes of this book, meetings were arranged, usually in the women's houses, at other times in pubs or cafés; once or twice, when the woman felt particularly threatened, in my home. They were tape-recorded, transcribed, edited and sent to the interviewee for checking. Responses at this point differed dramatically. Some merely wanted a few name or fact changes – all names, apart from those of women married to priests, and some details, have been altered. A couple sought major rewrites, claiming that what was written was too negative, or wishing to omit large areas of personal detail which they claimed were irrelevant but which, possibly, were just too painful to acknowledge as the truth.

Time and again, they would express a desire to stress the positive as well as the negative aspects of their relationship; to talk about the joys of intimacy and sharing, of working and praying together. Yet the moment the tape-recorder was switched on, what poured forth was a stream of hurt, anger, bitterness and unhappiness. Many had to think long and hard about any benefits.

As far as personal details were concerned, one respondent, during lengthy talks at her home, described the physical side of her lifelong relationship. She and her partner had had intercourse only three or four times. On each occasion, the look of guilt on his face afterwards had devastated her. Eventually, he told her he simply couldn't cope with that aspect, so they stopped making love. But they didn't stop sleeping together. The sexual frustration that resulted stamped their relationship with suffering, particularly because she, who had always desperately wanted children, had to reconcile herself as the years slipped by to childlessness.

When faced with this in print, she demanded a rewrite. 'I was exhausted when I spoke to you,' she protested. She is always exhausted. Twenty years is a long time to hide the most important adult relationship in your life. To pretend you're single, keep a vital part of your life secret, timetable it around clandestine meetings, look over your shoulder. In the end, she wouldn't accept any compromise. She withdrew her story.

That woman is not the only one who is cracking under the strain. There's also Judith, who contemplated suicide when she returned from a taxing trip abroad to discover she would not see her priest for a further month because of his other commitments. Linda has tried every therapy in the book to keep her going when she feels she can't stand it any more. Dervla, who lives in such fear of being unmasked as her parish priest's girlfriend that she has refused to tell anyone her real name or home town, is on the verge of anorexia and is having psychiatric treatment. Many other women are or have been in counselling in an attempt to understand why they have got involved in a no-hope relationship.

Because, in the starkest terms, many of these relationships do *not* offer any hope. Time and again, Pope John Paul II has stated that he has no plans to change the law on celibacy and, by implication, to introduce a married priesthood (apart, that is, from the handful of married Anglican clergy who have been ordained into the Roman Catholic ministry). This despite the continuing exodus from the priesthood – an estimated 100,000 men have left since the Second Vatican Council of the 1960s and some countries are now suffering an acute shortage of priests as fewer men sign up.

More personally, there is little hope of what these woman want most of all: that their men will leave the priesthood so that, even if they don't marry, the relationship can at least come out into the open. They can go to the theatre together, or to dinner with friends, or on holiday, or even just to the supermarket, without fearing the unexpected encounter with someone who knows what he is.

That continuing fear cannot be underestimated. Few of the women interviewed, apart from those married to priests, have told their partners that they have spoken out about their relationship. They know they would be horrified and threatened. Even belonging to Seven-Eleven is seen by many of the men as a betrayal. At least one woman said her involvement in the group had rocked the relationship. So they keep quiet: to their partners about the group and their involvement in it; to outsiders about their very private lives.

As a result, they collude in their own oppression. Time and again, respondents stressed the importance of the subject, the need for open debate, yet emphasised the personal difficulties of standing up and being counted. This convention of secrecy can be inordinately frustrating for anyone trying to investigate the issue, and there were times when I wondered whether I would have undertaken to do so had I realised all the problems involved.

For instance, I know of at least one woman with a grown-up son by a priest; a woman sexually abused as a teenager by the man she then discovered was her father; a woman whose priest partner, in therapy at the time, committed suicide after she miscarried their baby; a woman who discovered her priest was having affairs with at least two other women during their ten-year relationship; another who attempted suicide when her lover returned to the priesthood after living with her and their child for eighteen months. Yet none of these women would agree to be interviewed for this book. Some were still dealing with the pain of their situation, one or two were considering writing their own stories, the rest were too plain scared.

It is an understandable fear. But as long as women remain silent, protecting themselves and their men, the Church will be able to say that these are isolated cases which need to be dealt with on an individual basis, rather than regarding them as symptomatic of a widespread disorder which needs proper, organised investigation.

Because these are *not* isolated cases. Every one of these women knows someone else in a similar situation. For every sensational case that hits the headlines, for every Annie Murphy and Bishop Eamonn

Casey, there are scores that remain hidden because the women lack the desire, the courage or the anger to speak out.

The stories in this book, then, amount to only part of the truth. But they bear witness to the bravery of those who are prepared to testify, even if not totally openly, and, by doing so, to try to effect some change within a powerful and conservative Church unused to having to account for itself or question its procedures, despite all the documentary evidence that compulsory celibacy simply isn't working.

It's impossible to know just how many priests are in relationships with women. According to a survey by American psychiatrist Richard Sipe, himself a former priest, at any one time 40 per cent of priests in the United States are not celibate. Of those, around 30 per cent are heterosexually active. There are no similar statistics for British priests, but a glance at the Catholic press, or a conversation with any priest, reveals that it *is* an issue.

One priest who has left the formal ministry told me, 'Go to any golf club in Ireland and you'll hear priests talking about their mistresses.' Another, who married after fathering a child, said, 'Some priests would go away for the weekend and you'd know they were going to see their parents. Others would go away and you wouldn't ask them any questions. You'd just know there was a woman involved.' And one woman active within the higher echelons of the Church believes: 'There is a general and non-judgemental acceptance that more priests are in relationships with women than are not' – a statement subsequently confirmed by a senior Jesuit.

Bearing in mind that many priests do remain true to their vow of celibacy, those in relationships with women can be loosely placed in six categories: those who manage to sustain chaste friendships; those who are in the experimental, adolescent stage of sexuality – dating, necking, not 'going all the way'; those who are in a more or less stable relationship with one woman; the serially monogamous, who have had a succession of partners; the promiscuous; and those who marry.

All, to a greater or lesser degree, are victims of a distorted theology of sexuality stretching back to the third and fourth centuries, and to the concomitant idealisation of celibacy. There are many, confusing, definitions of celibacy. The common understanding is that of sexual non-activity. In fact, as Richard Sipe points out, celibacy 'is not simply sexual abstinence any more than honesty is simply not stealing'. Abstinence, or chastity (keeping oneself sexually pure), is embraced by celibacy, which properly is an holistic way of life.

However, the Church's law of celibacy decrees that a priest should not marry, not that he should abstain from sexual activity. Obviously, given the Church's moral stance on sexual intercourse – that it should occur only within marriage – the one is seen to include the other. But the fact that they are not one and the same is where priests with elastic consciences – or with genuine objections to, or difficulties with, the distinctions – discover loopholes.

A sin against chastity, after all, can be seen as a sin of the moment, a temporary fall from grace. Celibacy, for a priest or a member of a religious order, is a lifelong commitment. So a celibate who decides to marry is making a premeditated decision to exchange one permanent commitment for another. Hence the belief among some priests that sins against chastity are less serious than the abandonment of their celibacy, and that the priest who leaves to marry is more of a failure than the ones who remain, even if they are conducting clandestine liaisons.

Hence the reason why those priests who tire of waiting for dispensations – which can take years to come through – and who, therefore, marry in register offices, are effectively excommunicated from receiving the sacraments, while those who stay in the priesthood, no matter how promiscuous, not only receive the sacraments but are regarded as sacerdotally worthy of administering them.

Much continues to be written about close, chaste friendships between priests and women in the tradition of St Francis de Sales and St Jane de Chantal, St Francis of Assissi and St Clare, the Jesuit theologian Teilhard de Chardin and a number of women, chief among them the American sculptress Lucile Swan. Teilhard was an advocate of the Third Way, a philosophy that suggested it was possible for a man and a woman to sublimate their love for each other in their love for God, like a marriage without the conjugal rights.

I have met women who have struggled long and hard with this ideal. But all the evidence seems to point to the improbability, not to say impossibility, of success. Either one partner ultimately desires a natural consummation of a loving friendship, which upsets the balance and, perhaps irrevocably, breaks the relationship, or both parties desire consummation, which leads to the problems described in this book. Alternatively, the woman, whether young and inexperienced or older, more mature, idealises the man's priesthood and her supportive role and accepts the platonic model only to discover, at a damagingly late stage, that the Church doesn't. 'We abided by every rule in the book,' said one woman bitterly of her four-year romantic friendship, 'but it still wasn't acceptable.'

At the other end of the spectrum, some priests choose to interpret the law of celibacy as a carte blanche for adolescent sex, without commitment or responsibility. A psychological profile of the American priest in the early 1970s, quoted by David Rice in his book *Shattered Vows*, showed that only 6 per cent of priests were fully mature and developed. Some of those who have missed out on the adolescent stages of sexual growth because of their sense of vocation and/or seclusion in a seminary may start catching up in their late thirties or forties, often causing untold damage to women who are several stages of human development ahead, but who misinterpret physical maturity for its emotional counterpart.

Mark, for instance, has now left the Church and has a steady girlfriend. Before that, however, and while still in the priesthood, he had three affairs. He admits himself that he was catching up on his teenage years. The third relationship was the most serious and brought to a head the conflicts between his vocation and his desire for intimacy. After many months of anguish, he left the priesthood, but made it clear to his girlfriend that they would need to start afresh. When, after six months, he told her he wanted out, she killed herself. She couldn't cope any more with his endless vacillations.

Then there are those priests who genuinely believe they are being faithful to their promise of celibacy so long as they don't go 'all the way'. A not altogether surprising conclusion to draw, given the Church's seeming obsession with genital sexual activity. In today's seminaries, for instance, distinctions are drawn between 'affective' relationships and 'genital' ones, between such physical intimacy as hugs and kisses and genital activity. But when does a touch or a kiss move from the platonic to the sexual? 'How far can you go?' to echo the title of one of David Lodge's novels on Catholicism. Is sex just about a biologically defined area, or is it an holistic, emotional and physical dimension? As

11

much about tenderness and loving as about penetration?

Who is drawing the line, anyway? For women, a cuddle may move beyond the emotional boundaries of celibacy, while a man might define sexual contact more explicitly. And what is more harmful in the long run – a three-month fully sexual affair, or a long drawn-out intimate friendship that stops short of sex, despite both parties' attraction to each other?

Out of all this confusion, some priests and their partners do manage to negotiate a workable, mature and stable relationship. Yet even here, where the man's priesthood may be almost as important to her as to him, there are elements of inequality and dishonesty. He is still a priest, she merely a parishioner. He is 'Father', the *pater familias*, 'kind, firm, wise, and the ultimate local representative of moral and religious authority', as Richard Sipe describes it. She is just another woman, doubly subordinate. He has access to sacred mysteries which she – even if herself a member of a religious order – can only assist with. No matter how much position and responsibility she acquires outside or within the Church, there will always be a power imbalance because he is 'holy', 'other', 'chosen by God'. Once he starts believing his own publicity, it's no wonder he is reluctant to give up that image.

All the real power in the Church is invested in men. Despite a vocal movement for women's ordination, it is still men who are popes, cardinals, bishops. There are still more men than women involved in reading the lessons, organising major church events, acting as Eucharistic ministers (one friend, the head of a Catholic primary school, insisted she was not 'worthy' to become such a minister when approached by her priest). Despite the increased profile of women in the Church and the growth of organisations like the Catholic Women's Network, women still have to defer to a priest, no matter how intellectually, organisationally or emotionally inferior he is.

Sometimes this power can prove a strong aphrodisiac, especially for women brought up with an ideal of feminine subservience, humility, sacrifice and self-abnegation; women convinced of their own worthlessness; women to whom passivity is a virtue. 'He may be a priest to the rest of the parishioners,' as one woman told me, 'but he's a man with me.' A heady mix of the sacred and the sensual. So there can be unconscious collusion to maintain the status quo.

In other cases, the woman's exclusion from the power base can, initially at least, keep her in awe of his sacerdotal ministry. A situation reinforced by the fact that, no matter how involved she and the priest are, as long as he remains in the formal ministry, she will always come second to his job.

At first, that knowledge might enhance, rather than unsettle, the relationship. The fact that he is not just a priest, but a good priest, caring, compassionate, sympathetic, devoted to his people, may be at the very heart of the relationship, particularly if she shares his spiritual beliefs. It is only as the years pass, and the strain of being unacknowledged and invisible becomes harder to bear, that what started as a bond, drawing them together, becomes an enemy, tearing them apart.

'Sometimes I want to take the scissors to his clerical collar,' said one respondent. 'He knows better now than to bring it with him.' Another, herself a religious education teacher with a strong sense of personal vocation to ministry, said her partner's priesthood was now a taboo subject. 'I used to love hearing him talk about what he'd been doing. Now I hate it. I know it hurts him very much, but I just can't do it, because it's his priesthood that means we can't be together.'

This is where similarities to married men emerge. After all, the priest is 'married' to the Church. He is theoretically unavailable in the way a married man is. He plights his troth to the Church at his ordination, promising to be available to all her people, not exclusively to one person. One woman told how her priest lover left her one day, waving his breviary (prayer book) at her, saying, 'This is my wife.'

So, if he becomes involved with a woman, even genuinely and deeply, it has to be as clandestine as an affair – a word, like 'mistress', deemed offensive by many of the women. They prefer euphemisms like 'particular friendships' and 'special friends', and they prefer to see their relationship as a 'gift from God', something more spiritual than physical. Which, on one level, perhaps indicates the extent to which some women have assimilated, consciously or not, patriarchal assumptions of female sexuality as something that needs to be controlled, rather than as something that can be freely and mutually expressed.

Yet there *are* similarities between a woman in a relationship with a priest and a mistress with a married man. In both cases, they meet on her territory, not his; she hangs up if one of his colleagues answers the phone; he never puts anything in writing; she can't be with him at the important times like Christmas, Easter, his mother's funeral; they're always worrying about being seen out together, so they don't walk arm in arm and never kiss in public; she can't share his public life, and only small portions of his private one; she remains single while her friends marry and raise their families and wonder why she can't find a nice husband, try to match-make, talk to her about their relationship problems, not knowing she has any of her own. It is an aspect of secrecy particularly difficult for women, for whom love and relationships are more usually a major topic of conversation. Even if she confesses to her closest friends, unless they are Catholics themselves, the chances are they simply won't understand: 'My non-Catholic friends just can't see what all the fuss is about,' as one respondent said.

Why do women put up with it? Why do they stay in relationships that are at best unsatisfactory, at worst exploitative and damaging? Are they mad, dysfunctional, inadequate?

In fact, the reasons are many and complex. Some women formed their friendships in the wake of the Second Vatican Council, when priests left the official ministry in large numbers, disillusioned with clericalism, and when others remained among widespread optimism about the possibility of a married priesthood. As a result, they quite reasonably believed their men would follow suit and either leave the priesthood *to* marry, or stay in the priesthood *and* marry. By the time they realised this wasn't going to happen, that Pope John XXIII's liberalism had been succeeded by Pope Paul VI's conservatism, it was too late; they were too involved.

Yet still they hope against hope, not least because of those magic words 'I love you'. Love is the reason to end all reasons. For love, women will put up with a lot: with exploitation, manipulation, even downright abuse, no matter how unconscious. They will put up with having their lives disrupted, their sexuality distorted or frozen, their integrity compromised. Maybe, as one psychologist put it, they need to learn to love themselves a little more, their men a little less.

Those words, 'I love you', can propel a woman from emotional into physical intimacy. From being a forbidden act, sex becomes a metaphor for commitment and permanence – from the woman's point of view, at least. And, contrary to popular belief, most of the relationships I have come across were initiated either mutually or by the man. Very few were consciously instigated by the women – which is not to say that unconscious instigation did not take place.

For some priests, a relationship with a woman is a unique thing, a once-in-a-lifetime experience which they either fight against or incorporate, with much rationalisation and compromise, into their lives. The traumas they undergo can act as proof of fidelity and strength of feeling, and both parties can find elements of spiritual as well as emotional and sexual satisfaction in a relationship forged from such bitter struggles.

Other men have several consecutive relationships. Each time, they have to negotiate their way through the minefield of Church policy and individual conscience and needs. But there are those who, having developed a taste for intimacy, including sexual intimacy, establish concurrent relationships. One woman who had a five-year relationship which she believed was exclusive, was shocked to discover that her partner had had three other relationships during that time. 'But you'll always be my number one,' he told her. And she, like many others, before and since, believed him, excused him. After rebuking him for abusing his power, not over her but over the other women, she blamed his inadequacies on 'the system', and remains with him.

Why? On the face of it, she is not a weak woman lacking in self-esteem. She does not, as some others do, feel 'chosen' by a holy man – she is a member of a religious order herself. As a non-Catholic, she has not absorbed the Church's negative teachings about women's second-class status. She does not feel undervalued. But, as she says, 'I feel as good as married to him. But he doesn't see himself as tied to me as I am tied and faithful to him.'

Perhaps she is psychologically impaired. Perhaps, underneath her poise, she does have an unhealthy sense of self. Perhaps his availability to other women relieves her of the need for total emotional and sexual involvement: certainly, she views it as a 'friendship in the Lord', one that espouses non-possessiveness. Maybe that can work to a woman's advantage as much as to a man's – and maybe the motivations of human beings are indescribably complex.

In some cases the law of celibacy, combined with the power imbalance and with the confidential nature of the ministry, becomes a licence for male promiscuity. The clerical garb, by proclaiming unavailability, can act as a cloak of invisibility, as can the seal of the confessional. 'He says I have no right to ask him what happens when someone goes to see him,' said Moira of her ten-year relationship with a man she has since discovered to be promiscuous. 'But I think, if I'm in this relationship with him, surely I do have a right?'

Beyond all these hidden relationships lies the open road to marriage. No one, least of all those who are married to priests (they reject the label of ex-priests, preferring to say they no longer serve in the official ministry), would say that marriage is the perfect solution. As Margaret Ulloa, married to Luís, says, 'In some ways, marriage is just the beginning of your problems.' But at least a decision has been taken, a positive choice made, ending the agony of indecision, circular arguments, endless discussions, reflections and retreats. At least the couple have a chance to discover if theirs truly is a marriage relationship, instead of endlessly speculating about the strength and endurability of the feelings experienced.

If a man is going to leave the priesthood, it usually happens early on in the relationship. Margaret and Luís Ulloa decided within half an hour of realising they loved each other. Angie and John Crawford-Leighton made the decision overnight. Although it is essentially the man's decision, it's often the woman who, by proclaiming her support, dismissing any anxieties, and taking a firmly practical approach, propels the decision forward. The longer a man is paralysed by indecision, the more difficult it is for him to leave – and the more hurt the woman becomes.

Not everyone can accept that they have missed that chance, possibly that vital 'crunch' moment. One woman told me that, after eighteen years, she simply could not believe that her partner would not ultimately choose to leave the priesthood for her. She seemed blind to the fact that he had been in the priesthood for thirty years, and presumably felt an even stronger commitment to that – his security, his job, his community, his life. She had invested so much time, energy and hope in the relationship that she simply couldn't face the idea of failure. But neither could she come to terms with the relationship as it was –

secret, deceitful, ultimately unfulfilling.

Is she a self-deceiver, then? Or a masochist? Certainly, there is a strong seam of suffering and punishment within the Catholic Church, with its images of Christ crucified, virgin martyrs, sin and retribution. And many of these women will have been brought up in the vale of tears tradition, where negative experiences are to be 'offered up' to ensure redemption, where personal sacrifice is required for the greater good.

The greater good here may be seen in the widely held belief that a woman is serving the Church of which she is still a member by 'servicing' the man, making him a 'better' priest, while he potentially immobilises her as a woman. The knowledge that she has helped him rediscover his vocation will be of little comfort if he finally deserts her for 'his first love, the Church'; or, more likely, if he dies without ever being able to publicly acknowledge the important role she has played in his life. Then, what started out with such hope for a bright new model of priest-partner relationship will be seen as a relationship preserved – possibly fossilized – in secrecy.

So are these women Jezebels, hussies, scarlet women? Very few of the women I have met, or the stories I have heard, fit those stereotypes. Only a handful would even admit to the appeal of the forbidden fruit yet, to their critics, that's exactly what this issue is all about. Women setting their caps at men who are unavailable, temptresses using female wiles as weapons in the battle with God for the man's body and immortal soul, seductresses wanting the ultimate sacrifice, and then complaining when they suffer.

There is no denying the power of the priestly challenge to some women's sexuality. Many priests are, indeed, familiar with this syndrome: with giggling schoolgirls asking for their autographs, young women haunting their Masses, older women taking every opportunity to speak to them, ferry them round, cook them dinner. It's an occupational hazard, part of the charisma of the dog collar. And there are women who regard every priest as a sexual challenge, who cannot form healthy adult relationships and prefer to flirt with or even seduce unattainable men.

But for some women, it may be more about non-sex – the safety of the celibate, the projection of a fantasy on to a real human being, a substitute lover who won't demand anything that you are not prepared, willing, or able to give, who will satisfy your sexual fantasies without challenging your sexuality. It may also be about comfort, companionship, security, healing. And it's what the priest, literally the father figure, chooses to do about these fantasies that matters – whether he chooses to ignore, deal tactfully with, or exploit them.

Peter Rutter has written powerfully about abusive, exploitative relationships in his book *Sex in the Forbidden Zone*. An American psychiatrist, he cites many examples of such relationships between male psychiatrists, doctors and therapists and their female patients; male lawyers and their female clients; male clerics and female members of their congregations. And he concludes that there is no excuse for any of them, as all are relationships of trust, and all, therefore, contain hidden power dynamics that work to the disadvantage of the 'client'.

Sometimes, a woman in need of counselling or advice is betrayed by the very man she has consulted. Because of the emotional intimacy of the situation, a close relationship can form which, by its very nature, she is often powerless to control. In the case of a priest, she may have gone to him for advice on a bad marriage, or on religious doubts, or on some other intimate area. She goes to him because he is her spiritual leader. He has privileged access to her spiritual wellbeing. He represents holiness and the possibility of healing, of redemption. He can restore her to herself. He is 'safe'.

Often, he is. But sometimes, hampered by inadequate training, he likes that image reflected back at him from the eyes of a dependent woman. Perhaps he is seduced by his own power. Perhaps he decides, unconsciously or otherwise, to exploit that power, gently at first, then more overtly. By which time she may be half in love with him anyway. He's so different from her husband or any boyfriends she might have had. There's an element of spirituality there that is missing in everyday life; an empathy, real or imagined. She's told him things she would never have told any other man. That draws them closer. Then the physical intimacy begins.

In a second scenario, as the relationship of counsellor and counselled progresses, the roles subtly shift. She proves to be a willing and sympathetic listener. She has gone to him with her troubles and now he is honouring her by telling her his. It is not uncommon, after all, for

18

priests to suffer a mid-life crisis, especially if their parents are dead and their friends are busy with their families. Life can be very lonely, for secular priests in particular, and the pressures on them have few compensations in terms of ordinary relationships. The man available for all has no support for himself. She feels for him, wants to protect him, care for him. After appealing to his priesthood, she appeals to his manhood. So vulnerability meets vulnerability. And a physical relationship develops.

To quote Peter Rutter, 'For women, the powerful forces underlying the sexuality of the forbidden zone emerge clearly as feelings of hope – hope that their deepest wounds can be healed and that their true selves can be awakened, recognised and brought out of hiding into the vitality of everyday life.'

Sex in this context becomes a metaphor for hope and healing. Sometimes, it does just that. One woman had a brief sexual relationship with a priest who was a lifelong friend. He was in crisis, she had just recovered from cancer. For them, sex healed rather than harmed. Once confessed, the friendship continued as before.

Two other women had affairs with priests while married. Both claimed the extra-marital relationship had enhanced their marriages: 'If anything, it helped us stay together,' said one, 'because it meant I felt loved, and I knew he wouldn't put any pressure on me to leave my husband, just as I wouldn't put any pressure on him to leave the priesthood.'

Such satisfactory arrangements do, however, appear to be rare – at least among my respondents. In most cases where the relationship has developed through a counselling situation, it would seem that these supposedly safe men, no matter how innocently, betray the trust invested in them. There is no institutionalised ethical body overseeing them, no official code of conduct or complaints procedure. They are protected from accountability – as from irate husbands – by the illusion that Catholic priests do not have sex.

For the priest, the clerical collar can be a visible restraint, a protection, not just against the advances of potential lovers, but against his own sexuality and, when necessary, against permanent involvement. He might caress this woman, he might even have sex with her but, come the day when her demands become unacceptable, he can put on his collar and say, 'You knew what I was. You knew I could never leave the priesthood.'

Even if he is found out, he can almost guarantee the continuing protection of the Church. He might be moved to another parish, or sent to a counselling centre for therapy, or told, as one priest was, to take the woman away for a dirty weekend and 'get it out of your system', as though a woman is only a means to self-gratification, not a potential partner. But it is very rare for a priest to be forcibly laicised and deprived of his priesthood.

The situation becomes more complicated when a child is involved. Most of the time, priests seem only too happy to leave birth control methods – in the main forbidden by the Church – to the women. But sometimes they are brought up sharply against the consequences of their actions.

If a woman becomes pregnant, there is no official Church policy. Each case is judged individually. In some cases, the priest leaves the priesthood and marries the woman, becoming an active father. In others, he remains in the priesthood and continues the relationship secretly, helping the woman financially. Sometimes, however, he panics, confesses to his superiors, is sent away – to another parish, another diocese, the missions – and never contacts the woman again, or only when she takes out a maintenance order against him. Thus he hides behind the very rules he has broken. But at least his priesthood is safe.

Even in paternity cases, there is no official policy on maintenance. One woman receives £60 a month from the priest who fathered her child, but his diocese refuses to accept any responsibility, claiming he is self-employed. In other cases, trust funds – hush funds, as they are more cynically known – are set up for these officially fatherless children.

Critics of the women say they have only themselves to blame. They've disobeyed the rules of the Church and have to take what punishment is coming to them. As one woman, now married to the priest who made her pregnant, said, 'Maybe it wasn't so smart to get involved with Chris. But people do fall in love.' Especially when they share a Catholic identity, a set of religious beliefs, intimate secrets; when they work together for the greater good; when they simply discover how compatible they are.

Such criticism seems to imply that the woman is as responsible for ensuring that the priest keeps to the promises he made at ordination as he is himself. Yet she made no such promises. She is nobody's moral guardian, nobody's spiritual director.

Admittedly, the inherent loneliness of enforced celibacy can make priests vulnerable, particularly those who are ill equipped for adult relationships. Here again there are two categories: the coldly distant and the inappropriately familiar. The former are those who, because of their own background and training, believe the only defence against attack is distance, and so refuse to engage in any human intimacy, even though part of their role is to talk about love and loving, to counsel the engaged and the married, to try to foster workable relationships within the communities they serve.

Other priests can give out confused and confusing signals. A recurring theme in many women's stories is the bewilderment they experience when a man who spent the previous night in their bed, or who in other ways was loving and caring, treats them the next day like a stranger. Or, worse, as a threat, refusing to speak to them on the phone, talking to them only with the door open or a desk between them, deliberately wearing his clerical clothes when they next meet, as though donning a protective armour.

Although seminaries today have introduced psychological testing and, in some cases, human development courses, many priests still don't know how to behave with women. Some still view the female sex as dangerous, sensual, ever ready to make a man of a god. During a visit to Allen Hall Seminary in Westminster, I discussed celibacy with a group of mainly older seminarians. One younger man, in his early twenties, admitted he felt it wise to keep the door open if he or a fellow priest was alone with a woman. I wondered what he thought the rector and I had been doing during our half-hour closeted together, alone, in that same room.

Because of their altruistic role, priests can inadvertently send out misleading messages of intimacy and understanding that we don't often come across in casual encounters – the held gaze, the warm handshake, the tender touch, which can be very attractive to a woman; the animus/anima appeal of a man with feminine qualities. 'He's such a good listener,' I was told. 'I really think he cares about people.' There are many instances of that caring: the ever-open presbytery door, the endless patience, the sympathy, the availability, the wisdom and comfort dispensed.

And most women in relationships with priests need an enormous amount of comfort. Because loving a man whose first responsibility is to the Church, as well as offering women the chance to share in his life and ministry at a very deep level, can be a lonely, isolated, threatened, unhappy, business.

That very isolation is what has propelled the women in this book to confide. For many, talking at all was a first. Others had never spoken at such length – 'I've covered more in these last few hours than in the previous twenty years!' said one. Occasionally, such a strength of feeling would emerge that the woman would break down. Yet no one ever questioned the sometimes intimate nature of my questions, or refused to answer them. It was only afterwards, when they saw it in stark black and white, that they felt uncomfortable. All very definitely felt these were 'their' stories – which indeed they are.

I would start by asking them about their upbringing, in an attempt to trace the roots of later relationships. We would then look at the development of this particular relationship. Even here, things changed as the stories continued to unfold. One woman kept updating her story as different feelings – of anger, primarily – emerged. No doubt her story has changed again since then.

Although the theme of the stories is the same, I believe they reveal some of the breadth and complexity of human experience; of human negotiation within inhuman constraints; and of some of the injustices perpetrated by the intransigent institutions of a Church which proclaims itself to be on the side of justice.

I have tried to avoid apportioning individual blame. Sometimes it is the woman who initiates a relationship, sometimes the man, often no one actually initiates it, it just develops naturally. But, given the unnatural circumstances, it's not surprising so many are harmed as a result. And it's those unnatural circumstances I – and the vast majority of those I have spoken to – would question. As the twentieth century draws to a close, is there a place any more for a law which was made 800 years ago, and which itself was based on a theology of sexuality that was evolving 800 years before that?

The men of these stories are very much an absent presence: the only priests who have willingly talked to me are those who have left the formal ministry. They have talked about the conflicts, the guilt and defiance, the excitement and depression, the knowledge that they are doing wrong in the eyes of the Church, yet fulfilling basic human needs – for companionship as much as for sex. They have informed my understanding of the priest's perspective without being directly quoted. Their stories will have to wait for another time, another book. Those men who choose to remain in the priesthood are understandably reluctant to talk, even in confidence. 'We must not underestimate the men's fear, their total identification with the "institution" as it stands,' as Felicity says.

So it remains the women's story. And, while there are those who are bitter about their relationships and who wish to damage the Church, the majority of those who have spoken to me would prefer reform. By that, they want to see celibacy as a choice rather than as a rule, one which enables both parties to evaluate objectively the importance and relevance of their relationship and, by so doing, to reach a mature decision about where exactly it is going and what role each has in it, as well as what genuine role each woman may have in the Church.

To end on a positive note: 'Being close to a particular priest,' as one woman wrote after that first meeting of Seven-Eleven back in November 1992, 'has given us all, in different ways, a personal insight into the mystery of priesthood, its spiritual power, its astounding generosity, its purpose and ability to convey to a desperate world the ever-present nearness of God.'

Teresa

Teresa is a shy, softly spoken nurse in her early thirties. We talked in the semi-detached house where she lives with her husband, who knows about Tim, the priest, though not the full extent of his continuing influence. Teresa started telling her story in a composed, quiet manner. But when she came to the part where Tim told her he loved her, she broke down. After that, the tears came at regular intervals, but she insisted she wanted the tape-recorder left on so that she could finish. Afterwards, she said that, although the memories are still painful, she was glad of the opportunity to talk. 'Thanks for helping me to do this,' she wrote.

I'd like to begin with my home background, because I think it's relevant to what happened to me. My childhood was a very negative experience, as my mum and dad had their own problems and their relationship wasn't a very strong or loving one. I think they loved themselves more than they loved each other or us children. My father drank a lot – he still does – and he's always been aggressive when drunk. My mother's response to that was to smoke herself into a state of chronic emphysema. I remember being shouted at and hit a lot and then hit again for crying. I was also sexually abused by another relative, so it wasn't any wonder I was the person I was when all this happened.

I was very shy, withdrawn and intimidated by the world. I remember feeling confused about life, and I had little sense of who I was or where I was going. I drifted into a number of platonic relationships with men, just because they asked me out and it seemed the thing to do. I didn't feel committed to any of them, so virginity wasn't a problem, but a comfortable state to be in. Needless to say, those relationships tended to

25

be short-lived and sometimes quite painful for the other person.

My mum's a traditional Catholic, but she can be surprisingly open-minded as well. My father's a lapsed Catholic and very critical of traditional Catholicism. Mum didn't always go to church but she'd always send us. Of course, we wouldn't go if she wasn't with us, we'd go scrumping or something. But I made my First Holy Communion and my confirmation and then, when I was about sixteen, I stopped going to church for a couple of years, the usual anti-Catholic fling, rebelling against forced worship and what seemed like an oppressive faith.

A couple of years later, I left home to do my nursing training and felt lost. I didn't feel I fitted in with the people around me. They were much more streetwise and confident and they seemed to be very together somehow. One of the other nurses was a practising Catholic and I started going to Mass with her. Catholicism actually had some meaning and value for the first time in my life. I went back to church then because I realised that I did have faith and it was important to me. That's when I met Tim.

Up to then, I was in no way in awe of priests. I certainly didn't hold them in any reverence. I saw them as people who had a job to do, and I was quite critical of the ones who say Mass as if they're commentating on a horse race. We weren't particularly involved with them as a family, though the ones I knew were supportive. I suppose there was a sort of parent figure there in a sense. I could talk to them about things, and I felt understood and accepted by most of them.

At first, that's how I saw Tim. Just as a very ordinary, likeable person. He was in his late twenties, about eight years older than me, and a curate in the parish where I was living. He was an OK bloke, popular, good for the crack, used to go to the pub a lot. He was very down-to-earth whereas I used to get worked up about things. I'd go to see him and he'd just say 'Do you want a fag?' I remember once a few of us had an argument with some other parish members and with one of the priests who was working with them. I was quite uptight about the whole thing, even though I felt we were in the right. I thought I'd done something terrible, but Tim said, 'You know, priests can make mistakes as well. Don't worry about it.' He put things into perspective for me and he was very supportive as well. At this time, he was nobody special. I didn't feel any special closeness or find him particularly sexually attractive.

While I was still doing my nursing training, he asked if I'd like to go to Lourdes on the parish pilgrimage. It sounded a bit religious, but he said it would be a good crack and he seemed a pretty sound bloke, so I went. We all had a good laugh together and a good time. The year after we went again, the same crowd, same crack. I'd decided by this time that I was going to work abroad and I was living at an overseas volunteer centre in London. It was disorganised and very cliquey, so I began to feel quite lost again. But I knew it was worth putting up with it, because I badly wanted to work in the developing world.

Meanwhile, Tim was also feeling miserable because of problems in the parish, and was living with a new parish priest, who was elderly and difficult. So neither of us were feeling very happy, and we talked about it in Lourdes.

When the patients were in bed, we'd all get together and get the duty-free out. This one night, I ended up sitting on his knee, quite innocently, just messing about. Maybe I was naive, but I didn't see it as anything bad or sexual. Gradually everybody went to bed and somebody turned the light out. We kept on sitting there, talking. He asked me why I was going away and I told him, and then he told me that he loved me and . . . Don't worry about the tears . . . it just changed my whole being, my whole concept of myself. I felt valued and accepted, affirmed and, for the first time in my life, I felt loved. And my response was to love him back.

It came totally out of the blue. I think it did for him, too. We stayed talking until the early hours, till about four o'clock. He wanted us to stay there and sleep together, nothing sexual. I said no because of tongues wagging, especially when we went home. But we talked for a long time, about ourselves and the people we knew. We shared our problems and our aspirations, our dreams.

It was then that I began to find him sexually attractive, which was part of this very deep love I felt for him. He was also attracted to me and I still believe our love was mutual. It was the way he used to look at me and speak to me. I don't think people can feign things like that.

At first, he seemed able to justify our relationship without any difficulty. He'd say things like, it was OK, that Jesus had also loved women, like Mary Magdalene – 'He didn't have her but he loved her,' that sort of thing. I don't think he'd had any other relationships. He said himself that he was immature for his age. He once mentioned a friend who was a nun, but I don't think it was anything more than friendship, though I never asked him.

I don't think anyone suspected anything at this time. Certainly no one said anything. Later, after we'd returned to England, he picked me up from London and drove my stuff home for me, and we met quite a lot. We just fitted in with whatever he was doing and what I was doing. There was a lot of chemistry then, a lot of feeling and emotion. That's when I learned to accept myself because, for the first time in my life, somebody else had done that, in a very loving and powerful way.

We spoke about our feelings – not a lot, because there wasn't the need for a lot of words, but our love for each other was certainly acknowledged and shared. We would hold and kiss each other, but there was no question of any sexual act. He told me once that he loved me too much for that.

If he'd wanted a sexual relationship, I probably would have consented, but I didn't want it at the expense of the relationship ending, which I thought it would. I didn't think he'd be able to handle the guilt, not to mention the thought of people finding out. He was quite paranoid about that, particularly the thought of other priests knowing about us. I don't think I would have felt guilty about a sexual relationship, as long as it was an expression of committed, mutual, meaningful love. I knew from the beginning it was important for me to respect his choice of celibacy and his commitment to the priesthood.

It was a few months later that I went to Africa. I never reconsidered going, because I felt we loved each other deeply and I believed our love was strong enough to sustain distance and any other eventuality. I know he had the urge to get on a plane and join me at one point, although he never did. I think one of his colleagues dissuaded him.

For two years, my life was just heaven. We wrote often, about our different lives and our feelings for each other. We shared so much in those letters – I can only describe them as love letters. It was like he was there for me, very much with me and an important part of my life. Meanwhile, I also loved the honesty and simplicity of the African culture. Their acceptance and openness, together with Tim's love, helped me so much to grow into the person I felt I really was. It was the happiest time of my life. I felt fully alive and whole, and I had so much love in me to share with others.

I didn't want anything else from Tim. I didn't want to marry him or take him from where he was at. I loved him as he was and I liked the freedom of our relationship. It was nice to have somebody there and to be there for him, to share love but also to be free. Can you understand that? There had been no sexual relationship, so I didn't see any reason why what I would call our loving friendship couldn't last for ever. I never gave the future a thought. I suppose our love seemed so perfect and beautiful that I just didn't envisage any problems.

It was when I came home that things started to change, not immediately, but two or three months later. Initially, we met, went for a drink, and it was great. I was quite detached, but I knew that was because I'd been away. He was quite attached, so in one sense the power balance had shifted a little. He may have felt threatened by that, because it meant he wasn't in control of things. He was no longer the adult in the relationship. However, my feelings soon returned, along with a deep commitment.

Tim was speaking much more sexually at this time. He seemed much more aware of the sexual implications of our relationship. I can remember the first time I saw him and he started to touch me. I said, 'Hey, cool it!' Perhaps he couldn't handle his sexual feelings alongside a vow of celibacy. That may have been part of it, but certainly there was a growing awkwardness. I think his biggest problem was the paranoia of other people finding out, which is sad, because celibacy is supposed to be about love, isn't it?

I could feel that he was becoming uncomfortable with our relationship and that made me anxious. I suppose I didn't want to think it could end. He was always worrying about his feelings. I don't know if we'd grown too close through our letters and he couldn't handle that closeness. I remember he was very preoccupied with what his mother would think, because she wouldn't have approved of it.

We saw each other a few more times, but neither of us could talk about the tension building up between us. I was still staying at the overseas centre in London, and one day he came to see me. He was an hour or two late, and some of my colleagues – I don't know if they'd picked up that I was waiting for him – made it obvious they were looking to see what was happening. That freaked him out, although he was uneasy from the start. I knew something was wrong.

That was when he said he didn't think he did love me, that it wasn't appropriate, he was committed to the Church, and our relationship had to stop. It was like it wasn't really him speaking. I wasn't strong enough to say, 'Why can't we look at this?' I couldn't begin to reason with him. I was just numb, devastated.

I remember walking him to the car and saying goodbye and not crying or anything. He said, 'Are you OK?' I said, 'Yes, fine.' Then, when I got back in, I got very upset. I took some tablets and some alcohol. I didn't mean to kill myself, I just wanted to get rid of the pain and go to sleep. I remember writing him a letter telling him what I really thought, how hurt and rejected I felt.

The next day, I felt really ill, but nobody realised what I'd done. I only realised myself the next morning. It wasn't a conscious attempt at an overdose, it was just like 'Get me to sleep. Get rid of this pain.'

When he got my letter, he wrote back before he went on holiday, saying he did love me and always would do. He just left things on hold, really. He went on holiday, came back and just stopped contacting me. He was stepping backwards, not getting in touch, very much distancing himself. He would speak to me when I rang him, he didn't say, 'I don't want to talk to you.' He would talk as if things were fine, say things like, 'You'll always be special. I love you,' then he'd change and become very non-committal. I didn't have the maturity to sit down and talk to him. I don't know if he would have co-operated with that, either.

He would never get in touch with me, never explain or give me any reason for why he stopped contacting me. There was never any formal ending of the relationship, he just left it open, and that was very hard to deal with because there didn't seem to be any reason why things should end. I feel quite angry about that, because he told me afterwards that he was 'given advice', presumably by the priest mafia. I was angry because we hadn't done anything wrong: it was all within the rules, within *their* rules. I knew sex was out of the question, I knew neither of us wanted him to leave the priesthood. I thought things were within the boundaries of Catholicism, yet our relationship still wasn't acceptable.

I left the centre and worked in a local hospital for a while. Each time I passed the drugs cupboard, I knew how easy it would be to die. I knew how to do it properly. I used to walk past this stuff every morning and think, 'Not today.' I used to think about killing myself every day and every night. It was only the thought of getting to God too soon, and the hurt I'd cause Tim, that stopped me.

We met just once after that. We went walking in the hills. Even there, he was paranoid, looking round all the time and obviously frightened and threatened. He told me to burn all his letters, and I was stupid enough to do it. I'd kept them all, and I just burned them. I nearly set the curtains on fire over the sink in the kitchen, there was so much airmail paper going up in flames!

I think part of his problem was that he saw our relationship as a threat to his ministry. He was committed to that and good with people. He was also very spiritual and prayerful, which was reflected in his liturgical celebrations. I'm cer..... , though, that other clergy had a lot to do with the breakdown of our relationship. It wasn't Tim speaking any more, it was the traditional voice of hard-line, right-of-centre Catholicism.

It didn't turn me against the Church, though. The Church was very much part of me, too. I needed the strength and the support, although actually it wasn't there. I didn't talk to any of the priests in the parish because, by this time, I didn't trust them. I did tell some of my friends, though, and I think Tim may have felt threatened by that. But my feeling at the time was that we were not doing anything wrong and it was a loving relationship that I needed to talk about.

He told me that he had grown through the relationship, that it had helped him to develop as a person, that it brought him happiness, an understanding of life and an understanding of himself. It gave me self-respect, self-esteem and the courage to be myself, at least at first. I always saw our love as something good and beautiful, which God had created within us, because God is love.

Some time after he sent me that last letter, I decided to join a religious order. I wanted to work abroad and I thought that would be the best way to do it. I also hoped it would make things work between us. You know, if there was an official demonstration by me of celibacy, maybe things could work out. I believed God would work through my experience in the same way He works in all people's lives. I joined a missionary order and, while I was at their formation house in England,

Tim sent me a Christmas card and a book, so I thought things were going to be OK.

When I first told him I was joining this religious congregation, he was euphoric. He offered to drive me back to their house, said it was great, the answer to his prayers. I felt so relieved. Everything was going to be fine. At the same time, there was so much tension when we were together – he was so wary and so guarded – that there was no real discussion. The day I told him I was going to the convent, he had the door open in the sacristy. He wouldn't shut the door. That was the sort of climate it was. Today, I would be able to sit down and talk to him about things, but then I didn't feel I had the skill or confidence to do that. I was confident by this time, but not with him. It was almost as though he was the source of my confidence, so I felt I couldn't challenge his behaviour.

I was in the novitiate for nearly three years. It was a very austere and rigid lifestyle, which in one way was good, because I was so depressed. I think I needed the discipline to pull me through. I don't regret doing it. I did learn a lot about prayer and spirituality, but the day was very structured and you weren't encouraged to be yourself. I felt I was losing my own identity and spontaneity. Much of the confidence and self-awareness I'd gained from living in Africa was lost, and I came home very timid and shy and withdrawn again.

During that time, Tim never wrote, which was hard, because there was no way I could get in touch with him as letter-writing was restricted. Somehow I was supposed to understand his reasons for that. I think a lot of my depression and lack of self-esteem was about the loss of that support and love, with no explanation.

In the end, I left before I took my first vows. It just wasn't working. When I saw him again, he was in a new parish. He was still frightened and threatened, sitting behind a big desk. He told me he'd 'taken advice' again, which was why he hadn't been in touch. I don't know if there was any feeling there then. I suspect there wasn't, that he was just frightened and quite detached. He didn't make any further effort to get in touch, and the last time I saw him was just before I got married last year.

I hadn't seen him for about ten years and I felt I needed to express my anger and resentment. Also, I still couldn't get him out of my head. I'd been seeing Pete, who's now my husband, for five years and yet this hurt was still there. I had this feeling that Pete was second best, whereas actually he's a different person altogether and the feelings can't be compared. I just wanted to get rid of all the hurt and all the angst. But it didn't help. I don't think that will ever go away.

When I saw him, I felt very much in control, fairly confident and together. He seemed older, wiser and more relaxed about seeing me than I thought he would be, but I still felt I'd moved on a lot more than he had. I'd worked through the fact that he couldn't cope with a relationship and I didn't think any the less of him for that. The deep feelings weren't there and I did feel quite removed from him in a sense, yet the hurt and rejection still felt very real.

I explained why I was seeing him and he said he didn't realise how much he'd hurt me, that he'd grown up and if it happened again he wouldn't react in the same way. Part of me wondered if it could still have worked, and we saw each other once or twice after that. I'm not sure why. I just thought, 'Why not? What the hell?' But there was no strong chemistry, no strong feelings, apart from the hurt and the rejection.

I'm still angry that he initiated our relationship and took the adult role, that he told me he loved me, let me believe that and that I returned his love. Obviously, I gained a lot from it, it was very affirming and it made me very happy. But then he rejected me, by being embarrassed and indifferent, without ever formally ending the relationship. In one sense, he can't take away the love that he gave me. I know that. Yet at the same time, he *did* take it away, with his rejection, which had neither explanation nor apology.

I don't feel bitter towards him. My anger and resentment is towards the institution, the Church. I think it's an example of where celibacy just doesn't work, even when it's applied. We kept all their rules, there was no sex and I never tried to persuade him to leave his ministry for marriage. It's obvious priests are going to fall in love, because they're human beings, so they should be able to handle it. If celibacy is about love, love shouldn't be a problem, no matter how deep the feelings. Celibacy is supposed to be about the perfection of love. How can it dismiss a deep, personal friendship? How can it include the hurt and devastation that I experienced?

Pete knows about Tim, but I don't think he's aware of the depth of the hurt. He thinks the Church abuses women anyway, and sees this as another example of that. I'm not that cynical. I do think the Church devalues and excludes women in many ways, but there are groups within it that are empowering. Prayer is very important to me, and my relationship with God is more important than the oppression of the institutionalised Church. I think God is a lot bigger than the Church and greater than all our religions put together.

I did hear that Tim has been very ill since our last meeting. I don't know if it was related to that or not. I hope not. He's made no attempt to contact me since then and I presume he doesn't want to. I'd like to think he's happy but I can't help wondering if he really is, and how different things could have been, for both of us.

Will I get over it? I don't know. No, I suspect not. I mean, fifteen years on and I still haven't got back all that confidence and self-esteem. I suppose he healed all the wounds of my childhood by loving the person I really was. Then he destroyed a part of that person, which is inaccessible to this day.

I'm reminded of that hurt every time I meet a priest who can't relate comfortably to women – and there are many like that. They look at you like you're a potential whore or else they don't look at you at all. They speak to you as if you count for nothing and they have countless ways of dismissing what you have to say, and of devaluing your gifts and contribution to the community. I have to remind myself that men like that are not true celibates, and that it's not Christ's love, nor do they speak for all priests. But there are still far too many of them.

Carmel

Carmel is one of the youngest women I have come across during my research. Now in her early thirties, she was just twenty-one when she began her affair – very much at his instigation – with a priest old enough to be her father. When I first met her, she was still angry about what she saw as his exploitation of a much younger woman and abuse of his position of trust. I talked to her again two years later, by which time she appeared to have worked through some of the negative feelings and reached some kind of understanding about her own role in the relationship. She no longer saw herself simply as a victim of a powerful male. Further analysis in the light of a commitment to feminism had shown her that some of her needs must have been met. Nonetheless, the in-built inequality of the relationship has had a long-term effect both on her religious faith and on her faith in the reality of romantic love.

I come from a family of rampant atheists. It's funny, because I really enjoyed religious education at primary school. I thought it was all quite intriguing. But my father insisted I was withdrawn from the class. They were all very anti-religion. My mother had been to a Catholic convent for a while, and then was taken out of it because her parents thought it was affecting her – she started building altars. Also, the nuns were particularly cruel and unpleasant to her. So, no, I didn't have any religious input whatsoever.

I first came across the Catholic Church when I was working for a New Age-type organisation and we went on a pilgrimage. It was actually the first time I'd come across Christians in any way, shape or form. I'd always been very anti because my dad used to make jokes about Christians – he used to tell us that nuns stole children! So I had been really indoctrinated the other way in that I thought anyone who believed in God was really stupid and obviously had no sort of logical, rational capacity whatsoever.

I remember ringing up the organisers of this pilgrimage and saying, 'Can I come? I'm not a Christian, I'm an atheist.' And they said, 'Yes, of course you can come, that's fine.' I still saw myself as the rebel and thought they were all stupid. I don't know why I wanted to go, really. I think it was the bike ride that appealed.

When I got there, the people didn't fit the stereotype in the way I had imagined. In fact, they were very inspiring people, in a way that a lot of fanatical people are when someone is very young – I was only twenty-one – and it all seemed very radical. I met people who were actually putting their money where their mouths were and, having a father who was quite political but also quite cynical about everything, it was like an antidote to that. His cynicism was amusing, but these people were actually doing things. It made me feel very optimistic, actually.

It was on the pilgrimage that I met Richard. He was a lot older than me – this all happened ten years ago, so he'd have been about forty-eight – which I do feel aggrieved about. I didn't know he was a priest and I was very surprised when I found out. I think, because I was an atheist, I wasn't in awe of him, so we got on well. I didn't know anything about religion at all and when I found out he was a Catholic priest and that Catholic priests were not meant to have relationships or get married or anything like that, I was surprised. Again, he just didn't fit the stereotype. He was good fun, not terribly earnest but obviously someone who was very highly motivated.

My boyfriend at the time was very scathing about him. He used to make jokes at his expense all the time; used to think it was hilariously funny that this man was a priest, and would wind him up. He was a Catholic, my boyfriend, though not a practising Catholic, and he used to do all this genuflecting and walking backwards out of the room when Richard walked in. I think he got a bit fed up with it, though we used to think it was quite funny. That's when I realised that Richard actually did take some of these things seriously because, when they were ridiculed, he got quite upset.

I don't know now whether I became a Catholic because of him or whether I fell for him because I became a Catholic. At the time, Catholicism seemed more intellectually stimulating than where I'd come from. I loved the ritual. It was liberation theology that I was involved in, and I met a lot of Christian feminists. So it was probably that as much as Richard that attracted me. It was also wanting to belong and to do the same as he did. I had instruction and was converted, but when I went to make my first confession, I couldn't tell the priest because he knew Richard. It was something I really wanted to do, but I couldn't even do that properly because of him.

I knew him for a year before anything happened. I had a serious motorbike accident and he came to visit me in hospital, I don't know how many times. I went to recuperate at my parents' house at the other end of the country and he came to see me, stayed in a chaplaincy nearby, took me out for my first walk, and that's when I started thinking, 'There's something going on here that I don't know about.'

I think because of my youth, I didn't realise I was in love with him until it became obvious. I'd previously dismissed him as a romantic attachment. I thought it just wasn't on the agenda. Yet it felt like he was pursuing me. How could it possibly be? It wasn't permitted, so how could it happen? Maybe he was just being caring? It felt really weird.

My parents were pleased that he came to see me, that he put himself out to do that. There was no reason for them to worry about anything else. As far as they knew, I had my boyfriend and we were probably going to get married, so that was it. But it was actually while I was recuperating that I decided I didn't want that relationship to continue. It had always been difficult and I just decided I'd had enough. I told him that and he found it very hard to accept.

When I went back to work after recuperating, it really did feel like Richard was wooing me, though I was still denying it. There'd be endless notes dropped through my letterbox at six in the morning because he was always racing off somewhere. Flowers left on my desk. He'd phone me up and say he was officiating at some wedding or baptism, and would I like to come and see him in all his robes? I remember thinking, 'That's a bit odd.' I couldn't understand what was happening, I really couldn't. At that stage I didn't realise I was in love with him.'

Then he invited me to the pictures and it was all very teenagerish.

God, it makes me feel so embarrassed when I think about it! It was like having a real schoolgirl crush on somebody, and he acted like a schoolboy as well. That's when we snogged each other in the cinema. It was all terribly passionate and that's when I realised how I felt about him and when he realised as well.

He admitted that he'd been very distracted by me, not that he was in love with me. I suppose it was lust, but he didn't dare admit anything as base as that. So that's when it happened. I had had this year of being very interested in him and thinking, 'I suppose I might be in love,' and then it happened really quickly. It was my accident which speeded everything up, really. That's when I realised he wasn't going to abide by the rules. I was pleased, but I was also shocked, when I realised his priesthood was not an obstacle to us having a sexual relationship.

I suppose what I liked about him was that he's very charismatic and handsome in a very English schoolboyish sort of way. So I was physically attracted to him – lots of women were, as women always are to charismatic people. I was quite fascinated by his class as well because he was the first person I'd ever met who was upper middle class.

I don't have any evidence of this but I'm sure he had a number of other relationships. I really have got a feeling that there was a woman in every port. There's at least one woman I remember whose behaviour was what you would expect from someone who had been dumped. He used to say there were three kinds of priests. The lonely alcoholic, the one who had affairs, and a few who were genuinely holy and spiritual and were totally involved in the religious life.

He was honest in admitting that he didn't believe in celibacy. He thought it was ridiculous and messed people up, and he didn't particularly want to be a priest any more, so imposing sanctions on himself would have been a bit stupid. And I do think it was all very exciting for him, this sudden discovery of sex. Having said that, the guilt was just terrible. He was very angst-ridden. That's what I got bored with, the guilt. It seemed completely inappropriate to me a lot of the time.

It was textbook stuff, in a way. He forgot all his wooing and everything, all the times he'd rung me up and sent me flowers – he couldn't cope with that. He was very into denial, so instead he'd cast me as the temptress who had led him astray and he couldn't control himself. That's how he justified it. He couldn't resist me. I remember him telling me once he'd had this important sermon to give and he couldn't concentrate because he kept seeing me. It was almost like a spell had been cast upon him. That was the sort of language he used. He would talk about what I meant to him in terms of being 'bewitched'. He didn't use that word but it was that sort of emphasis.

It wasn't like a normal relationship because, obviously, it wasn't a normal relationship. It was totally distorted. We couldn't have a deep and meaningful relationship with each other because we couldn't do the things that other people did, couldn't appear to be a couple. There was always this denial that we were together. We'd go to parties or social events or something and I'd just be there and obviously people would realise that something was going on. We went to a wedding together and a close friend of mine let us stay alone together in her flat, so there was that acknowledgement, but it was unspoken.

Things were snatched all the time. It was like a series of fairly unsatisfying liaisons. We always seemed to be running round trying to find places to have sex, so it became totally one-dimensional. Even when we went on holiday for a few days he was still paranoid. He could never relax. I can never figure out how much of that was his guilt about his priesthood and how much was his fear of the press finding out.

I made one big mistake. Because my previous boyfriend was so upset when we finished, I felt sorry for him and invited him to a party that Richard was at. And, of course, Richard and I left the party together – we must have already slept together at that point – and that's when my boyfriend, my ex-boyfriend as he then was, realised what was going on. That was awful, absolutely appalling. He smashed my bedroom window, basically, to get in, and Richard and I were in bed together.

That was a turning point for me in my relationship with Richard. My memory is that, OK, I was very young and naive, but they then went out into the living room to discuss what was going on, like what were Richard's intentions towards me and what was he playing at?

Thinking about it now, I can understand how my boyfriend felt because this man was very much older than me, and to a young man it must have all seemed awful. I remember thinking, 'This is great, isn't it? They're discussing me and I'm not included in this.' I felt like I was some chattel and they were making the decision about who got me.

It was resolved by Richard sort of fleeing into the night. It's quite funny, looking back. He said it couldn't continue, it was just too risky. We used to have that sort of discussion regularly, but it always would continue. I think he was very immature, actually. Any hassle, he couldn't face it. If ever he had to be confronted with anything, any reality, he couldn't deal with it. While things were all fantasy and he was doing all this wooing of me, it was OK.

After a while, I suddenly realised I was a mistress and, although initially it was all very exciting because it was forbidden, and I colluded in that, after a while it was just not much fun, you know. It's horrible, actually, and it really does affect your self-esteem being with somebody you love who suddenly gets up and goes home. All of that, and all this sneaking about – God, it's so tiring. I used to have fantasies about going shopping at Sainsbury's with him, something most women would find totally boring, but the thought of doing something normal together was really exciting to me.

But we never did do things like that. They just weren't part of his life. Everywhere he went, people would be desperate to cook for him – you know this thing about the poor, unloved priest who doesn't ever get a square meal? So he never had to go shopping anywhere.

It started to turn sour after about three months, because I declared my undying love for him and he freaked out. I remember him saying, 'Oh, my God! Why do people fall in love with me?' That's when he announced there was another woman in his life whom he'd promised to marry. I'd had this fantasy about being the love of his life but it turned out there was somebody else who had been around a long, long time. I don't know how he managed two illicit relationships at the same time!

His relationship with her had been sexual and wasn't now. I remember thinking it was like the virgin and the whore. He'd go to her for long, intense conversations, and come to me for sex. It felt as if intellectually and spiritually he loved her, and with me it was a very physical relationship. He was saying how distressing it all was for him, and again it sounded like he'd been 'done to', as if this woman had come and seduced him again and he was very passive. It was almost like he was something addictive that women endlessly used!

When he told me, I thought, 'God, he's really scared of any commitment,' which was strange, because I didn't think there could be any commitment. On another level, I felt reassured that he had had relationships and, I suppose, a bit disappointed as well. But he spoke about it in such dismissive terms, because at the time I think they were having a difficult time – she was getting fed up and he was feeling pressured. I don't think it's any reflection on how he really felt.

Even though he told me about this other woman, our relationship continued. And I still felt central. It actually lasted another five or six years. That's how long we were sleeping with each other. I was fed up with it, though, after a year. Then it became a nightmare, extremely depressing. Sneaking around became boring. But I was in love. And the fantasy of being in love was about being together against all the odds.

I believe now that romantic love is a destructive notion to keep women in their place. That's why I stayed with it. The fantasy was that we would be together till the end, even though I probably would have become tired of him because of the age difference. And he did feed that fantasy.

On one occasion I said, 'I've really had enough and I don't want to see you any more.' I went away, and when I came back he was very different in his attitude to me, very attentive and less paranoid. But everything was so difficult. It was so hard to be spontaneous, because yet again there was nowhere we could go. I was living in a shared house at the time, he lived in a presbytery, so we had important conversations on park benches. Maybe that was part of my resistance. I mean, I could have gone and got my own place in those days but I wouldn't do it. I did eventually, and that's when I started really feeling like a mistress.

Then I became obsessive, in that I was always waiting for him to ring and trying to arrange a time when we could be together. I think I'd been protecting myself before, and that's when it got hard for me, and when I did start telling my close friends. But, you know, I was involved with him for a long time and I could have stopped that and I didn't, which is why I can't easily say I was dreadfully exploited, because obviously there was something I was hooked into in that relationship. I think there must be lots of similarities with women who have relationships with men who are not available, whether they be priests or married men. I'm sure there's a commonality in all of that.

I wouldn't do it now. I'm far more protective of myself. I just wouldn't consider it. If you have some regard for yourself and you know what you want and you want your needs met in a relationship, you'd be pretty stupid getting involved with a priest or with a married man. It really messed me up. It was a deeply unhappy time of my life.

Once I thought I was pregnant. I was in a terrible state, but I also thought it was wonderful. I was so pleased because it was all part of this romantic fantasy. It was real panic stations for him. I remember him saying, 'I'll give you all my money to bring up the child.' And I said, 'I'll go and live with my parents and no one will ever know who the father is.' It was like a bloody Mills and Boon fantasy! He seemed to think that was a good idea, then he'd say, 'We'll probably end up together, anyway.' He was very confused. When I found I wasn't pregnant I was quite upset, but I told him and he said, 'Thank God.' He was over the moon. So that was another turning point. It seemed so callous. I felt he just didn't understand me at all. I thought, 'You rotten bastard.' That's when I started getting disillusioned.

The last time we slept together was just before he told me he was going to marry this other woman. I'd had sex with him after a party, and afterwards I felt extremely empty and sad. It was a very physical thing, nothing to do with being in love, and it's always sad when you realise you're not in love with somebody any more. Three weeks later, I got a photocopied letter through my letterbox announcing his marriage. I remember thinking, 'This is so typical of him. He's such a coward, he couldn't even arrange to see me.'

The other thing that annoyed me was that he thought I'd be so devastated. He was so full of his own importance by that stage. So I was irritated: one, because it was cowardly of him; two, because it was typically tacky, a photocopied letter that he'd sent to all his friends with a handwritten bit on the bottom for anyone who was a bit more important; and, three, because he didn't realise where I was at with him. I mean, I'd been encouraging him to get married to her for quite a while. It was, 'Oh, I just want this all to be finished, I'm so fed up with it all.' It really was for me a sense of wanting to move on, and not wanting him and my feelings for him to get in the way any more. So I didn't feel too upset about it.

I'd realised two years before that the relationship was going nowhere and I was fed up with it, but we would still sleep together occasionally. I just wasn't as bound up in it all. The other thing I did was, as I mentioned, to tell a lot of my close friends, which was a way of saving my sanity. Doing that somehow broke the spell, because there were people saying, 'Come on, this is just not on. What are you getting out of it?' That criticism was important. It made me realise I had to consider my own needs.

Looking back, I think I was very stuck with that relationship and very unhappy with it. It did take a real emotional toll of me which I can see now but, at the time, I just didn't realise it. Somehow I didn't feel quite part of the world in a way. That was a function of the secrecy. I didn't get on with the rest of my life.

I was vulnerable when he was wooing me because I'd just had the road accident. I used to feel it was quite an abusive relationship, because he was so much older than me and had so much responsibility, power and influence. Priests should realise that.

My perception has changed now. I feel there was something that kept me in that relationship; there was a part of me that needed to be in it. I'm less inclined now always to see women as passive victims in this sort of relationship. So I don't feel as exploited as I did a few years ago. I was more hard-line about him then. Now I suppose his emotional immaturity somehow evened things out a bit. Just because someone's twenty years older than you, it doesn't really mean much. Had he been a bit more thoughtful, he might have stopped to think, 'What am I doing?'; to realise there was a big power imbalance. In any other profession, like that of a doctor, he'd have been struck off. But I really cannot ever recall him saying, 'This just isn't fair on you.' It was always what it was doing to him, how it was affecting him.

There were quite a few people who never believed me, who thought I was making it up. They were all women who were apparently feminists, and I remember being annoyed about that at the time. There was one woman in particular who to this day doesn't believe that this happened. That's because she idealised him to such an extent that she really could not accept that this man was actually a human being and was fallible. I've heard from a close friend of hers that she still does not believe it, and this is a woman who's a feminist.

What this reveals to me is the power of people's emotions in all of this. Why do we have to have heroes? What function does it serve in people's lives? Because I don't think it's actually a particularly bad thing that someone wants to have a sexual relationship with someone else, another human being. I don't think it's particularly demeaning, but obviously to this woman it takes away from his godliness or whatever.

I've never felt that. I felt more that his guilt and his splitting the idea of what's spiritual and what's physical was more the issue, really, more the problem, and something that's maybe not confined to priests. I certainly know a lot of Catholics who would say that that's what they grew up with, and they were left with a feeling that those things were somehow wrong. A lot of them went completely over the top in trying to exorcise that from themselves.

I saw him only about a week ago, driving a car. I thought, 'Oh, God, how embarrassing.' But he didn't see me. I often think we're going to run into each other in Sainsbury's because I certainly see his wife in there and I have to hide behind the shelves. At least he bit the bullet in the end and did the decent thing by her. But I'm not really in contact with any of those people now, which is interesting in itself, because I was quite involved in all of that New Age stuff and I know they have regular little soirées to which I've never been invited. It doesn't annoy me, because I do think there's a slight embarrassment there with them all. They don't quite know how to deal with me. I don't know whether he still sees them. I suspect he doesn't.

It definitely had a long-term effect on me, yes. I felt I was very much in love with this man because it had all the ingredients. It felt very passionate, it was illicit, there was an excitement in the fact that it was illicit, all that stuff, and that's an experience some people never feel in their lives. I remember thinking, 'At least I know what real love is,' and all this sort of rubbish.

I feel very differently about it now. I'm very suspicious and wary about love and what falling in love really means. I don't know whether that's partly my age or what. As far as relationships go, I know there are far more important things than passion – that is something to bring you together, but what comes after that is far more worthwhile, and far more important. So, yes, it's affected me in that way.

As far as the Church is concerned, I no longer practise. I think celibacy in recent years has been shown to be a total farce. I do respect people who want to lead celibate lives, and I think there's a lot to be said for celibacy but, in terms of the priesthood, it's obviously not working, and it takes a terrible toll on priests and the people who are involved with them. On the one hand, there's this idea that, in being celibate, you dedicate your life to many people instead of perhaps one or two. So you are more able to give of yourself to your community, your parish. But there's a real need for human contact that's very spiritual as well, and there is a denial there which takes its toll.

It would be interesting to see how those who stay in the priesthood change their views from when they first go in to when they come out the other end. It also seems to be about people wanting to idealise priests. Again, it's part of this need to have symbols that represent something that no one else can be. Yet the revealing fact is that they, the priests, often can't be that symbol, either.

Felicity

Felicity is an attractive, very feminine woman in her early fifties, who favours embroidered Indian cotton dresses and colourful, dangling earrings. Softly spoken and highly articulate, she's involved in a number of lay groups within the Church, including women's groups. She also has a very busy work and social life, as well as finding time for her large family of siblings, nieces and nephews. Her house is neat and restful – except when her cats start squabbling. I've met her there a couple of times, as well as receiving various written versions of her story. Each time, the tale unfolds slightly differently. Despite its longstanding nature, it is anything but static. For someone who claims not to know herself, Felicity's approach to her story is surprisingly analytical and considered.

I want to start by saying how difficult it was for me to decide to contribute something to this book. I feel quite ambivalent about what I am doing. I know Andrew will find this very hard to accept, but at the same time I feel I have a need – and a right – to tell my story. Just thinking about how to try to describe our life has been quite therapeutic for me. I feel sad that he doesn't want – or doesn't feel able – to tell his and my story; doesn't want to tell everybody about these twenty-plus years of ups and downs but, overall, of faithful, loving and mutual care. The problem is of how to talk without implicating him or imputing to him thoughts and feelings he may not have. So what I can give is really only half or part of our life story.

I'm also anxious about getting the balance right between the positive and negative aspects. Because, although our friendship has been the most important thing in my life, bringing me much joy, growth, insight

47

and intimacy, there are also many painful and hurtful features.

I'm fifty-three now and I've had this 'particular friendship' for twenty-four years. He's a few years older. At first, there were many years marked by frequent agonising reappraisals and threats from me to leave him. Then there came a time when that was no longer an issue or a possibility. We then settled into a fairly comfortable and close middle age, but now it's all unsettled again.

We met through work in 1964. I'd had a very conventional upbringing as a white, middle-class, convent grammar-school girl. My commitment to the Church came alive in the sixth form when I joined a student Christian group, in which I remained until I left university. Then I did a year's voluntary work. The group I was with brought religion alive for me as something to be put into practice on a daily basis. It was about translating belief into action. I got excited about scripture and theology and by the notion that we could use our brains and didn't just have to be told what to think and do.

I then started working for a Catholic organisation which Andrew was also involved with. I was used to priests: I'd worked with many and had others as my friends, so I didn't see them as being on another plane.

Nonetheless, he was the first priest I knew who didn't always wear his collar. He was the first priest I knew who automatically wanted you to use his first name, not 'Father', and treated you as a human being. It seems odd to think how radical these attitudes were. But it makes some of his attraction clear.

We became friends, spending more and more time together when he visited the organisation I worked for. He invited me to visit him when I was in his area seeing relatives. As the friendship built up slowly, it didn't seem odd and I didn't see it as in any way dangerous.

Even though I was in my late twenties, I was very immature and inexperienced. I'd been out with men, but I'd rejected them all on some impossible model of perfection, and never felt I could spend the rest of my life with any of them. I'd never had any longstanding relationship, never lived with a man, never slept with one. So it took a while to realise what was happening – that I was in love. I had little insight into myself, didn't spend time questioning myself, didn't think beyond the present.

Like I say, I was naive. I saw him as a wonderful man who not only was extremely nice, loving, caring, outgoing, and treated everyone he met the same, from the cleaner to the chairman, but who was also very competent in the Church, very able. He was just good to be with, I guess. He seemed an ideal man and it was flattering to feel chosen by someone so wonderful. I guess I was looking for an impossible dream, but he seemed at the time to be the nearest thing to it.

So I suppose I felt that not only was I fulfilling my social role as a woman in looking after a man and helping him pursue his important job in the world, but, because that job was in the Church, I was doing something better, looking after a holy man. I had this vision of being this self-effacing, supportive partner, in true 'wifely' fashion, submerging my life to his, being the 'woman behind every successful man', bathing in reflected glory and in the satisfaction of a job well done. I don't accuse him in any way of encouraging or supporting this outlook – it was one I acquired from the culture of home and Church. With hindsight, I can see that the relationship between a priest – God's representative on earth – and a woman only serves to reinforce the dependency of the woman, her tendency to efface herself, to not be equal.

Understanding one's motives is difficult, especially after all this time. I know people talk about 'the lure of the forbidden fruit', but the phrase is a hostile and pejorative one. I didn't set my cap at Andrew, we worked and played together and gradually became friends. If anything, his being a priest let me relax in the friendship, rather than having to ask, 'Where is this going? Is someone expecting more of me than I am prepared to give?' I didn't feel that threat with Andrew.

He declared himself first. He said, 'I love you,' made a tentative effort to give me a peck on the cheek, then got terribly upset and nervous – largely, I think, for fear of what my reaction might be. He was a very intense young man. It took me a long time to declare my love. I just couldn't say the words. I'd never said them to anyone, and I was terrified of that implied commitment. But when he eventually got me to say, 'I love you,' it was a most freeing and helpful process for me.

We then went through a period of some major ups and downs as the reality of the situation began to dawn on me. Eventually, after seven years and one false start, we committed ourselves to each other. He marked this with his dead mother's wedding ring, which I wear all the time. When I die, it will go back into his family, though they don't know that. He does not and would not wear a ring or any token – which, looking back, was a foretaste of how we would live our lives.

We committed ourselves to not having other significant relationships with the opposite sex, to devoting most of our time and energy to each other, and to sharing our lives as much as we could, given the fact that we lived many miles apart. For a while, we wrote to each other every single day and he would want to know all the details of my life: where I was, what I was doing and thinking, even what I was wearing. Like I say, he was very intense, and very much driving our lives at that time, and I went along with it. The relationship took over my life. But we couldn't keep it up at that level, and that's when some of the harder aspects of having a love affair with a priest began to emerge.

We'd never had any relationship like this before, so we didn't have anything to compare it with. We didn't analyse or reflect. I don't remember ever having any great expectations. I didn't ever really want to get married or have children, and Andrew had no desire to leave the priesthood. He didn't have any faith or theological problems with it. He had the usual problem with the clerical state, but they weren't sufficient to make him want to leave, although he was always very supportive to priests who left – this was the late sixties and early seventies, when lots of priests were leaving in the wake of Charles Davis – and to their women, who, of course, were pilloried.

He would go through phases of talking about doing an ordinary job, like being a bus driver or working in a factory, and we'd joke about how useless he'd be at doing anything practical. But that was more about getting in touch with people, experiencing ordinary life, than about leaving the priesthood and getting married. He was always looking for new experiences, new challenges. But, right up to today, he's always said that being a priest is the only thing he is sure about and wants to be.

I think part of it was because he knew that if he left there would be such disappointment and distress. I don't mean to make him sound arrogant, but he had a high profile in the Church and had many people relying on him as a counsellor and for support, and others who were inspired by his thinking and his work for a renewed Church. There was an atmosphere in which it was felt that those who left were taking the easy way out. Perhaps he chose the hard way in.

Nor did I have any problems at that time with the Church as a faith or as an institution. I was a committed Catholic and I'd met the best of the Church, the liberal wing; people prepared to think as well as work for the Church who were prepared to question and discuss alternative approaches.

So I don't think we ever sat down and talked seriously about getting married. We just assumed we could manage our relationship in this other way.

At the beginning, we did see ourselves as married. That was the metaphor and image that we used, and it was one he chose. It was good in that it echoed the extent of the commitment we'd made, but in time I realised how misleading it was, because our life didn't have the characteristics of marriage. We were not in a public situation, we hadn't publicly committed ourselves to each other, we weren't displaying our love to the community at large. Also, in a marriage one would expect the marriage to be the first commitment for both parties. With Andrew, the priesthood is his first commitment.

I once suggested replacing the model of marriage with the model of two fellow priests, but that didn't fit, either. Now we no longer talk about how we relate or live. We no longer use any words, like 'wife' or 'husband', or models to describe our relationship. I now question whether our particular model – of a very intensive relationship with no secrets and everything shared – was helpful. After a while, I stopped seeing it as an ideal and began to feel it was potentially distorting and binding for a woman.

I began to explore, and to assert myself, often rather disastrously and insensitively and, I think now, very hurtfully to Andrew. But it was a sort of delayed adolescence, caused by changing jobs, working abroad for six months, and being challenged by what I found. The friendship went on being the most important thing in my life, but I did start finding irritations with it as a way of life.

He lived in a community with other priests, but had his own suite of rooms where I could visit him. I could never stay there overnight, though. I had to time my visits for when few people were about. He was always watching for people watching us – would the postman recognise my handwriting? Would the secretary recognise my voice on the phone? Would the porter recognise I was driving his car?

If other people were around, he'd introduce me as a casual

acquaintance, someone 'who drove me here' or 'who's helping with some typing' or 'who's just passing through town'. I was never there as a special friend. Even now, I share only a small part of his public life. Two close priest friends of his have become my friends, and so has one of his brothers. Even so, when that brother got married, I wasn't invited. I was really shocked. I'd even kept the date clear. Andrew couldn't understand why I was so upset. He said, 'It was only a small family wedding.' Precisely!

In the very early days, I saw these restrictions as a worthwhile sacrifice or 'surrender' – that was a word we often used. But there were still quite a few scenes. Neither of us appreciated the strain on me of not being recognised in his life, or on him of leading his life in a split way. I just used to freeze up and withdraw, stop talking to him or anyone else. Gradually, I learned the situations to avoid for my own stability and stopped meeting his friends, but even now there's a legacy from those times.

I introduced him to a few close friends and my family as the opportunity arose. My family have never to this day asked me about it, though I'm sure they've talked about it among themselves. Recently, though, I've confided in a favourite niece, of whom Andrew's also very fond. They all love him and think he's wonderful and occasionally he gets invited to family gatherings. And the positive aspect of our relationship was shown when he officiated recently at the funerals of two close family members. He and I worked on the services together.

The time we spend together is intermittent – it can be several days at a time, then nothing for a couple of months, then a passing-through weekend visit. We plan our lives separately now. We usually manage a holiday together, but that's been quite a battle for me, partly because Andrew works extremely hard and doesn't think holidays away are important, but also because of the logistics of where we can go so we're not seen. When we go away we go self-catering, we don't stay in hotels, all very much to take account of his fears of being seen.

He makes time to come here because his life isn't too tied to a particular pattern – it's usually what fits in with his time. It's very much on my territory, though, rather than on his. Having said that, he hosted a party for a significant birthday of mine in the place where he lives. Usually, we never have that long at any one time. There isn't time to adjust to him being here, to feel at ease with everyday routine so that we can start talking about things again.

In between times we phone frequently, so we have large phone bills. Sometimes I'd prefer to write, but if I do, he never replies.

We're not seen as a couple. There are only a few places where we would be seen as a pair with a history we could talk about and a future we can refer to. Even in areas where we feel most comfortable and accepted, like among my family and friends, we're still not automatically seen as a couple.

Some of these things have got easier as time has gone by. Society has got more accepting in terms of people living together in unconventional partnerships. But it's still been very difficult over the years, not being able to talk openly about our life together, not being able to talk fondly about his achievements, or about my worries about him or both of us. Many of my workmates and friends don't know I have someone important in my life. My words get very vague – I say, 'I'm going to see a friend,' 'I've got a friend coming this weekend' – in ways I'm sure must be very obvious, but I haven't worked out another way of talking about it. It's so silly, really. I doubt if my friends would blink twice if they did know. Nor would they be bothered about questions of what is a celibate lifestyle.

When we committed ourselves to each other, we also gave each other our bodies. It was the first time we had ever seen or explored anybody else's naked body, so we were both ignorant and curious. The immediate effect for me was like being given my body as a new gift. It made me confident and relaxed in it for the first time. I was fairly inhibited before.

Having said that, we have never had an active, full sexual life. We have shared a bed together – and we still would – but we haven't had sex. Partly because we were ignorant of what to do, mainly because we felt guilty and unable to talk about if and how we could express our love in a sexual way. We wanted full physical union because we wanted to communicate in every way, but I think we were influenced, almost in spite of ourselves, by the Church's obsession with the genitals, as well as by Andrew's concern about what others would think. Maybe if one of us had been experienced we would have gone ahead, who knows?

Instead, after a couple of fumbling attempts, we gave up trying and settled for general comfort and closeness. In a sense, we didn't know what we were missing. We both exercised a great amount of self-control and I think in those early days he was intrigued by how easy he found it. It's not been that difficult for me, either, because I haven't had experience elsewhere. The hard thing was when there was a lot of contact and caressing in the early days which then stopped. I would get angry about that, because he didn't seem aware of what was happening, and I wasn't very good at explaining, since we didn't have that language between us.

I do sometimes feel sad, sometimes angry, at the loss of the development of that aspect of myself. But it was as much my choice as his. I was brought up with conventional ideas about sex being something you didn't do until you got married. It was only when I changed jobs in my early thirties and moved out of a Catholic environment that I realised most people just didn't make a fuss about those things. If people were fond of and committed to each other, it was normal to sleep together in the fullest sense. If I had known that, or if I had been clearer about what to do, I might have been more demanding. I think Andrew would have liked to experience full sexual intercourse as part of his development and participation in human life. But he had all this guilt about the priesthood and celibacy. So we have lived our sexual lives within the limits the situation imposes.

In the early days it was a problem and caused quite a lot of tension. Now we've gone beyond that and it's a very quiet part of our relationship. We don't talk about it. Maybe because we both lead fairly busy and active lives, when we're together we plump for the easy way, being comfortable and at ease with each other, and avoiding some of the very difficult questions.

But I don't think of myself as a celibate being. At the beginning, I would never have contemplated sleeping with anyone else. Now, I wonder whether I would do it if there were someone else around of whom I was fond. In my head I would, but I have turned down the last two opportunities. I think it's the sort of thing where I should have closed my eyes and gone ahead and done it, then thought about it. Having time to think about it is fatal.

I suppose the decision isn't irreversible, but there would have to be changes in our style of relationship first. Having a full sexual relationship would have made Andrew feel hypocritical, but he would make a distinction between that and having a relationship now in its twenty-fifth year. Over the years, he's become much more relaxed about our relationship and about letting people in on it than he would have been if we had had a full and active sexual relationship.

I even had a proposal of marriage last year, from someone I had known for six years. I had no idea it was on his mind. There was no way we could live together – we're too different. In the end, I said I didn't want to marry anybody, which is true. I don't want to share my house and space and time. But it made me challenge my values and assumptions. Do I want to carry on living on my own as I get older? Would I like to share with a woman friend? If Andrew turned up on the doorstep willing to marry or live with me, is it what I now want? When I told him about the proposal, he didn't ask me what my reply had been, he just said, 'I have no right to ask you that.' It was infuriating. Maybe he'd have been relieved if I'd found somebody with whom I really could be happy, because it would have released him from the trauma and claims on his time and energy.

As far as celibacy is concerned, there seem to be many interpretations and definitions. But it doesn't mean living as a non-sexual being. I've met many priests over the years who seem to have entered the priesthood because they were not able to form relationships, particularly with women, and they saw priesthood as a haven where one had to love everybody equally, which meant loving nobody to any extent in particular. They thought being unavailable meant being on the other side of a glass screen, never making any real contact. I hope the modern selection processes mean there are fewer of those people around, and looks at their ability to form and sustain mutual relationships. Sadly, the feedback I get from friends in seminaries isn't very reassuring.

Once, many years ago, I heard a priest friend refer with some pride to a fellow priest who was counselling a distressed woman. He said, 'And he made her fall in love with him.' That was a terrible thing to have done, a total abuse of power.

I'd like to see celibacy as optional. It's widely seen as creating someone who is available only for God in some unreal and disembodied way. That's not how it's supposed to be. Close and sharing relationships between a priest and a woman can be extremely beneficial to both; can give whole new layers of appreciation to the priest about what his role is and how he is to live and help and teach and support other people. I'd very much like to see a married priesthood. It could bring new problems, but many priests who leave to get married do want to continue their formal ministry. And some do it clandestinely.

One of the sadder things about our relationship is how I now feel about the Church and Catholicism. This was what brought Andrew and me together, and it's been the place of some of our closest moments. We always used to pray together and celebrate the Eucharist at home together. But I've gradually become uneasy at what seemed to be a power imbalance. We can still pray together sometimes, in silence or in word and song, in ways which can be truly healing and nurturing. But not always. Sometimes something blocks it.

I've become outraged by the institutions and structures of the Church, so much so that I have difficulty sometimes in discerning the message it's supposed to be mediating. I find it harder and harder to accept the way it's delivered through the Church structures. Because I, as a woman, am invisible in his life as a priest. I'm more and more resentful of the way the sacraments are administered through structures in which women generally are invisible, and I'm infuriated by the men in black suits and white collars standing up there in front of us, representing a hierarchy and a patriarchy.

I find all the trappings of clericalism quite unacceptable now. If Andrew brings his stock and collar with him, I hide it away and find it hard to resist the temptation to get the scissors to it. Although he's fought all his life against the system, he still represents it, and it's in the exercise of his priesthood that I am most excluded. He finds this both hurtful and hard to understand.

Meanwhile, I'm struggling to retain a lively, deepening faith, to distinguish the essence from the structure, so to some extent I've abandoned the traditional structures and, through women's groups, I am finding a liturgy, a way of expressing communally and personally my way of understanding in a way which means something deep and sincere to me.

It's still changing, of course. But we still don't talk about areas that hurt. In some ways, it may have made life easier, but in other ways it has stopped us growing. I feel we could be a lot more together because of our particular interests and abilities, but because things have gone wrong in certain areas in the past, they're no-go areas now. Sometimes it feels as though there aren't many safe areas left. And anyway, when he comes here in a state of exhaustion, he doesn't want to get into deep and difficult areas, at least not immediately.

In the last couple of years there have been several occasions when it's all fallen apart – one or other of us on the doorstep, suitcase in hand. So far, we've just managed to drag it back together because neither of us, however angry and bitter we are, wants the whole thing to stop. And even if we don't continue at that level of closeness, we don't want a complete and utter break. So we bumble along.

There are two factors which have influenced my friendship with Andrew over the last couple of years. The first is that I booked myself in for some psychotherapy, which is still ongoing. I had a rather vague feeling that there were situations in my life I wasn't coping with adequately, and my relationship with Andrew was one of them. And it's proving very helpful in getting me to unpack various difficulties, particularly about relationships. I feel more aware now of my own rights, my own value and personhood, my own needs and wishes and how to express them. I think it would help Andrew, as well, to make time and space in his life for reflection. He says he can't talk to anyone but me, but he doesn't talk to me much, and I can't help him.

The second factor is more difficult for him to cope with. Recently, I've had the joy of meeting other women who have relationships with priests, and it's been extremely helpful to me in making me realise I'm not a freak. Or, if I am, that there are other strong, competent, apparently sane, normal and lovable women around who are as well! I can't tell you how much it has meant to me to be in this group, to be able to talk to them about things I haven't been able to talk about to anybody else at all.

But my going to the first meeting nearly caused the break-up of our friendship. It still threatens it. He hates me being in the group. He's used words like 'deceit' and 'betrayal'. He sees it as a great threat, feeling that he could be exposed through it, believing that anyone malicious or keen enough could pick up the trail back to him and that this would be the ruin of his life and work. Even at our age, he believes that people will put the most negative construction on our being seen together.

I have felt torn and guilty about that, as I do now in talking to you. I do recognise that he is vulnerable, but I believe the chances of him being 'found out' are extremely low – no one in the group knows who he is – and, even if he were, the effect would be much less than it would have been, say, twenty years ago. But he has suffered greatly in the past from what has at times been almost a persecution for his views, so I should perhaps be more aware of that.

But I also feel that he doesn't recognise that I have needs, and that I have suffered all these years from the isolation, invisibility and world of half-truths we live in. He doesn't recognise what a huge relief it is for me to talk to other women in similar situations and to realise that I'm not a neurotic, idealising, unattainable-seeking wreck; to laugh and cry and shout about my life with others who know what it feels like. I believe I have a right to a space like that for myself and that Andrew devalues me by trying to deny me it. So I've stopped talking to him about it and I don't tell him when I go to meetings.

He also says that being in the support group has made me more angry. Perhaps it has. Perhaps it's made me more aware of my anger and its legitimate, as well as its twisted, roots. It's also empowered me to begin to take control of my life, to see more clearly the positive and less than positive aspects of our relationship and to show that it's OK to have some strong negative feelings, to own them and work from them. It's given me the confidence to 'come out' to some close friends in whom I'd never confided before. It's also wonderful to feel there is someone at the end of a line. I've become very close to one woman in particular and we give each other a lot of support and consolation. And, through the group, I feel *action* is possible, to change perceptions and get issues like this on to the wider Church agenda.

Like I said before, there are positive and negative aspects to a relationship like ours. The benefits of our relationship? I shouldn't be speaking for him, but I imagine it has given him an understanding of people of another gender which he wouldn't have got any other way, from reading or study or the more superficial relationships which many priests have with women. And that understanding has given him insight

58

and enabled him to be the loving, empathetic, caring person he is.

The benefits for me? Um, that's interesting. What I've got out of it is a very close and loving partnership, because quite simply I do love him. I've had the experience of loving and being loved. It's brought me great joy and growth. I've changed enormously. And I've had that experience of closeness and support and sustenance. That kind of learning and experience is valid in the whole of one's life, I think.

I feel we've shared our lives at a very deep level which has been a revelation to both of us. Discovering and rediscovering who I am, who the other person is, and how I fit into his life and the world as a whole. It might sound ethereal but it's helped me with basic questions like this. It's given me stability and a place of safety from which to go out and do new things. So it's a constant sort of recreating process. It's changed my life completely.

The biggest negative aspect, of course, is the hiddenness. In effect, I've had a hidden life, one which couldn't be openly lived or shared, which could only be spoken of in very limited circumstances involving comparatively few people. So it's been like running my life in compartments, with one sealed off from the others and from outside. Those things tend to build up hurts and resentments.

Some of the constraints were obvious from the beginning, but this area of being invisible, of having to resort to subterfuges, of not having an identity as a couple, was not obvious to me from the beginning. They're better now than they were. Now, at least, at the airport or at the station, I can go up and greet him with a hug and a kiss as I would with my other friends. At the beginning, he was always looking over his shoulder to see who else was looking at us.

But I'm still not an accepted part of his work environment or community. I am not in control. I am, in a sense, kept at arm's length so as not to disturb the status quo of his life, and in this way I feel diminished. I read a phrase about the woman being on the 'shadowy unacknowledged margins of a priest's life' – at times, it does feel very much like that. And, in this exclusion, I can feel as though I'm doing something wrong and should be ashamed – yet I don't feel I *am* doing wrong. I feel the way we live is compatible with the place we each occupy in society and the status we hold in it.

He doesn't call it keeping a secret, he calls it his private life and says it's no one else's business. But I don't want it to be private. Most people share their close friends.

All this hiddenness which characterises the life of a woman in relationship with a priest is really to protect him. And I shouldn't be speaking for him today, he really ought to be sitting here being interviewed by you as well. Yet that's impossible even to contemplate. Andrew – and I know it's the same for other priests – is extremely fearful on this issue. He really feels that his whole way of life would be destroyed if people knew about our relationship and that they would be unaccepting of the positive aspects of our love. And it's true that there is discouragement and condemnation of any exclusive female friendships, usually against the women, though some men have been virtually persecuted.

About three years ago, I read an article which first brought it home to me that I wasn't alone and that I was in something of a mess as far as this relationship was concerned. I prepared a long letter to the woman who wrote it, but when I told Andrew, he got into such a state, begging me not to send it, that I didn't. So this time I haven't told him I'm talking to you.

He feels that any outside interest would be entirely prurient and condemnatory, as it was in the Bishop Casey affair. The fear is overwhelming. It has such a hold on men who are themselves confident in their work, often occupying high places in their orders or Church structures, and seems an extraordinary example of the power of an institution to restrict and limit the life of its members.

So life feels rather uncertain at present. After the last two years, I don't feel any security about the future, so I'm reluctant to take decisions many weeks ahead as I wonder if we will still be together. In theory, as we get older we should be able to spend more time together, yet our relationship seems more threatened than at any other time. I want to continue with it, but not at any price. I can't live with the insecurity of not knowing if it's all about to collapse.

To break my rule for a moment and make a statement about him, he has no doubt that being a priest is and will continue to be what he wants. So there is no question at all for him of any change in status. That is very hard for me to accept, and it's difficult not to feel bitter and marginalised.

One starts thinking, as the sixties start to loom, what do we do in the future? I'm not at all clear where elderly priests go or what happens to them, and he doesn't have any clear idea of what he will do. But I don't see myself moving from where I live, and he doesn't see himself moving from where he lives – at least, not nearer to me. So I guess we'll continue to live and grow old at the end of telephones.

What I would be nervous about is illness or disability in either of us and that we will not be able to offer the care that a traditional married elderly couple might be able to offer each other. A few months ago, Andrew was suddenly admitted to hospital. He asked his closest friend, who's also a friend of mine, to let me know, but he didn't do so for six days, by which time I'd heard from someone else. Andrew didn't seem to understand why I was so upset and angry.

In the longer term, there's that peculiar fear which I've found in other women in similar relationships. What will happen when he dies? When my closest relationship is broken? When suddenly I – whom he would have described as the most important person in his life – am relegated to being just another member of the congregation? Part of that hidden life, unacknowledged. Who will help me mourn, who am I going to talk to in the way a bereaved person needs to talk, about the person, the life they've lived and shared, the fun, all the good things that they want to be remembered? Who will be there for me?

I wish that we, and other people like us, could go public, come out of the closet about our relationship, be open and proud about it. It could demonstrate that mutual and equal relationships are possible within the hierarchical and male-dominated Church, and could make good role models for equal, sharing and complementary roles for men and women. We could have shown, in a society where many relationships are broken and maimed, and in the Church, that there is another way of doing things, alternative ways of living and loving, which would be good for the Church as an institution, making it a more loving place to be; good for the status and dignity of women in the Church; and good for him and me as individuals and in partnership.

Angela

I've spoken to Angela over the phone a number of times during the last three years. She has an attractive voice, light and with laughter in it, so I already had a very positive image of her before I met her. I also knew she was interested in goddess worship, and she'd given me the names of various books on the subject. We arranged to meet one day while her husband was at work and she picked me up from the station and took me to the detached house she shares with him and whichever member of their family is around at the time. There, we shared a late lunch in the conservatory after she had told me her story, which she did with such fluency that it was obvious she had gone over it time and again in her own mind. In fact, when, to my horror, I discovered the tape-recorder had stopped working twenty minutes earlier, she was able to repeat the story almost word for word.

I once read an article about a young priest who was in love with a woman. He went to the Pope and told him he wanted to leave the priesthood because of her. The Pope listened and then knelt down at this young man's feet and asked for his blessing. That decided him to stay a priest. But what I'd like to know is, what happened to the woman?

I was brought up by parents who were atheists, but I always, from being a very small child, had a sense of the presence of God, whatever that means. When I was about seven, I had a Catholic friend down the road who was about to make her first Communion. She was studying the catechism and I was doing ballet, and I remember sitting in her garden one day and saying that, if she would teach me the catechism, I would teach her ballet. So the only catechism questions I have ever learned I learned from this little girl, sitting under the bushes with her.

63

In exchange, I taught her my ballet steps. We thought it was a good exchange. So I was caught up in something even then. Eventually, I went to a Catholic convent school and it was when I started there that I got caught up in the whole atmosphere of the candles, the incense, the bells, the singing and the music.

I wanted to become a Catholic but my parents wouldn't let me. When I was about thirteen, I wanted to go to a Catholic mass, because at school we only had Benediction, which I loved. There was a French au pair living next door, so I asked if I could go along to Mass with her. I had to ask my schoolfriends what to do – I remember being by the phone writing things down, like how you have to genuflect when you go in, and make a cross on your forehead; how to kneel when the bells ring, and so on. I sat at the back of this church with this French girl, just knowing that this was for me. It was in the days of the Latin Mass, so we had the plainchant and the incense and everything, and I was totally caught up in the whole sense of mystery. Without knowing anything much about the teachings of the Church, I believed it all, every single thing, from the depth of my being, without doubt.

I was told I couldn't be received into the Church until I was eighteen, so the first thing I did when I went to London to train as a nurse was to visit the local priest. One evening, with two student nurse friends as witnesses, I was baptised. After the ceremony, we all went off to a party, and that's where I met the man who was to become my husband. He was a staunch Catholic and one of the first things he asked me was what religion I was. I laughed and said, 'Catholic, as of two minutes ago!'

He was the first boyfriend I had. I was brought up to believe that nice girls didn't have lots of boyfriends. I was eighteen, he was nineteen, and it was just the young stirrings of the flesh, not what I would call real love, though I didn't realise that at the time.

We were very devout Catholics to start with and did all the right things. We wouldn't have dreamed of using contraception, for instance. The Church said no, so we used the safe period. All my children, all five of them, were planned. I adore babies and small children – I'm a mother type, I suppose.

When my fourth child was born, the midwife asked me what I was going to do about not having another child – the 'What is it about you

Catholics?' sort of thing. In those days, if any ethical issues came up, I didn't think, I used to go and ask the priest and he would tell me what to think. I thought the priest had all the answers. But this was the first time I thought, 'What has the Church got against contraception, and why am I doing this?'

I decided to investigate. I got all the CTS [Catholic Truth Society] pamphlets – that's all that was available then – and I thought, 'This doesn't make sense. Why are we denying so much? It's so unspontaneous. It can't be right.' I talked it over with my husband, and decided it was all right to go on the Pill. That was the beginning of me being a thinking person as far as my religion was concerned.

What reinforced that belief is also the beginning of my story. We had recently moved and had a wonderful band of priests who had been trained in America and who were completely different from any other Catholic priests I'd met, much more open and enlightened, encouraging people to think and express their feelings. There was this lovely Irish priest, Pat. He used to come round every Monday afternoon because I was a very ordered person who washed on a Monday and ironed in the afternoon, and he knew he'd find me in. He'd get a kitchen chair and turn it backwards to sit on it, and I'd make a cup of tea and we'd just chat. When I had my fifth baby, he even went to the school to fetch the others every day and bring them home. He was very nice.

We were part of a group of people who used to get together regularly and discuss religion. It was a very exciting, stimulating time. The Pope was saying things that we as married people could see weren't right. It was complete ignorance of married life, let alone sexuality. I remember going to confession once, really mad, and saying to a visiting priest, 'I'm going to carry on with the Pill. I see no wrong in it. And if you say I can't be a Catholic any more, OK, I shan't be.' He listened to all my ranting, then he said, 'You must do whatever your conscience tells you to do. The most important thing is to follow your conscience.'

It wasn't because I didn't believe in self-control or even self-denial or anything like that. It was because I was being told to do something that wasn't logical or reasonable. And I just wasn't prepared to follow things that weren't logical and reasonable and which, in my opinion, were even positively wrong. My husband agreed, even though he was much more of a Catholic than me – he'd always been a Catholic and he'd never really stopped and thought about it.

I remember going to another Catholic church and the priest gave a complete sermon on the theme: 'If I can do without sex, you can.' I was mad. 'What a stupid man! He isn't even living with a woman, so what temptation does he have?'

Then a priest from the US came to the parish to help Pat. I'd never met anyone like him before. He was a darling man, about my age, in his thirties, very jolly. He transformed the presbytery. It was a forever open front door. You were always invited to their private sitting room – you'd just walk in and out he'd come with this enormous bear hug and give you lovely cuddles. That was Jack.

Then Sean came to join them, just out of seminary, with long, curly black hair – we'd never seen anything like it. He was a deeply introverted young person. Terribly shy, thin, pale, very quiet, deeply spiritual, highly intelligent. After Mass, Jack and Pat would always stand outside and hug everybody. Sean used to run away and hide. I used to say to him, 'Sean, you have got to stand up and greet those people.' I had a motherly feeling for him, and he would listen and come out of his shell. I loved him dearly.

Then they started to talk about this man who was to come over from the States, this wonderful man Dominic, who was in his early forties. We had this joke about when Dominic comes. I said, 'Two Fathers, one Son and one Holy Spirit.' Jack and Pat were the fathers, Sean was the son and we were waiting for the Holy Spirit.

At this time, I was often up at the presbytery because my aunt was their housekeeper. I used to go in and help her, do the shopping and take ironing home and so on. Jack would ask me to go up for coffee and a chat, and I used to love listening to them all talk. It was post-Vatican II when everything was being discussed and psychology was coming into spirituality. A lot of priests who had trained in the States were going off on psychotherapy courses and getting much more in touch with their feelings. They were coming off their pedestals and beginning to relate to people. I was totally fascinated by this.

Dominic, the new priest, duly arrived and said Mass for the first time the following Sunday. He shook our hands as we were going in. I just chatted and introduced myself and my family. The seven of us used to sit in the front row. And we had never heard a Mass like it. He transformed the whole thing. He was a wonderful preacher, had a terrific gift of words, a wonderful presence. Yet, although he was so charismatic, he was also shy and introverted.

After Mass, I and the group of friends I was with were totally bowled over by this amazing man. We wanted to tell him how much we thought of him. Other people were shaking his hand and, as we waited, another chap, a die-hard old-school Catholic, came up to him and let rip, saying the way he had said Mass was heresy, sacrilege; he'd never heard anything more disgraceful in his life; he was going to inform the bishop. I was very struck by the way Dominic took it. He was abused. Yet he just stood there saying nothing, head down, then said, 'Thank you for telling me how you feel. If you wish to inform the bishop, you have every right.'

Our group were so upset we came round him and said, 'We're sorry. It's not how the majority feel.' I was very upset. It wasn't because I had any special feeling for him; it was just an ordinary human concern for another person whom I felt had been treated abominably on his first day in the parish. I couldn't let it go. I was restless over the rest of Sunday. I decided that on Monday I would go down and apologise. I felt I needed to do it on behalf of the parish.

When I got there, Jack was there and I asked him to tell Dominic how upset I was and how the rest of the parish thought he was wonderful. He said, 'Why don't you tell him yourself?' Dominic was in the middle of writing a sermon or reading a book or something, so he came out not quite with it. He was polite, but I could see he was itching to go back. He was uncomfortable with me and with women in general, I felt, not as outgoing as Jack at all.

I used to go to Mass most mornings, then I'd help my aunt. One or other of the priests would usually invite me to stay for coffee. After a while, I was aware that Jack was encouraging Dominic and me to be together. For example, when there was something on at the children's school and I thought it would be nice for one of the priests to come along to meet the nuns, he would say, 'Why don't you take Dominic along?'

I remember the first time I said I would take him somewhere. I'd dressed up and felt I looked good and, as he walked towards me, he stopped in his tracks. I knew he was slightly embarrassed, because it was the first time he had been 'out' with a woman.

I was his sounding-board. When we had coffee together, I would sit and listen. I was a good listener. He would want to share the books and ideas he was having about his sermon. I thought what he was saying was fantastic. Sometimes I would come in with a few ideas of my own. But in those days I used to think that priests knew everything about God, and that they were the teachers. I joked about it to him afterwards, much later. He said we were bound to fall in love. We were talking about God, who was supposed to be love, so love was bound to happen between us. At the time, I wasn't aware of anything like that happening between us at all. I liked his company and he liked mine. We were completely on the same wavelength, spiritually, emotionally and psychically.

One day, Dominic, Jack, Pat and Sean were poring over the local paper, which had a picture in it of one of the parishioners in a swimsuit. They were saying, 'She's a bit of all right.' I said, 'Yes, she looks very nice.' And Dominic said, 'She's not a patch on you, Angela.' I remember being stunned by that unpriestly remark, especially in front of the others. They went quiet.

That same evening, my husband was away and Dominic brought Aunt Mary over. We chatted, and then Mary said there was something she wanted to watch on TV. I thought he might like to see round the garden – we'd just had a summerhouse put in. So we left Mary in front of the television and wandered round the garden. We went into the summerhouse and, while we were there, he said, 'You were terrific this morning.' I had been quite extrovert, dancing, laughing and joking about the flattering comment he'd made. I was a bit embarrassed about the way I'd behaved, so I said, 'I'm sorry, I was a bit over the top.' But he said, 'No, I thought you were terrific.' And then he leaned forward and kissed me gently on the lips.

I was utterly shocked and just stood there looking at him. He was saying, 'It's all right, there's no harm in it. We're not doing anything wrong.' Then he leaned forward and kissed me again. Of course, he was the priest and priests know what's right and what's wrong, so I totally accepted what he said. Time stood still, just like in romantic fiction.

Then my little son came running in. Mary had sent him over to find us. Whether she suspected something, I don't know. So we went back, had a drink, and then it was time to go home. He very cleverly packed her away in the car, came back to get some papers and then took me in his arms and kissed me again. I guess I responded more energetically than I had the first time because he said, 'I know how you must feel. It must be hard with your husband away.' As though I was doing it just because I needed it! I was angry with him for putting us both down. I said very firmly that what I was doing was for *him* not because I was missing my husband. That that was how I felt about him, and what I wanted to express to him.

I soon became aware that he had a sort of split personality, because sometimes I would go down to the presbytery and he would reject me utterly, while another time, he would cuddle or kiss me. I never knew how I would find him. Yet something deep was growing between us on a different level. Our meetings were encouraged by Jack, who was having an affair with someone else in the parish at the same time. Perhaps he was doing it to salve his conscience. He eventually left the priesthood and married her.

Dominic was very innocent. His sexuality . . . it was like watching a flower open up. Just seeing him stroke my arm for the first time was a very beautiful experience, and he would come out with some incredibly beautiful statements, like, 'I didn't know that two people giving themselves to each other could be so beautiful.' It's hard to describe the depth of the experience and how important, sacred and spiritual it was. It was very religious. But by actually saying the words, in a way I'm diminishing the experience, because there isn't the language for it.

I feel the most important part of what I want to say, the theme if you like, is that my life's experiences have been telling me something quite different from what the Church teaches. Our relationship was just a side issue of that theme.

I had all this confusion about the rights and wrongs of it. There I was, having so-called impure thoughts about someone who not only wasn't my husband, but was also a priest – sacred. Yet it was also life-giving, life-enhancing. I was becoming a better human being for it, more loving, more outgoing, more sensitive and caring because of the love I had for him. So I couldn't understand how something so 'wrong', according to the Church's teachings, could bring such good.

I used to ask him if he thought it was wrong, and he said no, it couldn't be, because it was love and the only sin was not loving. It was nothing he felt guilty about. He knew my husband and I didn't have a very good relationship, that we were now more like brother and sister, so he wasn't depriving anyone of anything. In fact, he was enriching all my other relationships.

He was confused too. I guess the confusion for him was that the reality was different from what he had been taught. I found out only many years later that he was a heavy drinker, so a lot of the way he was behaving, his 'split personality', could have been due to that. He was also a heavy smoker. It's funny, but I know of no priest who is not either a smoker, or a drinker, which doesn't seem to be proof that the life they live is emotionally healthy.

I began to get really screwed up by the whole thing. It was seductive, this coming and going with me. I was being wooed in a very strange, deep way because he was denying me, then wanting me.

Another thing about the relationship was that all my life I had had to negate my temperament. I have Spanish blood in me, and all my life I've had to turn down the volume control for the British. Even my husband would get upset if I blew my top about something. He's very quiet. But I find it healthy to let go and express myself freely. To keep that part of me down was like being half alive.

What was happening between Dominic and me was having quite a deep effect on us both, being passionate people. We were frustrated – pure sexual frustration because we wanted each other so much. At that time, we were both celibate: he by vocation and me not because I wanted to be, but because of my husband's lack of desire. We used to have violent rows but, in a way, my anger was acceptable for the first time in my life. My passion was acceptable. He loved it. He once told me that I was beautiful when I was angry.

One Saturday, we had a blazing row over something quite trivial. He said, 'That's it. I never want to speak to you again. It's over.' I remember going to a party that night and just crying the whole evening, drinking whisky to try to take away the pain. But nothing could take it away. Next morning I thought, 'I've got to talk to him about what's happening between us. We've got to be adult about it. We've got to make a decision – even if it means ending it.' When I got there, he was still angry. I said, 'We have to talk, Dominic. We can't go on like this.

You are destroying me.' He said, 'Come and see me this evening.'

When I went back that evening, Pat answered the door. Dominic was waiting for me. I walked into the sitting room, and he took me into his arms and kissed me. He didn't want to talk about ending the relationship, only about how much he loved me. That was the first time the sexual thing began. We didn't go to bed together, but we became more intimate, and we got quite nervous about what was happening. At a certain time, he said, 'I think you'd better go.'

Things didn't get any better. There was still a lot of coming and going. Sometimes he would say, 'We can't go on like this. It's got to end.' Then he'd say, 'You can't leave me.' It was always his decision. He never said, 'Let's talk about it.'

He then went off on holiday for three weeks. I couldn't bear being without him, so I asked if I could write to him. I wrote each week while he was away, pages and pages. He was sometimes worried that I was taking away from my family and husband by loving him, so in one letter, I wrote to him about this. 'I am the mother of five children. When I had my next baby, I didn't take any love away from the ones I'd got already to love the next one. Love isn't like that. The more people you give love to, the more you love.' I wasn't taking anything away from anybody. If anything, it enriched my marriage, and helped me cope with the fact that my husband no longer desired me. To love is surely the greatest gift you can give, and we learn to love not by being told to love but by being loved.

When he began to realise how seriously we felt about each other, he asked me to tell my husband. He didn't want anything hidden. So I did. I told him that Dominic felt about me in a special way and I felt the same way but it didn't mean I had stopped loving him. My husband said, 'Do what you like, but don't tell me any of the details.'

When Dominic came back from his holiday, the first thing he did was phone me. Could I go over straight away, he wanted to show me something. When I got there, he pulled out of his pocket all the letters I had written to him. 'I have carried these letters around with me everywhere I went. I can't tell you how much they meant to me.' He was radiant with what I was giving him.

The next thing I remember was that he was away on retreat somewhere. We had been feeling very passionate towards each other before he went, really hyped up. When he came back, I so desperately wanted him. He said Mass in the chapel on his return and, during the contemplation time after the Eucharist, he came and sat down near where I was kneeling, just in front of me. So close. I could feel him knowing I was there, near him. I could feel his whole body tense. He could hardly calm his breathing.

Afterwards, I had to see him. I longed to hold him. But there was a nun from the order who worked for him, and I think she was really in love with him herself. When I went to the house she was there, too. It was like a French farce – he had me in one room and her in another and he was going between us. Then he had a phone call from another nun. He was in such a state, wanting to be with me, the nun in the other room wanting to 'talk business', and now this other nun needing him. He chose to go to her, quite rightly really, but I was feeling very selfish at the time. I was angry because I felt that my needs were more important – quite wrongly, of course.

I followed him to his car, hitting him with my handbag, I remember, and shouting, 'Damn you. What about me? Go on, then. I hope you crash your car and kill yourself. Go to hell!' I heard the car going, and as soon as it had gone, I felt mortified. I felt I had sent him to his death. I went into Jack and told him I'd done something awful. Strangely, all he asked was, 'Have you been to bed together?' I said, 'No. But the way I feel now, I'd like to go down to his bed and wait for him to come back.' I think I would have done, too, except my son wanted me to fetch him from the youth club. If he hadn't, I think I would have stayed.

The next morning, all the fire had gone out of me. I just felt so full of remorse. I'd said such terrible things to him. I went to see him to ask his forgiveness, but he interrupted me and said, 'No, I have to tell you that something very important happened to me last night. I was very angry with you. I don't think I've ever been so angry with anyone in my whole life. I thought it was over between us, that I never wanted to see you again. Then, suddenly, in the middle of all this anger, I burst out laughing. That's when I realised just how much you meant to me. If anyone else had been like that with me, I would have hated them, it would have been the end. But I realised how much I really loved you.' And that was the greatest affirmation I have ever received. When I had been at my most evil, wicked, foul, he had loved me. That's the nearest you can get to the love of God on this earth.

I'd read an article in which Pope John had said, 'Dear God, you knew before you created the world that I would become Pope. Why couldn't you have made me more photogenic?' I often said to Dominic, 'God knew before he created the world that if you and I were put together it would be dynamite. Why did he do it?' He agreed. He once said that, with our fiery temperaments, our days would have been Hell but our nights would have been Heaven. He was 100 per cent male and I was 100 per cent female. That's what drew us so much together. It wasn't anyone's fault. We were being driven into this thing in so many different ways.

Soon afterwards, the time came for him to go. He'd been there over a year and his order wanted him to go to Ireland, to prepare for missionary work abroad. I helped him clear his room, pack his things, and drove him to the airport. I'd bought a Bible, and I'd said, 'Would you write something in it? Take it, sleep on it, open it, breathe your essence into it for the next few days, before you go, so that I have it of you.' He laughed and said why didn't he give me his Bible and take mine, which was better still. I got him to write something in the Bible he'd given me and blow some kisses into it. He was amused. This feminine way of being, what's meaningful to women, was a new thing for him. I was teaching him how women are.

I wrote to him regularly. I got a couple of short, sporadic letters back, promising to write more later, then suddenly nothing. I was worried, not knowing what had happened to him. Then I got a phone call from Jack saying Dominic was over here, was coming down to church the next evening and wanted to see me. I would have thought a lot more of him if he had phoned me himself.

When I got there, our body language was amazing. I dressed totally in black – I didn't recognise until afterwards what I was expressing – and he opened the door in full priestly regalia. Whereas before he'd always been casually dressed, he now had his black suit on, dog collar, the lot. He went to give me a priestly hug and I pushed him off. We went into the visitors' room, not the sitting room, which was significant. He sat on one side of his desk, I sat on the other. I was seething. He was treating me like a priest with one of his parishioners. He wouldn't let me near him. I was pleading with him to talk to me, tell me what was going on. He was being this cold, remote, distant man and making me feel like one of those women who run after priests.

There was a little bedroom next door and I could hear someone moving around in there. When I asked, 'Who's that?' he said it was another member of the order making up his bed for the night. Then suddenly he said, 'Don't you realise that, more than anything, I want to take you on to that bed and express all my love for you?' Why did he say those words? I reached out to him but, at that moment, there was a knock on the door and Jack came in and said did I want to go into the sitting room and have a coffee or a drink. I was livid. I realised Dominic must have asked him to come and get him after a set time. Just as we were beginning to communicate as two human beings again, Jack came in and broke it up.

We went into the sitting room, but I was out of my mind with grief. I can still feel the pain. We all sat there, four men and me, and the men were saying anything and everything, but I couldn't hear a word. All I could see was this man in terrible pain and agony inside, and I was crying, but neither of us could help each other.

In the end, Dominic said he was going back to London and Jack was telling him to stay and sleep on it and talk to me again in the morning, that he couldn't leave like that. I was pleading with him to talk to me, begging him to stay and let the others help us both. But Dominic was adamant. I was inconsolable, but he just walked away, left me without a word. On the way home, I had to stop the car I was crying so much.

I wrote to the address where I knew he was staying. I wanted him to communicate with me. I wanted to be treated like an equal, an adult, in our relationship. If it was to end, then it had to be a joint decision. But I heard nothing, except every now and then one of the priests who had seen him said he was asking about me.

Five years later, I went to Ireland with a group from the parish. I wondered if he was going to be there. I knew he was still in Ireland. One evening, we all retired to a pub and there were members of his order there. I asked one of them where Dominic was and he said he was going away in the morning, why didn't I ring him? He knew how much it meant to me to speak to him. He gave me his number and I rang him. It must have been getting on for midnight.

The response was amazing. He said, 'I cannot believe it. This is the most wonderful thing, to hear from you again.' I said, 'All I wanted to do was to say I love you and I'll always love you, even though we may never see each other again.' He said, 'I love you too, very, very deeply. I have always loved you and I always will.' I said, 'It's terrible to think I'm here and you're down the road and I can't see you because you're going away.' But he said he was only going away for the weekend and could we meet up on the Monday. So we arranged to meet in a quiet chapel attached to a convent where a nun friend of mine lived.

By a strange coincidence, the Monday was his birthday. I'd always remembered his birthday and sent him cards. I was sitting in the chapel praying when I heard him come in and call my name. I came running and went straight into his arms. He said, 'Let's get out of here quickly.' He took all my luggage because I was going back home that day and he was going to take me to the airport. We went back to his house, and that's when we made love completely for the first time.

On the way to the airport, I said to him, 'We didn't pray together.' He said, 'Angela, we have just given Communion to each other.' He said, 'Because you never gave up on me, because you love me so much, I know now that I can be a better priest to my people. You've helped me go out into the world and do and give so much more.'

Thereafter, I wrote to him regularly and we met once or twice a year. It was always good to be together. He never wrote, although I used to write to him, and we spoke on the phone. Then he went to South America for a few years. I carried on writing to him and, when we next met, he told me my letters had been a life-saver, because he was often frightened and lonely out there. Just to know that someone cared about him was very important to him. I feel I carried him through that bad experience.

The last time I saw him he was back in Ireland and I was going over to Cork for a wedding, so I wrote and asked if we could meet up at my hotel. It was such a long time since we'd been together. I spent the morning in church praying, asking for God's protection on our love. He came over and we spent the whole day together. Then he went off in the evening.

I don't know what went wrong after that, as he had seemed very happy and close to me that day, but I might have made a mess of it somehow. My husband and I hadn't been on holiday because he told me he couldn't get away, but he said, 'Why don't you go off on your own?' So I wrote to Dominic, 'Wouldn't it be great if we could holiday together?' I don't know whether that frightened him away or what, but the next time I phoned him, he came to the phone and said, 'Who is this, please?' – pretending he didn't recognise my voice. He was totally and utterly distant. 'I really don't want to speak to you. Just get out of my life.' I was saying, 'What's the matter? You can't be like that. What have I done wrong? Please tell me. Talk to me.'

It's many years since we met, and many years since that last phone call. I hate thinking how many years it is. I have written and written, but I've heard nothing. Why do I hang on? Because he told me, all those years ago, how important it was to him that I never gave up on him, however bad he'd been to me. Because he told me he was a better priest because he knew I'd always love him. Because I don't accept that he has the right to end the relationship without me being part of that decision. So I can't let go because he has tied me to him.

I have never loved anyone else this much, in this way. I doubt I ever will again. It was more than a physical attraction, it was a meeting of two minds and two souls. There were moments together, just sitting with him, when there was total transformation from this earth to something else. It wasn't sexual, it was much deeper, very spiritual. This sort of love only comes once in a lifetime and some people never experience it. In spite of all the pain, I feel I have been touched by God in a very special way, and I only wish that Dominic feels that way now, too. If he could say something like that to me, then it would make all the suffering worthwhile.

I'm not angry with him. He's merely a product of a Church that seems to me to have become more and more separate from the Christian message. Jesus had respect for women and tried to show they were equal in God's eyes. Dominic handled our relationship in a dominant way and never respected me enough to allow me any say in his decisions.

A very close friend of mine can't get over the fact that, when I start talking about him, even now, I'm transformed again. It's like the energy is still there. What we were for each other is still alive and still affects me, so how can I regret it? When we met, I was born again. I became me, the person I really am. How can I regret that? Because of our love, we were taken out of a frozen, inhuman sleep into a life there's no going back from. That's how I feel.

So much good has come from the experience. I have been able to give so much to others because of it. That's proved to me that it can't be wrong. But my sadness is about what it might have done to him. He had the opportunity to take a gift from God and he refused it. He has to live with that. These men stand up and preach about love. What are they talking about? I loved him so much that if he had asked me to end it, I would have done. But he never asked. Why? I'd have done anything for him. Maybe he didn't have the courage; maybe he still wants me in his life, even from this distance. Will I ever know?

My friend the nun eventually told me he had been sent home from South America because he was drinking heavily. I was full of hope that at last he was going to get some help and, if he had a good therapist, he would start facing up to the reality of our relationship, talk to me, discuss it with me and, if it had to be, say goodbye properly. But I've heard nothing.

All these years later, I'm still with my husband. I never thought about leaving him. I still care for him. He's been a very loving father. I really believe you can love more than one person at a time. Also, Dominic was a good priest and I would never have wanted to take him away from his vocation. I just can't see why we couldn't go along as we were doing, meeting up once or twice a year. It would have been enough – better than this.

He did once say that if he had met me before he became a priest, he would have seriously considered whether he wanted to be one. He also felt angry when he realised what a beautiful thing his priesthood was making him miss out on – not just sex but real love. It was so good, why should he have to deny himself that? Did he ever think about what he was doing to me, and does he ever wonder now what he has done to me, ending it like this? *That* makes me angry.

His biggest fear was that he wouldn't be able to live without me. But now he has to, and it was his choice. So it's like a bereavement, except that I have something the bereaved don't have – the knowledge that he is still alive and the hope that he may come back to me some day, somewhere.

Now I can't bear to go to church. It hurts too much and, anyway, it doesn't mean anything to me any more. My sons are atheists but very good, caring men. My daughters believe in a spiritual power, but don't like the Christian Church expression of it. They are good, caring women. I lost my faith, but I suppose that provided an opportunity for my own personal spirituality to grow. I see it as growing up and not needing a parent faith any more.

I was very angry with God at first. I couldn't accept the God of the male-dominated Church any more. Then I began to think about God as a woman, a mother, a creator and nurturer, who is peace-loving, gentle and all those other rich qualities of the feminine. I'd like to see more partnership between men and women in a religion. Then this world of ours would be in balance and maybe the Garden of Eden would come back. It would be a religion where the feminine qualities would be as valued and respected as the masculine qualities. Our planet Earth would be respected and nature would be cared for and enjoyed. Our sexuality would be a cause for celebration!

Why have we got as our symbol Christ on the cross? This awful, bleeding, broken, horrendous violence? Surely the birth of Christ should be the symbol, not his death. Isn't there enough suffering, hurt and pain without looking for it? Our symbols should be around creation and companionship.

I see the love between a man and a woman, including the sexual expression of that, as a wonderful gift from God to help us through the ups and downs of life, to comfort and sustain us. But the Catholic Church denies this gift to its ministers and looks down on the rest of us because of it. We should be celebrating life, not denying it.

I miss the companionship of church, and the Catholic Church still has the best 'incantations' – the good old Catholic Mass and Benediction take a lot of beating. But now I meditate for twenty minutes twice a day and, after my morning meditation, I pray. I ask that I may stand by Dominic's side as he offers up the mystery of the Eucharist – whatever that is or whatever it means – and I share it with him. I see the Eucharist as a celebration of birth rather than death. A moment when Heaven and Earth meet.

There's a prayer which was written in the twelfth century which says that when you love someone you are in the presence of God and therefore in the presence of the one you love. That's how I feel. That's what I believe in.

Bernadette

I first met Bernadette three years ago, at the start of my research. A small, middle-aged woman, she works as a social worker in a large Midlands town. Although I have met her three times over the years, I have never been to her house. On each occasion, she would take me to a café or wine bar – there was always somebody else at home, she said. For our last meeting, because I wanted to tape-record her using a dictaphone and lapel mike, we spent half an hour trailing from place to place trying to find a private space. In the end, we sat unofficially at a table in a corner of the town's large public library, fending off the occasional curious employee and suspending our conversation if anyone got too close. Bernadette likes to be flippant, maybe as an antidote to the responsibilities of her job and her other counselling work, or maybe as a defence against possible further unhappiness.

I was quite religious when I was at school. I joined all the usual societies – the Children of Mary and Legion of Mary, that sort of thing – and I used to go to Mass in the mornings before school. My father used to tell me off about that. Actually, he used to hit me a lot. I was physically abused from when I was very small, and my Catholicism was another stick to beat me with. He was brought up a Catholic himself, but because he and my mother married in a non-Catholic church – my mother is Church of England – my father's sister fell out with him. And, although he decided to have me baptised and brought up a Catholic, he was actually quite anti-Church and used to hide in the toilets in the yard when the priest came.

When I was about seventeen, for some reason he returned to the Church. So he and my mother were married again in the sacristy and I was standing there with the holy water and the brush. Then he started going to church all the time. I kept on as a Catholic. I married a Catholic in a Catholic church, a full nuptial Mass, all the trimmings. I was twenty-one at the time and my husband came from a staunch Catholic family, but the marriage didn't work as I discovered he was bisexual. So I threw him out.

I'd met him at a ceilidh, and I knew him for a year before we married. I'd no idea at that point that he was bisexual – I was a good Catholic girl and you just didn't know about such things. But I didn't divorce him on those grounds. I divorced him on the grounds of mental cruelty and failure to maintain. It was very difficult. This was 1966, remember, and we were both practising Catholics. And I had a daughter. I got pregnant on honeymoon and I'd been married only nine months and three days when my daughter was born. It wasn't long after that that I threw him out. Then my daughter and I went back to live with my parents. Two years later, I went to Latin America, on the missions.

At the time I was nursing. I wanted to do something different and I saw this advert in *The Universe* for volunteer missionaries. We had three weeks of training and then we were sent to various places. I went out to Bolivia, leaving my daughter with my parents. And that's when I met Vin.

He was about forty-six and I was twenty-seven. When I met him, he was in charge of the student nurses and social workers. There were four of us who flew out to Bolivia, and two mission helpers there already. My jobs were to look after the house, supervise the cook and the cleaner and the gardener, do the shopping, and do a bit of teaching. There were thirty-five students in residence and I had to keep an eye on them as well, make sure they were eating properly and so on.

It was funny, really, because he'd come home from the college and I'd be there to greet him. He said it was like coming home to a wife – 'Oh, it is nice to come home.' Then Christmas came and he said, 'This is the best Christmas I've ever had in my life.' It was just a matter of somebody to care for. There wasn't a real, what you might call sexual, relationship at that time. I mean, I'd kiss him when he came in, but just like the rest of the community. It just developed naturally.

I'd had one or two involvements with priests in the past, before I was married, but only on a superficial level, no emotional attachment. There was one who was upset when I married and who went off to America. He's still there – I went to visit him a few years ago. It turned out he's had a lady friend all the time he's been there, though I don't know whether or not sex is involved.

Then one year, on a pilgrimage in Rome, I met a priest from Wales, Tom. We ended up having an affair for a couple of years. I'd go and see him or he'd come up here. We did sleep together, yes. I was very naughty, I suppose. But I didn't have guilt feelings. I don't know why. He did. He even once deliberately drove his car into the back of another one on his way back from seeing me. But he was all right.

Vin, though, was the serious involvement. We'd spend a lot of time talking and sometimes he'd take me to meetings. After a while, the others got a bit jealous, and when we went out once or twice to friends of his for dinner, one of them in particular would be sitting up waiting for us when we came back. 'Oh, hello, Marie. Doing night duty?' we'd say.

One evening we were just talking and the others drifted off and we sort of drifted into his room. We started kissing and cuddling and it went on from there. Sometimes, at night, I used to creep past the servants' quarters into his room and yes, OK, we'd spend some of the night together in the same bed, but we never, ever had intercourse. He was afraid of sex. If he thought he was getting too excited, he would get really upset. I've never seen anybody so brainwashed. Sex had evil connotations for him. It was the way he'd been trained. And he was absolutely petrified of having an orgasm. I mean, that would have been the end of the world for him. And to my knowledge he never did.

There was another priest in the house as well, so we had to be very quiet, but I'm sure he knew. Eventually, after about nine or ten months, it got too much for Vin. He felt scared, distressed, so he went and told his superior. He didn't tell me he was going, he just went, so of course, I was sent for, wasn't I? I said, 'Well, we haven't done anything wrong.' But the superior said people in the house weren't happy about the relationship; it was too personal, and it was upsetting Vin's spiritual development. I insisted that we hadn't done anything to be ashamed of, that there was no question of us having been indulging in illicit sex, and that I for one was happy with the relationship.

I'd have been happy staying in Bolivia with him. I had no problem with the relationship spiritually, though psychologically and from a human point of view, it was a problem. But in the end I agreed not to extend my year out there as I'd planned to do. So I resigned.

As for Vin, I didn't speak to him again. They whisked him away, first to Columbia, then back to England, and I haven't heard from him since. I mean, I tried writing to him, and I sent back a couple of things of his. But I've had no further contact with him. He was probably forbidden to ever contact me again.

So I came back to England. I felt very angry. Very angry and very, very upset. I cried all the time on the plane. I was devastated, and it was quite a while before I gathered myself together. I loved him. And I suppose, in a way, I still love him. Any man I've been out with since has had to measure up to Vin. And it's impossible because he was an outstanding character, really, like a lot of his order. They're trained to be that way.

When I came back, I took up my nursing again, working nights, and during the day I went to college. First, I did my A-Levels, then I went into social work. I also got involved in the Samaritans, something I'd first heard about through Vin. Everything I did was for Vin, really. He changed my life. Going out to Bolivia, meeting him, living in the same community, it all changed my life completely.

On the downside, when I came back, I'd had enough of the Church. I lapsed for about twelve years. I took my daughter away from the Catholic school and sent her to a county primary and then to a state comprehensive. I thought, 'If that's what the Church does for people' – thinking of Vin, not myself – 'then I don't want anything more to do with it.' And, for twelve years, I didn't. Nor did my daughter. In fact, she doesn't go to church at all now. She just laughs at it.

When I came back, I took up again with Tom. For a while I worked as his housekeeper, living with him in the presbytery. It ended when he said it was too much like being married and he couldn't cope with the guilt. That's when – well, I took an overdose. It was very naughty of me. I did it there, in the presbytery, and I ended up in hospital. Tom took me. Or, rather, he sent for the doctor and the doctor got me into hospital, and between them and the psychiatrist they had me sectioned.

I was on a twenty-eight-day order for safety, for self-protection, but I didn't like it so I walked out, and they couldn't do anything about it.

I went to Scotland, which wasn't bound by the same Mental Health Act. I didn't stay very long, just long enough for the heat to die down. It was November, terribly cold and I was in this bedsit, frozen to death, putting money into the meter. It was horrendous, it really was. But my parents never knew. Nobody knows. I just told my mum I'd gone looking for a job.

Men, honestly, they're not worth it. When I first got back in touch with Tom, I told him about Vin. And he said that, while I was away, he'd had someone stay with him, a friend who was a widow and who'd turned to him in her trouble. So he'd decided to bed her, as another experience, and she had been absolutely shocked: 'Where've you learned that from?' So that was another reason for sectioning me, to keep me quiet – and, as it happened, the psychiatrist was a chaplain and the doctor was also a Catholic. So this was the Church closing ranks.

Anyway, that was the end of that. But at no time did I feel religious guilt. I just don't believe in celibacy, I suppose. A lot of priests like it because they have everybody running stupid after them. If they were married, nobody would take any notice. I mean, our parish priest has gone to Lourdes this week with a load of women, and they'll be all over him and making a fuss. If he had a wife, they wouldn't give a damn. That's why I think they're quite happy – and it's common knowledge that a lot of them have a bit on the side.

I've had other opportunities. There was a priest who came to our parish after years with an order in France. Now, our parish priest at the time was an absolute swine. He and the housekeeper didn't want anybody else, and they made Patrick's life so miserable that he used to go round in the afternoons to all the old folk's flats and sit there, because they'd give him tea and biscuits and it would be Father this and Father that. I was president of the Legion of Mary at the time, and he was made our spiritual director, so he used to come and visit me regularly. 'I have to come here,' he'd say, 'before I can face those two.'

Once he kissed me and there was a little bit of silliness – nothing deep, no intercourse or anything like that. He thought he was being very daring, but I was just looking after him.

Then he was given a parish miles away and he couldn't cope with the responsibility. Looking back, I think he was a bit unstable. He was so depressed, I ended up trailing backwards and forwards every night and sitting with him. In the end, I told him to go and see the Bishop, and the Bishop sent him back to France for psychiatric help.

Now he's in another parish with a priest around his own age, a really kind Irish priest. So he's quite happy, though he still toddles round to see the old folk. I haven't had any contact with him for a while.

He was quite a holy man, a good man, and I think, where I was concerned, he probably thought, 'Here's my chance to know a little bit about life.' He was so unworldly, really, and he'd never had an experience of anything like that before. So it was just friendship, really.

I suppose people would say I'm the villain because it's always the women that tempt the priest, isn't it? It's not that the priests should know better, that they've got greater spiritual resources than the rest of us. It's always the women who do the bad things. Maybe I should have felt guilty that I'd taken them away from God temporarily. But it's no good feeling that. That was yesterday and tomorrow is another day.

I try to do good to balance the bad. You've only one life, after all. I've enjoyed the experiences, though I've paid for them, too, emotionally, in terms of anguish. It's just like virtue being its own reward: sin is its own reward as well – if you can call it sin. People don't use that word nowadays, do they? One priest said to me a few weeks ago, 'The trouble these days is that we've forgotten about sin.' I said, 'Oh, there's still plenty of sin about.'

I can't remember if I ever confessed them. I might have done, but like anything else, you come out and do it again, don't you? If I wanted to talk about it, there's a Cistercian Abbey in Leicestershire I go to a couple of times a year, and I'd tell them. They hear everything, and they don't bat an eyelid.

But I wouldn't do it now, not again, because I remember the pain, and at my time of life I can do without it. I wouldn't want to inflict that pain on anyone else, either. If I thought someone was thinking about it, I'd try to counsel them out of it. I'd be able to give what you call a forcefield analysis – these are the pros, these are the cons, let's weigh them up.

I know an awful lot of priests and they're very, very selfish. They're taught in seminary to care for people but when it comes down to it, it's the individual soul that counts and they must guard their soul against all comers. It's always *my* soul, *my* priesthood that's most important.

I eventually went back to the Church because my mother was very ill. You know how you turn to God when you've got problems? Well, I prayed to Our Lady saying, 'Give me my mother back,' and Our Lady was saying, 'But I'm your mother.' So when my mother recovered, I started going back to church. I do the readings, I've even become a Eucharistic minister, taking Communion to those who can't get to church. I've got some Eucharists in the car at the moment, actually. But I don't feel there's any contradiction there, not at all. It's funny, Vin once asked me if I'd ever been baptised. Maybe I'm just amoral, or maybe I just didn't take on board any of the brainwashing. But, oh, gosh, no, no one knows. They'd die!

I don't follow the teachings of the Church slavishly. There are lots of things I disagree with. I mean, it doesn't matter to me whether Our Lady was a virgin or not, or even whether Christ was married. So I'm not traditional. Not at all. I take from the Church that which can lead me nearer to God, and I leave the rest.

For instance, I think birth control is a matter for the individual. With Tom, I used the diaphragm and then I went on the Pill. I wouldn't like to see an Abortion Act because of the trauma it causes to the women, but I think divorce should be allowed, though only after a lot of counselling. I've never wanted to marry again, though, not after Vin. I would have married him, oh, yes. And I'd certainly like to see celibacy being optional. Although, on the other hand, if there were a married priesthood the wife might get under the feet of those involved in parish work. Also, our priests live on what comes in from the collection plate, and they wouldn't get as much help from the laity if they had wives, because they'd think she could do the work. So I do have mixed feelings about it.

Thinking about it now, with all the experience I've had of counselling, I think having had a very cool relationship with my father, and the fact that he abused me, probably explains why I've been attracted to priests. Because, in a way, they are nice people; they're not likely to hurt you in that sense, they're likely to be kind and understanding. And the fact that they're quite a bit older, as well. So for me, it's friendship and maybe a father figure. Also, because we're both involved in counselling, it's like you're on a similar wavelength. Both committed to helping people.

Some people make a joke of it, say they're missing sex, but it's not just that. It's the warmth and the comfort and the companionship and the understanding, what they would otherwise get from a wife. That's what they're looking for. If a priest needs sex, he'll go down to the red-light district and pick someone up. People are people and no one's a saint. The Irish say the temptations for a priest are Punch and Judy – drink and women. And there is a bit of excitement in it.

But it's got nothing to do with a woman's lack of self-esteem. If anything, having a relationship with a priest bolsters your self-esteem, to know that someone so educated and intelligent cares enough, and thinks you're worthy enough, to have that relationship with you.

Angie Crawford-Leighton

Angie and her husband John are secretaries of the Advent Group for married priests and their wives. They live on a housing estate in an area of high unemployment in Essex. John, now seventy-three, is increasingly housebound through ill health. Yet both he and Angie, a warm and lively woman in her early fifties, do their best to be cheerful and welcoming, sharing fish-and-chip lunches, bottles of wine, and their thoughts on social, political and religious issues. Like so many couples in the same situation, they have had to face numerous hardships – financial, emotional, physical and social. But they have faced them together, publicly. They can present a united front to the world because John left the active ministry when he and Angie fell in love. They have been together nearly twenty years, and still obviously love and care for each other. During our long conversation – and in subsequent telephone calls – Angie was anxious to stress the positive nature of their story. 'I want to give a bit of hope and encouragement to people in an impossible situation,' she said.

My first encounter with John was on my daughter's First Communion day. Long before that, from my late teens, in fact, I'd been at odds with the Church and its teaching. I couldn't help but balk against the blinkered doctrines of my childhood. It was only when my own children reached school age and were accepted into the local Catholic school, even though they weren't baptised – it was the nearest school to where we were living – that I began to have any contact at all with a Catholic community. With a broken marriage and divorce behind me and a new house in a new town, it was a new start on my own with the little ones. It was an idyllic period.

After my daughter had been at the school for about a year, it started. She used to come home and ask, 'What's a Catholic? Why don't we go to Mass?' Through all their baby years, I'd never wanted them to be baptised into something I'd struggled with so hard as a child. I'd decided to bring them up to the best of my ability with a sense of fairness, to be kind to each other and to treat other people with courtesy. But when she kept coming home and saying, 'Mummy, Sister Josephine says . . .' I knew I'd got some hard decisions to make. So I went to see the local curate, because he dealt with school matters.

He was very good, very patient and sympathetic. So, after several meetings, I agreed to give it a try and take the children to Mass every week. Then, of course, all my daughter's peer group were going to make their First Holy Communion, and she couldn't, because she hadn't been baptised. I was beginning to feel that maybe the Church did have something to offer them, so I agreed to have them baptised. There was no fuss, no celebration, just an ordinary day after school with my sons' shirt-tails hanging out, and a lot of dirty knees. They held their own candles and grinned at each other across the font. And, in a way, it meant something to me, too. It seemed right.

That First Communion day was the first time I had received Communion for about seventeen years. It had a tremendous impact on me. When I stepped into the aisle behind my daughter in her lacy white dress, I wanted to cut and run, but there was no escape. The parish priest, John, was standing in front of me, greying temples and half smiling. As he said, 'The body of Christ,' I thought he looked rather benign and reassuring. I had no idea then how much he would change my life. But that day was a turning point and, although I wouldn't go as far as to say that it was like a great light on the road to Damascus, I did begin a tentative journey of faith.

When my youngest was five, I decided to get a job. I wanted a bit of independence, and I wanted to support my family. While I was looking for one, I had a winning ticket in a church raffle. The prize was to be collected from the presbytery. When I went there, the housekeeper came to the door looking dreadful. She had a migraine and was ashen-faced and wearing dark glasses. I asked if I could do anything for her and she asked if I was any good at washing up. That was the start of a friendship that's lasted to this day. It also provided me with a part-time job. Frances, the housekeeper, needed extra help in the house and it was absolutely ideal. The house and church adjoined the school and the hours fitted in perfectly with school.

I loved working in the presbytery, answering the telephone, greeting visitors at the door, even everyday cooking. It was a happy, busy house and no two days were ever the same. I saw John briefly each day, usually at mealtimes, but he was something of a whirlwind, in and out all the time. He never seemed to do anything at half-speed and ceremonies, meetings and parish activities seemed to take up all his time. When he did sit down occasionally for a coffee and a chat, I enjoyed his company. He was interesting and friendly, so *ordinary*, not a bit like the sanctimonious, aloof priests of my youth. We had a lot in common as well – a love of painting, music, books – so we never ran short of things to talk about.

One winter evening, on a rare trip out with a girlfriend, I met a man she worked with. He was pleasant, single and Catholic, and we met regularly after that. The children liked him and, after a couple of months, we decided to get married. I *thought* I loved him. But I married him for all the wrong reasons, really, because I was looking for a father for my children.

I said to John, 'I'd like to be married in church. Would you do it?' He agreed and, because he knew money was tight, he offered the use of the presbytery for guests after the ceremony. It was just a small wedding – the only guests were my parents, my brother and his family and two friends. My mother-in-law refused to have any part of it because she didn't think her only son should be marrying a divorcee with children.

After the ceremony, we gathered outside for photographs and I looked round for John. He'd taken off his vestments by this time and he was leaning against the porch door, lighting a cigarette. I caught his eye and, just for a second, I saw this strange look there, a sort of haunting sadness. Then it was gone. That look was my abiding memory of the whole day. I can still see him there, keeping himself apart from it all, lighting a cigarette and just looking at me after he had conducted my marriage ceremony.

I suppose the marriage never really started. Life went on, but I soon realised I should have done the honest thing and not married my husband because I had such a feeling for John. By that time, he was my very, very dearest friend. He became my confessor and counsellor, and I could trust him with my innermost thoughts, and often did. He was always there. He of all people knew how fragile my marriage was and he tried ever so hard to advise and encourage me. He even put me in touch with the Catholic Marriage Advisory Council. But I didn't realise how fond of him I was until he had a bad road accident.

Frances often stopped at my house for a coffee on her evening walk with John's dog, and this particular night she was late and came in looking very worried. John and a parishioner friend had gone out for the day to Burnham-on-Crouch, where John kept an old boat on the river. He used to go down to it on his day off. They had been due home hours ago, and she'd just had a phone call to say they'd been in an accident and they were both in hospital. I simply wasn't prepared for the leaden feeling in my stomach. I felt absolutely desolate. Frances said, 'It's OK, Father's only got a broken nose.' In fact, he was quite seriously hurt. He not only broke his nose, he completely smashed his face. The nose was missing, his jaw was smashed, he had swollen black eyes, everything. He'd broken some of his ribs, and there was a massive haematoma on one side where the gearstick had gone into his thigh. He was really very poorly.

Frances was a bit phobic about hospitals, so the following morning she bargained my share of the housework in exchange for me visiting the hospital. That first visit was a dreadful shock to me. John looked awful, unrecognisable. After twenty-four hours, it was decided to transfer him to another hospital where there was a facial surgery unit. I offered to accompany him. All the time I was conscious that there was more to this man than I was letting other people see. Yet there was never a word said between us, not a look or anything. It was only afterwards that he told me how much my visits meant to him.

The day he was transferred, we waited in his room for the ambulance. He lay on the bed, I sat on the chair. We were both reading in silence. And the feeling was one of tremendous peace, not speaking, no contact between us, just being there.

After a few days in the new hospital, the surgeon said to him, 'We're going to rebuild your nose. What did it look like before?' Anyone else would have said, 'I'll show you a photograph.' Not John. He just said, 'Oh, any nose will do.' So they did the best they could with what was left – and the nose he has now is not a patch on what it used to be!

Eventually, he came out of hospital, facing a long convalescence. He was weak and handicapped by this awful contraption to keep his jaw in place. Teeth cemented together, rods coming out of his mouth attached to a steel 'halo' screwed into his skull. He could only eat with a straw and had lost a lot of weight. For the next few weeks, my shifts at work were taken up with liquidising his food and making him comfortable. Once the metalwork was removed, he began to slowly get back into the routine of parish life. Celebrating Mass was difficult at first as he found it very taxing to speak and, for a while, he was unable to preach.

It was the beginning of the long hot summer of 1976 and, one gloriously sunny morning, he decided a visit to the boat might be good for him. I offered to go, along with another parishioner who was going to share the driving. It was an ideal day for tinkering around and tidying up the boat for the summer.

We had a pub lunch, and on the drive back home I had the most awful indigestion – probably from stretching across the boat engine all afternoon to remove a stubborn bolt. I was doubled up in the back of the car, hugging my middle. John was in the passenger seat and, at some stage on the way home, he leaned across the back of his seat and said, 'Are you all right?' As I leaned forward to reply, I felt the briefest brush of his hair across my forehead and it was just like an electric shock. I shook all over. It was the first real physical contact I'd ever had with him and it felt so intimate. Just his hair and the smell of boat oil on his jumper. I felt this closeness, this realisation of how I felt about this man.

After a few moments, he reached back between the seats and felt for my hand. His was warm and strong, and I remember thinking, 'Why is he doing this? It's only making things worse.' But I wouldn't let go. I just held on to him until we got off the dark roads and it was light again. And as I sat there listening to them talking in the front, I thought, 'That's all I'm ever going to have of him. And it's all I need. I'll never forget.'

When we arrived back at the presbytery, John said he would drive his friend home. To me, he just said, 'Let yourself in and get your bike. I'll see you tomorrow.' I went in and walked through to Frances's room. She'd gone to bed. I was shaking like a leaf and couldn't get warm, even though it was a lovely warm night. All I could say to myself was, 'I can't go home. I don't want to go home.'

I put the fire on and sat there smoking cigarette after cigarette. Then I heard the key in the door. John came in and he was like a sheet, absolutely white and visibly trembling. He slumped against the wall and said, 'We've done it now, haven't we?' I could hardly speak. I just whispered, 'Yes, I think we have.' I remember I stood up as he came towards me, and his exact words were, 'I haven't kissed a girl for twenty-eight years and I'm going to do it now.' And he did. And the world turned upside down. There was nothing else in the world. There was no husband, no kids, nothing. No priesthood, no 'What about the rules?' There was just us.

Yet before that time, there hadn't been a word or hint of love between us. Not a word. We hadn't planned anything, we hadn't worked it out: 'This is silly. I'm fifty-six and you're thirty-five, you've got three little children and I'm an old celibate.' We hadn't figured it out because we hadn't realised there was anything to figure out. It simply happened in a moment.

We sat and talked for what seemed like forever, and suddenly the enormity of it all hit me: 'What am I doing? We can't do this – he's a priest. I have to go home. My husband and children are in bed and I have to get them up for school. I have to be normal.' John had to be up for seven o'clock Mass. I was still in a state of shock when I rode my bike home at five o'clock. When I got there, I thought, 'This isn't happening. I'm imagining it. I'll go into work at nine and he'll pretend nothing's happened, so will I and we'll just carry on with our lives.'

I took the children to school as usual. My husband went to work. I went very nervously into the presbytery and found that John had collapsed at Mass that morning. He'd got halfway through the service and he'd passed out. I found him sitting in the kitchen. As soon as we looked at each other, I knew it was all real. He came over to me, put his arms around me and said, 'We have to tell the Bishop.'

Later that day, we drove to Bishop's House and I waited outside while John went in to see him. He refused to see me. Apparently, when John was telling him, he puffed so much on his pipe that he nearly set himself alight: 'Midsummer madness, John. I'll give it six months at your age.' He wanted John to go away for a while to a monastery and rethink, but John made it clear we'd made up our minds and nothing would change that.

That evening I told my husband. He had a large whisky and went straight to his mother's, where he stayed. We had been married for eighteen months. He didn't try to talk me out of it. He made it very easy for me, no arguments, no questions. He took off his wedding ring, went into the garden and buried it. In a way, I think he was relieved. I hope he was. I don't know if he ever forgave me. I never saw him again after that.

John and I told the children the next day. They thought it was rather exciting – 'Father's going to live with us!' Before we moved, my daughter had all her little friends in the garden saying, 'Yes, he's in there. Go and look!' Squealing little girls would come in – 'Oh, look, he's in there!' It was a great adventure for them.

As for my parents, my mother took an awful lot of stick from people in her parish when it became known, but she understood why we'd done it and gave us a lot of support. It was harder for my father. It took him a few days before he could bring himself to accept what had happened. Then he came over to see John, to shake his hand and say, 'We're on your side,' even though they knew it was going to entail an awful lot of problems.

Within a week, John had moved out of the presbytery and into my house. We lived among packing cases, boxes and clutter during this really hot weather. That first week, I felt as though we were under house arrest because the press were virtually camped out on the doorstep. I never spoke to one reporter, but it was all over the papers, with quotes supposedly from me – 'My Hell, by Priest in Love' was one headline, and 'Priest in a Crisis'.

The oddest thing was that a lot of the comments from John's parishioners were along the lines of 'I could understand it if she had run away with the curate, but to run off with the old fellow!' They couldn't believe it. Some of them reckoned the trauma of the accident had affected John's judgement, and nearly all of them saw me as the villain. I think there probably would have been the same reaction even if I had been single. The biggest crime seemed to be that I was responsible for taking him away from the Church and his priesthood. Scarlet Woman, Jezebel, Eve – all these labels are stuck on a woman who has a relationship with a priest.

So it was a very stressful time. Naively, I thought it was going to be simple – love will conquer all. In the event, it has. If I hadn't had the love that I have for him and the love he has for me, we would never have survived.

Individual support was patchy. We had some genuine support from a few priests, friends and neighbours, but we also had anonymous offensive letters and phone calls. As far as the Establishment was concerned, we were beyond the pale. The Bishop's spokesman told us we had to go to Mass outside the area, where we wouldn't be recognised. So every Sunday we drove to Bow in the Westminster diocese – an hour there and an hour back, which unsettled the children. They couldn't really understand why we had to do that.

We also had to move house. Everyone knew us where we were. The local authority – I had a council tenancy – were very good. They arranged an exchange. That's when we moved here. We liked the house and the place. We never realised then that it was an unemployment blackspot.

I had no job any more. John was unable to find a job at his age, though he tried very hard. He did do voluntary probationary work, which was very rewarding in its way, but it was only four years until he was sixty and classed as unemployable. So, no, it wasn't easy in the beginning, and sometimes I wondered if I'd been quite fair to uproot the children. I felt confident that they were secure, happy little people so long as we were all together, and that's the way it's turned out. But they all had to move schools, make new friends and start afresh.

In the early years, it was difficult for John, adjusting to family life and the strange ways and demands of little ones. It was all so new to him, a whole new way of life with different worries and responsibilities. He's often said, 'It's a long, hard road from Father to Daddy.' There's a distinction between Dad and Father. I mean, even if he has no part in your birth, Dad is the one who will sit up with you all night when you've got measles, and hold the bowl while you are sick. He's the one who runs you back and forwards to school football, and he's there when your first girlfriend or boyfriend lets you down. Against all the odds, John *earned* the name Dad, and gradually we all gelled together. The children love him dearly, and our great bonus now is our granddaughter.

Quite early on, the local parish priest heard that we were having to travel to Bow to worship and said he couldn't see any reason why we couldn't attend the local church. My parents had moved nearby so, when we started going, we always sat with them at Mass. They were delighted we could all be together. Two of the children joined the choir and, gradually, over the years, we became part of the community and were accepted just as we were, making no secret of our past. People were kind and non-judgemental and we made a lot of new friends.

Then we had a bit of a bombshell. After nearly ten years in the parish, one morning, before Mass, the priest called John into the sacristy. He was very upset and hardly knew where to start with what he had to say. He told John he had been ordered by the Vicar General to refuse us both Communion. He had protested strongly and tried to reason with the VG, but to no avail. He said, 'Johnny, this goes right against my conscience, but he has left me no choice.'

Apparently, there had been a letter to the Bishop from someone in the parish complaining that our very presence at Mass was a scandal. After that, it seemed the best thing we could do was to quietly withdraw from parish life. Neither of us could bear the idea of going to Mass without receiving the Eucharist, so we never went again in this parish except for my father's funeral in 1986 and my mother's six years later.

John decided not to apply for a dispensation. I gave myself an annulment from my second marriage, and we married nine years after we met. Why did it take so long? We couldn't see the point of doing it any earlier. I had my divorce through pretty quickly, so we were free to marry civilly, but we were never free to marry in the Church. Instead, we got married at the register office. The one thing I insisted on was that on my marriage certificate, I would not have some euphemism like clerk, retired or social worker. I wanted John's occupation to be put down as Roman Catholic priest, which it is.

How hard was it for John to give up his active ministry? At first, it didn't seem hard at all. Yet, with hindsight, I can see it was like a bereavement. If you don't deal with it at the time, it becomes a great grief pushed to the back of the mind. There is a tremendous sense of loss: of friendships, of recognition and status, and of priesthood as you were ordained to practise it. If you don't grieve for those precious things at the beginning, they become suppressed and come out in other ways, like moods, unaccountable sadness, depression. We experienced all of those in the beginning. We've had to work through a lot of anger and resentment as well as bring up a family and survive.

The year of our excommunication, we made contact with the Advent Group and, in many ways, that's been our salvation. We've found kindred spirits there, like-minded people with a common bond yet a great diversity of views, all of whom have given up one life for another, very different one. It's helped us so much, not just as an organisation but as a network of people who can say, 'I know. I have been through this. I have cried, I have howled, for what I have lost. But I have moved on. This is a new life, a new direction, a new and renewed priesthood.'

So now we've moved on to a new ministry. The narrow view of priesthood as we knew it doesn't exist any more. Ours is an ongoing ministry. I don't call John an ex-priest. He's a priest who has resigned his official position to marry and take a new path. He'll be a priest till the day he dies. An ordained man never loses his priesthood. You can't have it taken away from you by authority any more than you can be 'reduced' to the lay state. What an insult to the laity that is! Once you have realised that, you can move on to a new and renewed ministry.

If a person or a community were to say, 'We have no priest to say Mass with us. Will you come?', of course he would, and he has done in recent years. This is taking the Church back to the way it was and the way it should be again. We have lived in the same neighbourhood now for eighteen years and, when friends or acquaintances call on John for counsel, advice, or to ask him to call on a sick or dying person, it's because they have come to know us well and recognise his unswerving commitment to his priesthood. It is his sacramental ministry they call on, married or not, and that means a great deal to us and our hopes and visions for the future Church.

It has been, for us, a learning and growing experience, and we feel the Holy Spirit is with us. Our ministry is not about what you read in a book but about what you've lived, and all the theory in the world doesn't give you that. Through the Advent Group, John and I are now able to offer other people the same love and encouragement we received. It's a privilege to be at the end of a phone and hear someone making the first tentative steps on the road to their new life. To be able to say, 'I understand. You are not alone, but among friends.'

Through all our years of turbulence and change, through the good times, the bad times, the indifferent times, the difficult times, there is one factor in our lives that has never altered. And that is our love for each other and for the family. That has never wavered. Through that, we have been able to be strong for each other. We have never, ever had any regrets – not even tiny ones. I suppose at the time we must have appeared an odd, ill-matched pair. Only we knew how very right it felt from the first moment. And, from such different starting points, we have slowly arrived at the same place on our journey of faith.

I'd like to feel ours is a story of hope and conviction even though, in the beginning, we were afraid of our own shadows. John is content now. I am very content. Because – it's like this picture I painted [*a painting of a woman and child bathing*]. My paintings are beginning to reflect our life now. This baby – this is new life. The water of baptism is calm and clean and pure. This new ministry, this new life, is ours to live, and it's very precious, and *nobody* can take it away from us.

Julia

Julia is an area sales manager for a computer firm. Attractive and well groomed, she's nonetheless slightly unnerving as the kind of person who wouldn't suffer fools gladly – probably the result of being a single mother bringing up two children, and having to hold down a busy and demanding job at the same time. She is rightly proud of her achievements – and bitter that the Church of which she is still a member has done little to help her, financially or otherwise. It's six years now since her affair with Eamonn ended, though she still occasionally sees him in court, for maintenance hearings. It's even harder for her to let go of the past than for most women who have had relationships with priests, because for her the past is ever-present in the form of Rosie, a pert and pretty six-year-old.

We met through Mass, really – he was just the parish priest. We started speaking and obviously got on very well and it just developed from there.

I'd been divorced a few years and had Hannah, who was then about six. I had a good job, a house, and I'd been involved with someone, so I wasn't looking for another relationship. Not at all. As for priests – well, I didn't have any particular feeling about priests. They didn't really figure very much in my life. They were there, they said Mass and that was the end of it. I didn't really know them. I'd known our old priest for fifteen years and I was actively involved in the parish but there are lots of parish activities that don't involve the priest. But when I moved parish, the priest there – Eamonn – was involved in a lot of things.

My first opinion of him was formed when we were at a meeting for

Hannah's First Holy Communion. The meeting went on for so long that I got bored and walked out. And Eamonn, who had made no contribution to the whole thing, followed me out. He said, 'Why are you going?' And I said, 'No way am I going to sit listening to this for the next couple of hours. I've got other things to do.' So he said, 'Well, I've been wanting to speak to you, anyway, about Hannah. Can I have your phone number?' There was no need for him to ring, I could have told him what he needed to know there and then. But he did ring.

Like I say, I had been involved with someone for a couple of years. He had cancer and he'd come out of hospital very ill. Because we'd been involved, I felt I ought to have him stay with me – he lived on his own in a flat. But I was also apprehensive about having him live with me because of Hannah. I didn't want any conflict with her, so I was in a dilemma. I asked Eamonn what to do, and he said, 'You can't live with him here, as man and wife.' So I didn't.

Another day, he asked me to play guitar at Mass and I said I couldn't, I was going away. In fact, I came back in time to go to Mass. Afterwards, I told him we'd just stayed overnight and left early, and he said, 'You've never asked me to stay overnight, have you?' And one evening I had toothache and didn't go to the CAFOD [*Catholic Fund for Overseas Development*] group, and he rang me at about midnight and asked where I'd been. He said, 'I went specially to see you.' So there were all these little signs.

At the time, though, I didn't take it seriously. I really didn't. To me, he was just a bloke. I didn't see him as a priest. I mean, I've got a good friend who's a doctor and when I talk to him, I don't think about my body all the time. You know what I mean?

I have to accept what people say, that maybe some women fall for a priest because of his position of power and authority. But I deal with men all day – managing directors, accountants, company owners – and I don't find them attractive just because they're what they are. I may find *a* company director attractive, and it's the same with priests. Priests aren't attractive because they're priests. It's the person behind the priesthood I might find attractive. And that's what happened. After many months of speaking to him, I found him attractive and he found me attractive – but not as a priest and parishioner. What I always say is, if they're behaving as a priest, they will not get involved with a parishioner. It's only when they stop acting as priests that they get involved.

I began to think it was a bit strange when he'd ring up and say, 'Shall we go out?' But we were just platonic friends – I've got lots of friends who are friends with priests, priests who become part of the family, you know? So it wasn't any big deal.

I remember at one point him saying, 'I've been in twenty-five years now, it's time I was let out. Then I could marry you, couldn't I?' I thought he was lonely then; deep down there was an unhappiness in him.

Another evening, after a meeting, he pretended he'd got some concert tickets for me, which he wanted me to pick up from the presbytery. But I knew I'd got them at home. He said afterwards he just wanted me to go back for coffee. I said, 'Well, why didn't you say so?' So the next time, he invited me back for coffee and that's when it started.

At first we just chatted and laughed and got on very well. When he kissed me, it seemed inevitable. But we didn't sleep together for a long time after that, about a year after we first got friendly. You see, he didn't take it lightly. Neither did I. We got close, but I said, 'Look, you're the priest, you have to be sure.' And he said, 'I'm not sure.' So we didn't do it. But the following week, he said, 'Now I really am sure.'

I can't say whether he'd had a relationship before or not. He would always maintain that he didn't, but I don't know, I honestly don't. He always used the withdrawal system, which I thought was fairly well controlled. That was his decision. But maybe it's a natural thing to know what to do.

He rang me the next day and said, 'Last night was really lovely, but ours can never be a marriage relationship.' I said, 'Did I propose, then, in my passion for you?' And we started laughing. But he was unhappy about it, so I said, 'Well, the best thing to do is make sure it doesn't happen again.' Then, the next week, it happened again. He came round, he was sitting next to me and I said, 'No, you must go and sit over there so we can have a nice chat.' And he said, 'I don't want to chat to you tonight.'

I'm sure he felt genuine love. But afterwards . . . it's like if you have an affair and you still love your partner, you'd feel guilty, wouldn't you? You'd maybe try harder but all the time you'd want to be with the other person. It's a conflict. You see, the thing is, priests are just men. But sometimes they're badly behaved men.

At the outset, I don't know how he would have reconciled what he did with God. He did say to me once that he wasn't happy because I wasn't going to Communion. I said I couldn't because we were having sex, and until I went to confession about it I couldn't go to Communion. And I said I didn't know how he did it. He said, 'I tell God I'm sorry, so that's OK.' I said, 'In that case, why do we have confession?' That's how he reconciled it. He'd say he was sorry, then he'd do it again.

As for me, I didn't feel guilty. I really didn't. I mean, I loved him very much and I *think* he probably did me. I think it was unhappiness that made him form a relationship with me, and we'd both have been happy to carry it on. If he hadn't been a priest, we'd probably still be together, because we were able to be that close to each other. So I don't feel guilt. But it was always going to be a tragedy, we knew that.

The way I look at it, I was six when he entered the seminary, I was thirteen when he took his vows, and I was thirty-six when I met him, so I'd have thought his vows were a bit more important to him than they were to me. *I* didn't take the vows. *I* didn't spend seven years in a seminary preparing for them. If his vows were that important to him, he wouldn't have pursued a relationship. You can't put the onus for that on to a woman. It's not the laywoman's job to make sure the priest keeps to his vows.

We have to accept – and it may be hard for some people to accept it – that priests are quite capable of initiating a relationship. This may have been his only affair, but there are far more priests having multiple relationships with women than there are women having multiple relationships with priests.

I knew I was pregnant a fortnight later. I got pregnant the second time we slept together. He was in Ireland. When he came back, he rang me and I was quiet, to say the least. When I told him, he said, 'Oh, Lord! Can you come over?' When I went over, he said, 'It's hard to believe there are three of us here.' Then he said to me – I can laugh now but at the time I was so angry – 'I gave you that book to read. You should have known.' It was a book on the Catholic birth control method, and he'd given it to me before there was anything sexual between us. 'Oh,' I said, 'did you want me to read the book before you started sleeping with me?' I'd honestly thought he'd given it to me simply because he taught the Catholic method of birth control and he wanted me to read about it.

I knew he wouldn't leave the priesthood. I didn't want him to leave the priesthood. So I booked into a clinic. I did it, not really to have an abortion, but because there was no one else I could tell and I didn't know what to do. But he made me cancel it. He said, 'Don't go, please don't go, we're in this together. I'll take full responsibility.' So I didn't go. Then, when she was born, he was all for me having her adopted. He said she needed two parents. I said, 'But she has two parents.' And once, when we were having a row over it, I said, 'When Rosie grows up I'll tell her you wanted her adopted.' And he said, 'Yes, and I'll tell her you wanted her terminated.'

I never intended to bring her up on my own. He told me he was going to do everything he could for her and be the best kind of father he could. I said, 'There's no way this child isn't going to know her father when I've got another one who does know her father.' He reassured me he would always be there for her, which is why I'm so angry about the way he's behaved. If he'd told me the truth, that he couldn't be there, I could have made a better decision about going ahead with the pregnancy – which is difficult, now I've got her. But when I think of some of the hurts she's had, not from me and probably not from him, but from the situation, with Hannah seeing her dad, it might have been the best thing to do. But he told me that would never, ever happen.

All through the pregnancy he was marvellous, making sure I was looking after myself, very supportive. And he was happy. After all, he didn't have to bother withdrawing, did he? I do remember one occasion when we'd been to bed and made love and I came down to make a cup of tea, and he said, 'You just don't understand me, do you? I've got to be on the altar in a couple of hours. You don't understand how I feel.' I said, 'I could understand it more if you said this *before* we went to bed, when we could do something about it. But I can't understand it when you promote sex, you actively want to do it, and then you say this.' I did get quite angry with him then.

I didn't talk to anybody about the pregnancy. Any anxieties I had I confided to Eamonn. I was always fairly discreet about everything. I wasn't a gossip, so I don't think people would have asked me about my private life. It came up with my family, of course, but they just thought, 'She'll tell us when she wants to.' They weren't going to harass me. So I kept a lot of the anxiety inside. I was seven stone when she was born – I'd been nine stone before – so that's how badly it affected me. But it's difficult for me now to remember that. It probably affected me more than I care to remember.

Eamonn was on holiday in Ireland when she was born. He wasn't going to change his plans just for me. She was actually due the day he came back, but she was six days early. Someone else told him I'd had her. He came round straight away and picked her up and started telling me where I was going wrong – you know how they are. He was just a dad, really. He was very good when she was born, very attentive. He really loved her. He was always ringing me about her.

I was far more practical than him. I knew it couldn't go on, that really he was not going to be involved with the little one and at some stage he'd have to do something about it. He thought he could carry on being a priest and for us to carry on as well. He was always going to have to face it at some stage.

I remember, very early on, when she was about five weeks old, she'd been in hospital with a bug. I brought her home, and after Mass he came to the house. I was in the back with some people, so Hannah let him in. She came through and said, 'Father's just come but he's gone upstairs to Rosie.' He hadn't realised there were other people there.

Rosie was so like him. If you had a doubt, once you looked at her, you knew. My mother knew the day of the baptism – Eamonn baptised her. She said, 'I know who Rosie's father is, because you've only got to look at her.' She quite liked Eamonn, actually – she blamed the Church for his attitude. She said it was ridiculous, them having to be celibate because obviously they don't all want to be. So she doesn't think it's his fault.

He once said, 'I'm very fond of you but I don't know if I know what love is.' And I said, 'Yes, that's the tragedy, isn't it? You go round telling everyone to love God and you sit there and tell me you don't know what love is.' I've thought that more and more as far as he is concerned. I mean, if a man is incapable of caring for and loving his own child, he's certainly not capable of loving and caring for his congregation, is he?

106

The relationship remained sexual for over a year after Rosie was born. I had the coil fitted. He really objected to that. He said to me one night, 'Will you go to the bathroom and take that out so that we can make love?' What do you say to that one? I said, 'Well, no, actually, because, first, I can't do that, and second, do you want another one?' And he said, 'Well, I wouldn't mind a boy, so long as you don't get me up for the two o'clock feeds.' It was a very irresponsible attitude towards the whole thing, when you think about it. All I can think now is, 'Thank God I didn't marry him.' That was the luckiest escape, because when I look back at how weak he was . . . Yet if he hadn't been a priest, maybe we would have married.

When Rosie was six months old, he celebrated his silver jubilee. I went to the do because he said he couldn't get through it without me. I had to go, really, or people would have wondered why. He was going on about all the great events in his life, and I thought, 'You forgot one, didn't you?' His young nephew was there, too, and someone turned round to me and said, 'We know who Rosie's father is,' because she was the double of the nephew, who was very like Eamonn. I didn't deny it. I've never denied it, and I never would.

The trouble was that after that we couldn't keep it secret. Another parishioner said to me, 'We can't carry on pretending we don't know who the father is. If he doesn't tell the Bishop, we'll have to.' So he had to tell the Bishop, who said he could carry on as a priest as long as there was no gossip or scandal. Eamonn probably told him the relationship was over.

I went to see the Vicar General and he said they'd move Eamonn right away, to a new parish twelve miles away, so no one would know. I was told, 'He wants to continue being involved with the baby. He wants to be recognised as the father and we don't want to make things difficult for him. We're hoping he'll do what for him is the right thing.' I think they were intimating he should leave, but they didn't want to tell him to do that, which is fair enough. But there's no way that child could not know her father when they were in such close proximity.

The last thing the Vicar General said to me was that I should never, ever let Eamonn's family know. I said, 'Oh, shouldn't I?' There was no way. She's part of their family. I thought that was ridiculous. In fact, his family have had nothing to do with her. They don't want to know.

Their attitude is, what kind of woman would go with a priest? Rosie could have gone to the same school as her cousin, Eamonn's nephew, but I didn't want that. So she doesn't go to her nearest Catholic school, because that's where he goes. But at the school she does go to they know anyway, because she's told them.

I didn't realise she knew. I've never told her. But a friend of hers showed her a picture of a friend of their family who's a priest, and Rosie said, 'My dad's a priest as well.' But I'm not going to be honest with her at the moment because they don't really understand at that age. Maybe when she's fourteen or fifteen. I've just told her her daddy's working in Ireland.

My employers were absolutely marvellous throughout the pregnancy. They were quite happy for me to carry on working, but a nursery for Rosie was £2,000. I was only earning about £9,000 at the time, and my mortgage was over £300 a month, so it just wasn't viable to go to work. Then I got into trouble with my mortgage repayments. I told Eamonn I might lose my house and all he could say was, 'I'm losing mine as well.' But they were going to give him another one. I mean, he's 50 per cent of the problem, and he was given another house, all furnished, all paid for by the Church, and the mother and child were going to have their home repossessed.

There was no provision for us. There isn't any support whatsoever for the mother and child. I accept my share of responsibility for having the affair and for having Rosie but, having said that, I've looked after her, done the best I possibly can for her, and he's run away and they've supported him. If he was Joe Soap on the street, he'd have been taken to court, not protected by his employer. I've never asked for any provision or assistance from the Church. What I have done is ask that he does what he promised during the pregnancy and never abandons his child. He said she would always have a father. But he hasn't fulfilled that promise, and until he does, I shall object.

I'd also like to know how the Church reconciles the fact that, if a priest gets a woman pregnant and is prepared to do the Christian thing and openly support her and the child, he is likely to lose his job and be excommunicated. Yet a priest in exactly the same position who abandons the woman and child is allowed – encouraged, even – to stay in the priesthood.

Anyway, before the birth, I said I wanted his name on the birth certificate. Then, when I was in hospital, I got depressed and I thought I'd leave it six months to see how I felt. He said OK, then he started being funny, saying he had to ask the Archbishop's permission. I said, 'Please yourself, but the Archbishop won't tell me whose name I can put on the birth certificate. If you've got any qualms, we'll go to court and you can have a paternity test to prove you're her father.' But he never denied it. So we went and registered her birth, and the next day he went to Ireland for a fortnight.

While he was away, Rosie was ill and had to go into hospital. The day I came out with her, there was a journalist and a photographer on the doorstep. They said, 'We've known for six months but we haven't had any proof. Now we've got a copy of the birth certificate and we're going to run a story.' They were asking where Eamonn was, so I rang his brother-in-law and he said, 'I'll stop him coming back.' And he did. Eamonn never came back. That was 1990, when Rosie was sixteen months old.

They told me he'd had a nervous breakdown. Maybe he did. When you're stuck here with two kids, you can't afford to have one. We were quite good friends at that stage. We had parted amicably. But we'd stopped sleeping together three or four months before that. I was very bitter with him really, with his lifestyle. He came round here once, played with Rosie, did the dad bit, then he said, 'Got to go now, I've got confession.'

It was splashed all over the newspapers, but I hadn't told them. The journalists wouldn't tell me who had, but I think I know. It had to be someone who knew I was going to the register office, because the press knew within hours. All the time, it seemed like it was all OK with Eamonn, and with the Church, until the press found out. We could carry on our relationship, he could carry on being a priest, the Church could carry on covering it up. But as soon as the press reported it, no one wanted anything to do with Rosie and me at all. So the biggest sin, it seemed to me, was telling the press. Even though it wasn't me who told them.

I was offered £15,000 for photographs of Rosie but I wouldn't take it. I wish now I had done. I was even offered an advance of £25,000 to write a book. I never had any desire to ruin his life. But he shouldn't have run away, and he shouldn't have abandoned Rosie. The only thing I'd say is, you wanted me to go ahead with the pregnancy, you carried on with the affair, you insisted the child was born, you insisted she was baptised, the Archbishop knew all about her, but the minute you were found out, you left her. That's why I'm pursuing him through the courts. He's not treating my child like that and getting away with it.

When he ran away, I said I wanted a maintenance order but no one would tell me where he was. I tried to get him to court five times, so in the end I served the papers on the Archbishop instead. The diocese had always denied that they knew where he was, and they'd always said they couldn't take any responsibility for him because he was self-employed. Yet the very next day Eamonn rang me, pretending he knew nothing about me speaking to the Archbishop – he just happened to decide to ring me. They still pretend they don't know where he is, though I know he's in Ireland. He won't give us an address.

His solicitor finally said he'd come to court but he had no money, no income, because he was unemployed. I knew he was getting a stipend from the Bishop, and his friends were sending him money. Initially, though, his solicitor said he'd only pay 5p a week. I said, 'That would make nice headlines. I'll see him in court.' And he wrote back, 'Do you want a publicity campaign or £5 a year?' Well, that did it. There was no way I'd talk to him then. If I'd wanted a publicity campaign, I could have hounded him. But I didn't want that.

So he came back from Ireland for the court hearing, because he knew otherwise I'd be after the Archbishop. And when we got to court – it was the first time I'd seen him for four years – he said he was prepared to pay what he could. It started out at £10 a week, and now it's £15, though I'm still after a proper maintenance order to get it on a legal footing. At the moment, it's a voluntary agreement. But it's not the money I'm bothered about. All I've ever wanted is for him to do his best by Rosie.

He met her that weekend, but he's never bothered since. He wrote to me saying he'd still got a calling from God and the only way he could work was on the missions, but he wouldn't go if there was any more publicity. And he said he'd write to her at Christmas and for her birthday and when she was older they'd talk. I said, 'There is no way you're going to have access to this child when she has no access to you.

There's no way you go on the missions until you start acting better by her.' The first card he sent just said 'Father'. Now he writes 'Daddy'.

Does he love her? How can you love someone when you never see them? He keeps pretending that he can't see her, but he won't. I'd hate her to think he didn't care for her. He's seen her just once since, a few months ago. She told me that, when I went out of the room, he said to her, 'I love you very much.' So she said, 'I told him I loved him, but I don't really. I just said it.'

I feel very sorry for him. It's a great loss to him, because he's never going to get a relationship with Rosie, is he? She calls my solicitor Dad, and if anything happened to me, he and his wife would have her. Deep down I think she's very hurt, because she reacts very angrily about Eamonn. She's the only one in the class without a father and it's very hard for her. She's a lovely little girl but she's very bitter. She hates his name being mentioned because she sees Hannah with her own dad a lot.

There's no way I would ever entertain him and me. There's nothing there now whatsoever. But I shall keep on reminding him that this child – this person – is here. I don't let it rule my life, though. You're the first person I've spoken to about it for years.

I don't go to church now. The more I think about it, the less I want to do with it, though I'm still involved on the social side, running the club and everything. For a long time, I separated his actions from the actions of the Church. I didn't involve them at all in the beginning. It was something between me and him. But now I feel that, really, his behaviour is no different from theirs. At the end of the day, he's protecting them by not getting in touch with the diocese, and they're protecting him.

Originally, people were split in the parish, but as time has gone on and they've seen Rosie, they've grown more hostile to him. They say he could at least have kept in touch with her. His new parishioners were furious because the Archbishop had told them he'd moved there because their parish priest was ill, but really it was to get him away from the parish where people knew.

I'm not sure whether or not to bring Rosie up as a Catholic now. At the moment she's in a Catholic school, but as a non-Catholic. And I'm worried about her doing her First Holy Communion. She wants to do it, but I'm trying to talk her out of it. It just seems like the Church has no interest in children. I mean, if the Bishop is the priest's father, as he claims, then he's the child's grandfather.

How can the Church answer the fact that, if a child is a gift from God, then so is Rosie? As such, she should not be abandoned. Also, if parenting is as much a vocation as celibacy, the mother shouldn't be abandoned, either. But the sin doesn't seem to be the fact that priests have sex. It's the fact that they have a child.

The Church isn't living Christianity. It's all male-dominated hierarchy. At the end of the day, I'm of very little importance to them compared to a priest. So I don't want much part of it any longer. There are times when I've been really angry with God, thinking, 'It's no good speaking to you because you're on his side.' But, while the Church have no credibility as far as I'm concerned, because they don't practise what they preach – it's 'Do what I say rather than what I do' – I've still got faith in God. And I can still pray.

One priest said to me, 'She's better off without him. Forget it.' I said, 'I can't. This is a life.' I won't just forget about it. I shall carry on and on until the Church does something about it. I'm not asking for financial assistance. What I want is recognition for my child that she exists, that he's her father, and that in the end she is more important than the priest.

If celibacy is going to cause so much heartache and become such a burden to some priests, and destroy children's lives, they should look again at making it optional. Otherwise, we're going to lose some very good priests who can't live with it. As it is, the law of celibacy has ruined a lot of people's lives. It's ruined my life, it's likely to have a very bad effect on my child, and it's certainly had a catastrophic effect on the often very good priests who've been led to leave the priesthood because of it.

Matilda

Matilda is a bright and bubbly young woman with pretty dark, Irish looks and the Irish gift of the gab. I met her a couple of times in her pretty terraced house, and we've spoken often on the phone. The first time we met, she insisted a friend of hers was present throughout – 'to give me strength, and to help me if I forget anything'. In the event, once the tape-recorder was turned on, Matilda needed no help to remember. The only time her fluency failed was when, talking about her father's death, she began to cry. Although her relationship with Chris officially ended three years ago, it still causes her grief, anger, and not a little puzzlement. She blames it, too, for stopping her from forming another relationship. 'I don't think I could ever trust a man again,' she says.

When I told Chris I was going to talk to you, he said, 'Good, I'm glad you're going to tell our story.' I said, 'It's not our story, it's *my* story, it's completely different to yours, and you can't appropriate it.'

I was at university. I'd been with my boyfriend, Simon, for over three years and I got pregnant, as you do, just to break up your second and third year. I was completely flummoxed by the whole experience, so I dropped out and decided to go to another university where they had childcare. I was also unhappy with my course. I was doing theology and English and they had a very traditional theology department – I was still a Catholic girl in those days.

I changed to a university which had a better religious studies course, and which had a crêche on campus. Simon had graduated, so he got a job in this other town, and we decided to buy a house together, even though by this stage we were starting to split up. In the meantime, he rented a flat, but his landlord wouldn't let me and Charlotte stay there, so I had a three-month-old baby and nowhere to live.

In the end, some friends of Simon's said they'd got this friend who was the priest at the university, and I could probably stay in the chaplaincy. I just retorted, 'In your dreams!' I'd never been friends with a priest, ever, and it seemed a really weird idea. But after a week, I was so desperate that I rang up and asked if I could go and stay there for a couple of weeks. He said, 'Yes, OK.' That's how I came to live with Chris.

At the time, I had really short, really spiky hair, and wore trainers and sloppy jumpers all the time. I was quite a rebel. Then I walked into this place and met this person and thought, 'Oh, my God! I'm not staying here for long.' He had on a pink shirt with a long seventies collar on it, black crimplene trousers that were slightly flared, a red V-necked jumper with a little lion motif in the corner, a haircut that was just like nothing on God's Earth, with really long sideburns, and these thick, old-fashioned bottle glasses. He was about thirty-five, fourteen years older than me. And I just didn't like him.

I was so depressed that first night. I thought, 'This is horrible. I don't want to be here, living in the same bloody house as a priest!' After a couple of weeks, our house sale came through, and Simon and I moved in together. While I'd been in the chaplaincy, Chris had been really nice to me. He brought me cups of tea, constantly checked on me. He loved having Charlotte around. At the same time, there were all these weird students around who were all religious, into prayer groups and stuff, and I was thinking, 'I don't want to be here at all.'

So Simon and I got our house, moved in, had a complete nightmare two weeks, with some violent confrontations, and then I left him; just walked out, literally in the middle of an argument. I said, 'That's it, we're finished.' I just knew there was no way it was going to work. I didn't know what I was going to do, where I was going to go. Chris said, 'Come and live here,' so I did. I didn't think yes, no or maybe. I just thought I hadn't got a choice.

And, basically, in the end, he did this really big come-on. He initiated the whole thing. I went out with him one night, got really drunk because of the situation between Simon and me, and slept with him. I can't even remember what happened, to be honest. I just woke up the next morning and thought, 'Oh, my God!' That's how confused I was. There was no way on God's Earth I would have thought of having a relationship with a priest. It was just something that happened. I said to Chris, 'I hope you used a condom.'

I suppose what I was drawn into was somebody being very kind and protective towards me, somebody saying, 'I'm here for you whenever you need me, whatever time of the day or night.' I hadn't thought about being involved with him at all and, basically, sleeping with him was a comfort thing rather than having feelings for him that I wanted to develop. What I needed was somebody to look after me. So I stayed there and got stuck, because we then got involved in a relationship. I wasn't even sure I wanted to; I just kind of fell into it, like down a rabbit hole.

At first it was very much a dependency thing. I didn't have any friends at all in the town except Simon, so I felt really isolated. I couldn't drive, couldn't go anywhere – even my family weren't nearby – so I didn't see anybody from one term to the next.

After a while, I did tell two people what was going on, because I didn't know what it meant at all. One was another student, and she was so horrified that I thought, 'I shouldn't be telling people about this.' The other person I told actually said, 'Have you thought about what you are doing to his relationship with God?' I thought, 'Well, I'm buggered if I'm telling anybody else if that's the sort of reaction I'm going to get.' So the whole thing was incredibly secretive.

I can't remember him ever saying, 'Don't tell anybody.' I just knew I couldn't. So, very quickly, I became secretive and lived in a private world where I stopped contacting people. I'd got a really wide circle of friends and I just stopped talking to them. I knew priests were supposed to be celibate, so that was the big reason he wouldn't tell people. I knew I couldn't tell my family as they would have gone bananas. But one of my main reasons for not telling anybody was because I wanted Chris to love me.

On the one hand, I had this guy telling me I was this incredible, special person, and I felt I must be because he was supposed to be celibate and was therefore breaking the code of conduct of his order for me. He was also building up an intimate relationship with my child, the child he couldn't have. I've got photographs of him feeding her, changing her. He was there when she said her first words and took her first steps, all those important moments.

Yet there were many strange things going on that I couldn't make sense of. Like why would he be all right towards me one minute and then, when other people were around, be quite cold and distant? I learned to accept that and, you know, since then I've sat down and realised I've always had low expectations of relationships with men, and therefore I have accepted some very negative behaviour towards me. Although we lived in the same house, the times we were actually together were few and far between. It was very much behind closed doors. We'd spend time together in the mornings, but it was quite furtive and felt horrible on one level. So then I came to question whether he really did love me or whether he just wanted to have sex.

I hardly ever had penetrative sex with him. I've just never liked contraception. I think it's fine to stop yourself from having babies. I don't think it's fine that all these devices are invented for women to rip their bodies apart with or inject themselves with, so I've only ever used condoms. But it became a real issue between us – not the contraception, because he understood that I didn't want to use it, but the penetrative sex. I was quite happy with other forms of making love, but he was permanently frustrated. At one point, he even accused me of making him so frustrated that it encouraged him to have other relationships, which was amazing, really.

I wasn't his first sexual partner, oh, my God, no! He'd had loads of sexual relationships. He'd been in the seminary since he was ten, and when he was a teenager he was a homosexual for about six years. He would say other people led him into the relationships, but he liked to evade responsibility for his own actions by saying, 'It was you who did this to me.' That's basically just an excuse. He probably played a pretty active part and got quite a lot out of them as well, because he wouldn't have engaged in them otherwise.

Just before his ordination, he spent a year out, and he had a couple of relationships then. And the year after he became a curate he had a relationship with somebody and was even going to leave the priesthood for her. But he went and told his parents and everyone made him realise he wouldn't have a life outside the priesthood, so he just dumped her one day.

One of the reasons I didn't like having sex with him very much was because he wasn't a very good lover. I think he'd been so used to casual sexual encounters that it seemed natural to come within about three seconds. To give the guy his due, as the years went on, our sexual relationship did improve a lot, and we really did have some nice and intimate times. But I did have a bar on having penetrative sex with him, not so much in the beginning but as everything unfolded.

What I felt happened to me over the space of the two years in the chaplaincy was that I lost my identity completely. I came out of it with a long bobbed haircut and wearing flowery dresses from Laura Ashley. Evidently, I was partaking of this exercise but there were some really strong influences on me, like him saying how much he hated women with short hair. So the day he left, I went and had my hair cut. That was symbolic, but now I have it short because I really love having it short. It's not a statement any more.

For those first two years, I submerged myself into his agenda, became very much the person behind him. I was always waiting for him to come home, to come back from holiday, to visit me, to finish something else before he could talk to me or sleep with me or whatever. I found myself in some ridiculous scenarios, like sitting up until 1.30 in the morning until he came back from wherever he'd been, usually getting pissed in the name of pastoral duties, just so I could see him for half an hour before I went to bed. I got trapped in that way of behaving and that way of relating to somebody.

The issue there is about being involved with an unavailable man who's got something bigger than you in his life, so you become very much a peripheral consideration. I also felt that he was a very demanding person, emotionally, sexually and psychologically, and I was always having to sort things out for him. He'd give Sunday lunches for students, for a hundred people at a time, and I took that over. I became a master chef. And I'd go into his office and sort it out because it was always a mess. His life generally was a complete mess. I look back on it now and think he just didn't know what he wanted, who he was or what any of it meant. He knew he wanted to be a priest and have the authority, but he also wanted to have a relationship. Or, rather, at first he wanted to have sex – that was his driving force, and initially he was reluctant to take the relationship anywhere.

There were some weird things happening at the chaplaincy, some strange relationships and some very needy people, which all seemed abnormal to me. But because I was enveloped in this relationship, I got enveloped in all those politics as well. It was only when I got out that I realised *I* wasn't abnormal, I was the normal one in an abnormal world. It was normal to him to behave in a manipulative, secretive, devious way and then stand up and say Mass on Sunday and perform as an actor, knowing that he'd left a trail behind him and that there'd be another trail the next week.

Even domestic normality was too much for him. He was used to working a twelve-hour day and doing things like going out to students or parishioners at 1 a.m. That was normal to him, which it wasn't to me. He gave too much, because when he had a day off he'd be exhausted and completely depressed. He couldn't function and he'd become very negative about himself. He couldn't pace himself. He'd have a discussion group and then they'd all go to the pub, or he'd have a college dinner and invite students back and they'd stay up drinking until three in the morning.

After about six months, I got some really bad vibes from one particular female student, one of the hangers-on at the chaplaincy. She hung on to his every word and was totally enamoured with him. I felt as though I had become a defender of my territory. There were several women students around like that. They used it as an open-house chaplaincy and it was very much focused on the charismatic characters of the chaplaincy: Chris himself and the lay chaplain.

He also had a housekeeper who hated me with a vengeance because he was her darling. She certainly wrote him some very weird letters. There was a lot of antagonism between them in the end because she couldn't accept that he would leave the priesthood for me. She used to write me reams of letters about how I was leading him astray, how I shouldn't be taking him and how I was just going to leave him penniless and alone in the streets. The fact is that he did end up penniless, because he left me, the house and everything, but he left it all by choice.

That summer, about a year after I'd moved in, I nearly had a nervous breakdown. I was stuck in with Charlotte while he was always out. I thought we were going to have some time together, but he went off to Italy for three weeks instead with the students, including this particular student to whom he'd been giving advice. I spent most of the summer trying to find out if he was having a relationship with her.

She had been around a lot that summer, and he'd go out for an evening with her. I'd say, 'Why are you going out with her? Why aren't you staying here with me?' And he'd say, 'I have to because she's one of the students and I'm the chaplain.' That was part of his job, but he had been sleeping with her as well. One particular night, he went out with her and when he came back I went mad. I'd sat there all evening thinking, 'I am going mad.' I could feel myself going over the edge of this precipice, because I just didn't know what was going on. I didn't even have the language to articulate how I felt any more. All I knew was that I loved him, I was in love with him, and he was hurting me. But when he got back, he denied everything and said I was paranoid and I needed to see a psychiatrist. I lashed back at him but he got really angry and threw me to the floor, pinned me down and said, 'Don't you ever accuse me of anything like that again!' He was outraged that I should accuse him of being unfaithful.

Yet when he came back from this holiday, there were two photographs with her in them, including one of her in her swimsuit. There was another one of him in his hotel room, and I said, 'Who took this? Michelle took it, didn't she? Why are you doing this to me? What's going on?' He denied it emphatically. He made me believe there was something seriously wrong with me. I'd sit there and think, 'This is divine vengeance.' I blamed myself for getting involved with him, I blamed myself for being jealous. All of a sudden, every woman was a threat to me, because most of them were in the running for him or he flirted madly with them.

So eventually we had this confrontation. I said, 'Have you slept with Michelle?' And he said, 'Well, yes.' I said, 'You're supposed to say no, you're supposed to say no!' I felt this incredible sense of injustice. After he admitted being unfaithful, I said, 'For God's sake, it's not enough for you not to be celibate, you have to be screwing around as well!' He had no answer for that at all. He said, 'She chased me and eventually I gave in. I don't know why. It won't happen again. It's you I love.'

But Michelle wasn't the only one. I'd become quite good friends with one of my tutors, Judy. We'd go to exercise classes together and have dinner together, and one evening she got completely drunk and decided she was going to sleep with Chris that night. There were twelve of us sitting round this table and this woman was so drunk that she was putting her arms round him, putting her head on his shoulder, really going for it, and he wasn't objecting at all. I was so angry, I said to him, 'If you sleep with her tonight, I'll kill you.' In the end, I ran a risk because there were other people staying in the flat, but I insisted on staying in his room. I said, 'You're not sleeping with her.'

She knew about us, not from me but from him. That was another issue. Apart from those two students in my first year, I hadn't told anybody, but, by the end of my time there, a substantial number of students knew about it. Some people had inferred it but most had got it straight from the horse's mouth. He confessed to every bugger on earth, I think!

He even told my family, on my graduation day. He was washing up in the kitchen with one of my sisters and he poured out his heart to her about this relationship we were having. I'd never breathed a word to any of them about it. I'd kept silent for two years and then he told my family. I was so angry. My sister was funny. She just said, 'All this time we thought you were on your own and you've been getting your oats all the time!' But from then on the rest of my family found out, so I had to deal with all of that, yet his family didn't know anything. That's about the power of disclosure. I didn't have any power to disclose any details about our relationship, because I would have been dropped or punished in some way by him. Yet *he* did. It was a confession thing. He'd pour out his heart and ask for forgiveness.

That's what he did through some of the students as well, which was entirely inappropriate. So, by the end of my second year, this student opposition from a few select people, including my tutor, became really strong. One day a delegation, which included a person with whom I had been briefly involved one Easter, came to the house and basically said, 'We think this is wrong and we're going to go to the Bishop about it.' It was terrible.

But Chris wouldn't let me go. He was determined I was going to have a relationship with him. When we had the graduation ball, I went with this other person, very definitely saying to Chris, 'I'm not putting up with this any more.' At that same ball, Chris asked me to marry him. He said he was going to tell his parents, he was going to leave the priesthood, he really wanted to be with me. He cried and protested and I had to believe him so I said, 'Yes.' I was completely floored. Three days later, he said he didn't actually mean it, and that he shouldn't have asked me.

By the time the delegation arrived, the Bishop already knew about us. Chris had told him. The Bishop had been quite understanding – his actual words were: 'If you or that young lass of yours ever need to talk, then you know that I'm here for you' – but once the students were involved it became a scandal. Chris was threatened with being thrown out, but I think he must have promised he wouldn't see me again. So, instead, I had to leave town. Luckily, I'd got my degree by then – I got a first, God knows how – and I went to London, which was the farthest away I could get. I'd intended not to be with him any more because I'd had enough, I couldn't cope with it. I saw Judy before I left – I didn't know at this stage that she'd been sleeping with my partner – and she said, 'Well done, you've done very well. But let me give you two words of warning. Don't get pregnant, and keep your mouth shut.'

Within a week of me going, Chris came down to see me, 'I can't cope without you.' Yet the day after I left, he had slept with Judy! I didn't know for about a year, when someone told me she'd seen them out together. I asked him if he'd slept with her and he said he had. I wanted to pin him against the wall, I was so angry. He'd been having an affair with two other people for a year and a half of the time he was with me. I thought I was in a relationship with one person and one person only and he was sleeping with three women at the same time. Both the others had their own partners – we could have got AIDS or anything. Chris ended up marrying Judy to her fiancé. I couldn't believe it. She had been unfaithful to him for a year.

I moved to London and did an office job for a while but it didn't work out, so I moved back to the West Country, near my parents, got a job, a lovely house, just me and Charlotte, and started building my life again.

Just before I went back home – this would be the summer of 1990 – Chris and I went to Ireland for two weeks. While we were there he bought me a traditional Irish wedding ring and said, 'I really do want to marry you.' We came back and, when I spoke to him again on the phone, he became quite cold towards me again and eventually said that he didn't want to marry me and didn't think it was a good idea that we should see each other. All the time, in the five years we were together, I was on a complete seesaw of emotions: 'He loves me, he loves me not.' I felt like one of the petals that has been plucked off the flower. I'd be glued back on but I'd need more and more glue each time.

After that phone call, I had to do something, so I got on the train, walked into the chaplaincy and just screamed at him. I was so angry that I smashed my ring with a hammer, and I took out a book I'd bought him just the week before and ripped it up in front of him. I became an hysterical, screaming woman. I'd never been as angry with anybody in my life and I don't think I ever will be again.

I remember having to defend him quite a lot when other people said, 'He's really bad for you,' because he was someone I cared about. Now I consider that it was quite an abusive relationship emotionally, and I had had to defend my abuser. I'd remember all the times he'd been good to me and to Charlotte – even Simon admired him for his relationship with her – and I thought, what would she do without him in her life? It's a terrible motive for doing anything and I'd never do it again, but I did feel quite driven by that because she'd been with him for two and a half years of her life by then, and he'd always had this very positive relationship with her.

After I'd lived in my home area for ten months, I started an MA at the local university, and the same week I started there I began going to counselling. I was in counselling with a lovely woman from the Catholic Marriage Advisory Council – sounds like an anomaly in itself – for two and a half years. It was my salvation. I remember that first week saying to her, 'One of the issues is I'm having a relationship with a priest, but that's not the problem!' Then I spent six months crying about it.

It was a real turning-point for me when I moved back home. I did my MA, made a lot of friends, wrote a book, became quite accomplished, and lived in my little house, furnishing it all for about £400. I started building things for myself instead of relying on him. It's significant that, as long as I was independent, Chris wanted to be with me. He'd come over, take from us, and then go back to the chaplaincy filled again. But when I needed him, he wasn't there.

The chaplaincy became quite a bugbear in the end because it always seemed that there was a battle between me or it, but it wasn't, really. It was a battle between me and his independence. I'd been very needy when I met Chris. I hadn't had any confidence in myself and I lacked self-esteem and self-worth. So I would put his needs before my own.

As I became more confident and assertive, we had a lot of quite bad times. He'd hit me and I'd say: 'How can you do this? How can you counsel people about all these different things when you're doing this to your partner?' He'd say I'd provoked him – 'If you didn't provoke me, I wouldn't hit you.' I'd reply: 'If you could control your temper, I wouldn't have bruises on my body.' It felt as if there was a real game going on between us to do with power.

I was always crying, in tears nearly every day. Now I can't remember the last time I cried. It only happens on specific occasions and at very intense moments. But then, all I can remember for the first three years I was with him was that I cried, because I was in a relationship that confused me completely and ripped me apart inside.

I still never knew what was happening. He let down me and Charlotte a zillion times, saying he was coming to see us and then not turning up, or turning up hours late, or I'd arrange something with friends and the same thing would happen. I was building up a circle of friends who saw me as a very strong person, very much in charge of my life, and then Chris would turn up and I wouldn't be able to do anything for a week after I'd seen him because I was going through a lot of trauma about what was going to happen to us. I didn't feel I wanted him to leave the priesthood. I didn't know what I wanted, except that I wanted to be with him because I cared about him. But even then I had inklings of 'Do I really love him or do I just care about what happens to him?' There's quite a lot of difference between the two, really, and I never knew which I felt.

In the middle of this, my dad died. We'd had notice about two weeks before, so there was a lot of trauma. The day he died, Chris was in Lourdes with a group of students, and to this day I feel angry about that. All my brothers and sisters were there with their partners and I was on my own. I rang him in France to tell him, but he was out, so I left a message to ask him to ring me back, but he didn't. I was really, really upset about this. I phoned the next night and told him my dad had died and he just said, 'Oh.' When he came back, he told me what a stink it had caused when I rang him where he was staying in France. My dad had died and I was being told off for disturbing him and for ruining his reputation.

I remember being really upset with him and saying, 'You knew he had only two or three weeks to live, and you still went and did all these duties, and you weren't there.' My dad really liked Chris, really cared about him, and I thought, 'I've even got to explain to my dad, who's dying, why Chris isn't here.'

We had this big discussion on the Monday about whether he could come to the funeral because it clashed with a chaplains' conference which he was supposed to go to. In the event, he did come to the funeral, but he got into a lot of shit for it. I do understand that these were pressures on him and on the situation in which he lived, but I felt I needed him there. And he was really good. He spent time with the family and helped put the service together, but he also had to ring the chaplaincy every evening, so – and he'd probably be upset if he heard me saying this – I was made to feel it was a massive sacrifice for him to be with me.

After the funeral, he went back to the chaplaincy and my mum and I went and stayed there for a week. It had been my home for two years, and I saw no reason why we couldn't stay there, but there were some politically important people who didn't like it. They caused a massive fuss. They went to the Bishop and he said he wanted us to leave. My mum was with me, for God's sake! I wasn't sleeping with Chris or anything. I know that Judy, my ex-tutor, was among those who instigated the big drive for us to leave. She had been sleeping with him, but she also wanted him to be her priest, this authority figure, and she saw me as a threat to that. I just wanted to blow them all apart and tell a newspaper or somebody what had happened to me. You know, why is everybody blaming me for this? Why are people looking at me and seeing this big, bad temptress who's done something wrong? When I think of the politics of it all, it really stinks.

But I had to leave. And, within three weeks of my dad dying, Chris was also asked to leave the chaplaincy by the Bishop. When he told me, I said, 'Does that mean you have to leave the priesthood?' And he said, 'Well, it's as good as, because the best I'll get is some Godforsaken parish.' He was quite lost so I said, 'Come and live with me.' He said afterwards he hadn't wanted to do that, that he felt forced into it by me. He said he'd really wanted to travel round the country and do a bit of thinking. But he came.

I had my exams for my MA finals about five weeks after he moved in with me, and my dissertation to write, and he was a nightmare. He wanted to turn my house into the chaplaincy. It was 'Get your stuff out of there,' and 'Stop doing this.' He was driving me bananas. He'd brought quite a lot of icons with him as well, lots of religious pictures and a picture of himself in his ordination garb.

He registered at the same university as me to read architecture, and got a job delivering pizzas, but he only lasted two days at that – it was too menial for him. So we lived on my grant. I wasn't materialistic or anything but he did things like going out and spending £80 on food – I'd spend £25 a week, if that – or buying half a crate of lager because he'd always had lots to drink at the chaplaincy. I was dead careful with things. I'd say, 'We can't afford that.'

So I felt I was having to deal with all the practical issues as well as all the emotional and psychological ones. He couldn't cope with normality at all. He couldn't cope with going to the supermarket, cooking tea, being ordinary, Mr Nobody. It wasn't enough that he was special to me and Charlotte. He wanted to be special to a lot of people who weren't that close to him. That was another thing. I remember the first time he got angry with me: he said he couldn't cope with somebody being close to him. He just couldn't deal with that level of emotion.

It's funny, but my impressions of the relationship are most strong from when we were in the chaplaincy, because that's when he was at his most potent. He became a bit of an insignificant character after that in some ways, which is not to say that *I* saw him as insignificant, because I still invested my heart and soul into it all, but in terms of the world he was. When he walked down the street, no one would say hello to him, or ask, 'Can you come round to our house to sort something out for me?'

I remember once walking down the street with him and we saw a woman who had been his parishioner some years before. He had his arm around me and we turned a corner and met this woman. He was shocked, but he was also really effusive with her because he was so pleased to be recognised. He even introduced me to her as his partner and said he'd left the priesthood. I think he was quite proud of me that day. A lot of the time, though, his frustration with that lack of recognition would come out in anger towards me, because he couldn't cope with the transition.

I was still going for counselling once or twice a week. For the first five weeks, I just talked about Chris, about what was happening with him and how depressed he was feeling and what I was going to do to cope with this depression of his. Nothing about me.

One day, after I'd done my first exam, he was driving me to my mum's and we had an argument. 'Right, that's it! I can't stay in the car with you. I've had enough!' So I got out, and he drove off, with Charlotte in the car. I learned not to do that again. I had to walk seven miles home. I had no coat, it was raining, I had no keys to my home, no money on me, and when I got home he wasn't there. I rang up this friend who lived about a mile away and said, 'Are Chris and Charlotte there?' She said, 'Yes, but Chris is just going.' I ran round, shell-shocked, and she said, 'He's gone.' That was it – no word, nothing, he just walked out. I think something had snapped. I was devastated.

A week later, just after I'd done my second exam, I was beginning to feel better. I got home and there was a letter. He'd written to tell me how beautiful I was, how sorry he was, how much he loved me. I didn't have a clue where he'd been all week. He'd actually gone to the Bishop and said, 'I want to come back to the priesthood,' and the Bishop had said, 'You can't. Go and get yourself psychologically sorted out.' He sent him off to a retreat centre. He lasted two and a half days and then he escaped through a bedroom window. He couldn't cope with it at all. So he came back to me. He said he had been treated very badly at the centre but I think it was because they'd uncovered some problems that he didn't want to deal with. It's a very American style of counselling, apparently, very confrontational.

We then decided to buy a house together and, within ten minutes of seeing this house I'm in now, we'd made an offer for it. But I had big problems about us buying a house together. It seemed a big step to make. What if it didn't work out between us? He was deeply wounded that I could even suggest that. He was really sure about it and, although I wasn't, I wanted a house of my own, so we bought it.

He was very good that summer, actually. We spent a fortune on the house – it was ridiculous. As a chaplain, he'd had all the money given to him all his life. So he had about £5,000 in savings, and in one day he managed to write something like twenty-one cheques for things for the house! He had no concept of money at all and he found real life incredibly hard, whereas I'd only ever known this world and it felt nice and comfortable and safe. He worked really hard on the house and looked after Charlotte in the school holidays while I was writing my MA dissertation.

Even so, in the end, I got behind in my work. I finished the dissertation in the November and started my PhD in the October, so you can imagine what I was like – not because of the academic work, because I really love that, but because of trying to balance the two things and having to give to Chris all the time. I was used to giving to Charlotte and dealing with her demands, but I felt that I'd come home and, if he needed me to talk to him, I had to listen otherwise we'd have sulks and rows. He was going to counselling himself at that stage, but he was seeing a priest, which was not exactly the healthiest of counselling situations.

In a way, it was re-enacting the chaplaincy days. He still did all the things he'd done in the chaplaincy, like causing an argument and driving off on me, and I'd be sitting there thinking, 'Is he going to come back?' Gradually, though, I acquired more and more resources and friends of my own, so I'd say to him, 'Go then, if you want.' He didn't, but it became hard to live with. I know it must have been a difficult time for him as well, but I was knackered all the time.

The first time he left, Charlotte didn't seem particularly upset, because she wasn't really part of it. He wasn't angry with her or anything. She just saw him packing his stuff, he took her round to my friend's, said, 'I'll be back later,' gave her a kiss and left. So she was all right about that, though she was perturbed when she saw me upset.

We moved here in the August and he left in the November. There was a lot of resentment going on during that time and he was quite aggressive towards me. In fact, a week after we moved in, a friend came for the weekend and we went out for a drink and Chris came back and just flipped his lid. I said something to him – I can't remember what – and he threw a glass at me, and a chair, all sorts. My friend had gone to bed but I'm sure she must have heard. I was too embarrassed to talk to her about it the next day.

Another time, we went into town and started having an argument about a chair. We walked out of the shop and he punched me and knocked me to the ground, knocked my glasses off. I was really upset. People came up and said to him, 'What do you think you're doing?' I hope I will never again in the rest of my life hear a guy saying, 'It's nothing to do with you, it's a domestic situation.' I couldn't believe that he'd dealt with so many people over the years who had gone through domestic violence and he could actually say that.

Afterwards, I told him it was completely unacceptable and if he ever hit me again . . . and he didn't. But he did walk out one day when we were at university together. I went to the car to meet him and it wasn't there. I had the car keys because I'd driven in and I thought, 'The car's been nicked.' No sign of Chris. I got a taxi to Charlotte's school. No sign of Chris. The teachers must have thought I was mad because I said, 'Oh, God, I think my partner's left me.' When I got home, there was a brick through the back window and the door was wide open. I thought, 'I've been burgled.' There was an incredibly venomous note from Chris about how awful I was. I can't remember some of the words he wrote in it. I don't want to remember, it was horrible. I was shocked, and Charlotte was upset because I was upset.

I rang his parents up and they said, 'Serves you right. You shouldn't have set up home with him.' He'd gone back home to them and said he didn't know what he wanted to do, that I'd forced him into the situation. I was really depressed for about a month, quite suicidal, because there seemed no point in carrying on. I just thought, 'I've got myself into an utter mess and now he's completely let me down.' I felt I had sacrificed so much. I'd sacrificed friendships, I'd sacrificed my integrity, I'd sacrificed family approval, and he'd just walked out. For a month, I functioned normally during the day, but every night I was completely out of it, just didn't deal with anything.

Finally, I decided on a new start. I still saw him at university and he did some incredible things. He'd meet one of my friends, pour his heart out about why he'd left and all the time this friend would be ready to punch his lights out because he'd been there picking up the pieces with me.

He still had this great need for confession and what he wanted me to do was to forgive him. So I did. I was stupid. He came back in the April and said it was really going to work this time. But I'd changed in those few months. I'd stopped crying at counselling and was feeling quite strong. My book was taking shape, I'd been offered part-time teaching, I'd lost a lot of the weight I'd put on when I lived with him. I'd also started thinking I was never going to be with a man again for as long as I lived, because I came to believe that all men were like Chris. But he came back and I serviced him all the way through his first-year exams: sat down and helped him revise, typed up essays for him, cooked all the meals, even though I was supposed to be doing my PhD. I couldn't even get in the bloody study because he was using it all day.

I also held a massive surprise birthday party for him, all because I still cared for him, even though something at the back of my mind said, 'I can't imagine being with this person for the rest of my life.' That was the point at which I felt I had a choice. Up to then, I hadn't thought I had. It was always on his terms; even making love was when he wanted to.

He was here for another three months and then I went to give a talk at a conference, the first time I had done this. I did it really well, and I rang him up to tell him, and when I came back he'd left. He did exactly the same thing as before. He dumped Charlotte on someone, saying he was going to the dentist. But this time he left peacefully. He'd ironed all the clothes, he'd cleaned the house, everything was spotless, and I came home and he'd gone.

I was dead upset. It was like being let down yet again. He'd taken from me and Charlotte all over again and then gone on his way. But I also felt, 'That's it, it's finally over.' So I was quite calm, and I think that meant that Charlotte could express what she was feeling, because she just stood at the top of the stairs and howled at the moon. I've never felt so helpless in my life. I must have held her for about forty-five minutes while she just sobbed her heart out. She couldn't even tell me what was wrong.

She talked about him for weeks afterwards and the explanation I gave her was, 'Chris doesn't know what he wants. He's a very upset person and he isn't happy with his life, so he thinks it's better if he doesn't live with us because he'd make us unhappy, too.' One day, she suddenly said, 'I don't miss Chris any more, you know. I'm glad he doesn't live with us any more.' I said, 'Why?' And she replied,

'Because he always made you cry.' In this five-minute conversation, she'd sorted it out and said, 'I'm all right about it.'

So it was over, and I took steps to ensure that it would stay over. I got some letters from him to which I didn't reply. I also got some phone calls, so I had my number changed. Last year, he sent Charlotte £20 for her birthday, which I sent straight back. He also sent her a card at Christmas, which I didn't give to her. Why not? Because I don't want to encourage her to have a relationship with him. I don't think he's a very good person for her to have in her life. I've concentrated all my energies on making her feel secure, but it's been like a death, really, someone going out of her life. Even now, three years after he left, I still think if I gave him half a chance he would have a relationship with me. But he wouldn't have a chance any more. I think that's why he left the last time, because he saw that I had a life that was separate from his and I was making my own choices.

Do I miss him? Not at all, no. I actually feel quite shocked that I had such a long relationship with him. It was so ungood for me. The first year I was angry, as much with myself as with him, and that anger propelled me right away from him. After that came a lot of sadness, because evidently I did care for him. I put my whole life energy into the relationship, which I've never done before or since. But I feel he took so much away from me that that counteracted any of the good feelings.

That's basically my story. It probably sounds quite confused because there are lots of different layers and different issues and different times which made it quite traumatic. All the issues about power imbalance – he never saw the power as being his, yet he had complete power, all the time, for five years.

What he gained was a sense of himself, a sense of what he wanted, a confidence and an ability to go out and face the world. What I lost was trust in another human being and my faith. I hadn't really been to church for a few years before I met Chris, but I was a strongly religious person. Much of the relationship interfered with my faith. To be fair, I don't know what I believe any more but I know I still want to stand up in the middle of Mass and say, 'Do you know what the Church has done to me? Do you know how I was treated because I loved a priest? Do you know how much he was given by the Church and how much he was let off and how much I suffered because of your investing such authority and power into this person?' I don't think I ever will do it; the need will probably go away at some point.

The big issue now for me is that he's going back to the priesthood. He was given a special licence to conduct his sister's wedding and that was the first time he'd ministered as a priest for three years. He's in touch with his Bishop sporadically, but he's quite adamant that that's what he wants to do. Why? Well, it depends how you look at it, doesn't it? From my cynical perspective, I'd say it's because he can't cope with the real world. Because he became incredibly frightened, aggressive, cornered when he was out here in the real world. He couldn't accept being an anonymous person, couldn't cope without that authority, that status, that recognition and that ability to be a magician of the people, to perform rituals that make people feel better about themselves and their lives.

I think he now realises he can't be a magician architect, because he hasn't put the work in. When he started off, he was going to make the big time, but he's spent too many years drinking and abusing his body and not being very good to himself, so he found it hard to be a dedicated student.

He was a priest for so long, things have always come easily to him. Money's always been there, bills have been paid; status has always been there, he's never had to acquire it. People need an idol, a leader, so they choose priests, without looking at the personal qualities of that person or whether he's any good or not. That's not to denigrate Chris – he was a good priest, but he was good because he's good at acting out a role.

He did see the priesthood as his vocation. After he left, he would often cry and say, 'I was a really good priest,' but it was balanced by this almost overwhelming need to deceive and manipulate. He wouldn't see it like that, but he had a massive influence on incredibly vulnerable people's lives. I think he's one of those priests who get a lot of power out of the priesthood, which covered up some of his own inadequacies and weaknesses so that he could always be distanced from the issues involved in a relationship. Whenever there was an issue to be confronted, like infidelity, he'd retreat behind his priestly barracks.

The Church's advertising campaigns don't advertise for emotionally robust and healthy individuals. They want people who are prepared to be celibate and accept all the norms of the Church, which means they get a lot of unhealthy characters. How can you be a spiritual and emotional leader among a community of people without being spiritually and emotionally robust yourself?

Ultimately, our relationship didn't ruin me for life or anything, but it has made me wary of having relationships with men. I felt so negative about them that I even wondered if I was gay. So I guess I was in one of those destructive relationships with a priest, because there was so much secrecy and manipulation going on, so much hidden behind the mask of priesthood. What I thought was happening was that this priest had fallen in love with me, deeply cared about me, and was trying to find a way through that. But what was actually happening was that he was having relationships with several women and not taking responsibility for what he was doing.

I believe he violated my vulnerability and the position I was in. If he was sitting here now, he would disagree with me. He'd say, 'Matilda, that is not what I did at all. I responded to your needs.' He couldn't see what he was doing in that he was using other people's problems and vulnerability to feed himself. He gave and gave because he needed to be needed. And all these problems would come out because he wasn't dealing with his own problems, he was dealing with other people's. That's what he did with me. He dealt with my problems. Which wasn't what I needed. When I needed someone strong to help me set up on my own, he set up a very dependent relationship in which I became the dependant and he became the giver.

Talking to you has brought up a really significant issue for me. Namely, why am I talking about it now? Partly it's catharsis, and partly it's to give a voice to a lot of women who are in these relationships and who can't say anything because they are too frightened to speak out or too protective of their partner, or whatever.

I feel I should speak out about him going back to the priesthood as well. But how do I do that? I've thought about writing to his Bishop and detailing what has happened and why I feel that this person is an unsuitable candidate to be taken back into the priesthood. But I'm not sure it would do any good. Also, and this is the issue for me, would it be vengeance, or would it be speaking out for justice?

Some time after Chris left, I wrote a parable about a woman on a journey. She was travelling from a relationship to herself and she met this kindly old priest who wanted to look after her and help her get to herself. Through a series of twists and turns and stumbles, she realised he wasn't ever going to do that, so she opened her eyes and discovered she was in a cage. The priest spoke out and said, 'I'm leaving you.' She said, 'No, you're not leaving me any more, I'm leaving you. I've realised no one but me can let me get to myself.' So she walked out of the cage. She broke free.

Susan

My first sight of Susan was of a tall, grey-haired woman standing in the country lane outside a thatched cottage, flagging down my taxi. Immediately, she was solicitous – had it been too awful a journey? Had I had anything to eat? I must be dying for a cup of tea. Although it was a sunny day and her beautifully tended garden seemed enticing, at first we talked in her dark, but peaceful, study. 'I don't want the neighbours to hear,' she said sensibly. Afterwards, interview concluded, we took tea outside among the butterflies and bees, and she insisted on giving me an armful of freshly picked, sweetly scented herbs to take home. Although Susan's relationship with a priest ended nine years ago, it remains a significant event in her life. On the desk in her study is a tiny framed photograph of a handsome, fair-haired man. 'That's Carlo,' she said proudly. 'You can see why I fell for him, can't you?'

It strikes me that we never hear about the women in these cases. Or, if we do, they're held up as Jezebels. It never occurs to people that we might have the same spiritual leanings as the priest, and that's why we fall in love with them.

I was brought up in a very traditional Catholic family. Both my parents were Catholic, I went to a Catholic boarding school and, when I left school and went into nursing, I still carried on my religion. It's only been in the last seven or eight years that I've physically left the Church. Now, I have left it completely.

I got married in a Catholic church, although none of my family wanted me to marry my husband because they all thought he was not socially my equal. So there was this big family row and they more or

135

less disinherited me. None of them came to my wedding. It was an 'either us or him' attitude.

I was twenty-five when I married. My husband had been one of my patients. He came from a quite horrific background, terribly disturbed. His mother had left his father when he was very small and taken his younger sister with her. So he was shunted around from one member of the family to the other. When he was old enough to leave school and earn some money, his mother got him back and wouldn't allow him any further education, although he was very intelligent. She made him go on the buses instead, then he did his National Service. It was then that he became ill. So, when I first knew him, he wasn't doing anything. He did go back on the buses, and from there he met someone who trained him up as an inspector.

When my first child was born, my father allowed my mother to come and see us. After that, she would come and see us about once a year. Eventually my father came to see us, too, but they were never fully reconciled to my husband. In the end, of course, they were justified because he left me with four children, all under six – the youngest was six months old.

I should never have married him. It wasn't fair of me, because I knew he was grossly immature and so was I, for Heaven's sake. I mean, I was a green little convent schoolgirl who'd had few boyfriends and hadn't really kicked about in the world very much at all.

We were living in London at the time. When he left, my parents, the whole family, pulled together and found us a cottage in the country. My father had this very rich sister who said she would buy us a place, but I was to pay my father rent. It was on condition that I never got back with my husband or let the children see him. So there I was with four tiny children, no money because he'd taken all my money as well as his – he'd even taken my engagement ring to give to this blonde – *and* my Family Allowance book. He'd gone off with a succession of different women before eventually he got this woman pregnant. She gave up the child to be adopted, I heard later, but he married her and had another child by her.

He was very young when he left. For about eighteen months before, he was working away and just coming home at weekends, so the children didn't see him an awful lot. I suppose it was a development from 'Daddy only comes home at weekends' to 'Daddy doesn't always come home at weekends' to 'Daddy doesn't come home at all.' Even when he was with us, he never gave them a birthday present or card, never bought them anything. They did have a rough time with him.

So I had to survive with no money and on Social Security, all these little kids, the youngest a baby still, and no home. What would you do? I moved into the cottage with the children. But it's led to a lot of trouble because the child that was adopted decided he wanted to find his real mother and, about three years ago, contacted me to ask if my ex-husband was still alive. He wasn't – he died ten years ago. But then it all came out, the whole can of worms, and the children all blamed me for them not seeing their father. I came in for a lot of their anger. Some of them are still having counselling and therapy. I'm sure they'll work through it, but at the moment I'm having a bit of a terrible time.

Anyway, it was when I moved to the country that I started going to church again properly, becoming involved and bringing the children up in the Church. They were all baptised, and did all the Catholic milestones, but they didn't go to Catholic school.

At that time, the Church offered me something I needed, very much so. I started to teach a bit of religious instruction to them and to other local Catholic children. I played the organ, and my children grew very musical so they sang, and every year at Christmas we had a carol service. I suppose, because they didn't go to Catholic school, it was a case of making sure they were involved in everything that was going on in the parish.

The church in the village was just a small one, served by the local priory. Every summer, the brothers had a summer school for foreign clergy who'd come over for about eight weeks, learning English and so on. I became involved in that, giving informal lessons, opening my own home to them, lots of evenings with spaghetti and wine. It was great for the children, too, because they met people of so many nationalities. There'd be South Americans of every kind, Australians, Canadians, several from African countries, Europeans.

I was trying to think yesterday which year it was. It must have been 1983 or 1984. I had had four years of clinical depression and I was in a vulnerable state, though I was finally recovering. This particular summer, there was a little gang of us who used to go round together –

parishioners and visiting priests. Carlo was a member of a Spanish teaching order. Whenever we went out anywhere, it was always us together. We got on really well and had so much in common – literature, poetry, music – he played the piano wonderfully – and our political and social outlook was very similar.

One of the reasons we identified so strongly with each other was because I was then studying liberation theology and working at the same time for Amnesty International. He was a philosopher inclined to Marxism, and we shared the same opinion that the Church should get politically involved where human rights were concerned.

When he went back, he started writing and we had quite a correspondence. Then, suddenly, the following summer, a new lot of priests arrived and, to my astonishment, he turned up again. He hadn't told me he was coming and I was completely, utterly surprised and shocked. That was when it began to get serious.

In his letters, there had been hints about how he felt, odd things he'd written. But I was wary, because I felt so vulnerable after the depression. I really didn't want any complication in my life. I felt I just couldn't cope with anything else after that, and with the children going through adolescence. At the same time, yes, he was special to me above all the others, my main friend, and I was tremendously attracted to him. But I still thought, 'No, no, no, this is terrible. I can't get involved with a priest.'

Yet I still kept answering his letters. It was nice to get them, it's as simple as that. Everybody likes to feel they're loved, don't they? But I still couldn't reply in exactly the same vein. My letters were affectionate, but they weren't as deep as his. Yet I still never thought, 'No, I must stop this.' I've burned them now. All of them. I bitterly regret that.

When he came back the next year and I walked into the room and saw him, that was it. Bingo, bingo! I no longer fought it. I loved him and that was the only thing that mattered. We both instantaneously recognised it.

The day after they arrived, the priests went to the priory to concelebrate Mass. Afterwards, we were all to go into the big refectory and have a welcoming party. I got there a bit late, so I sat at the back, where I couldn't really see the altar. After Mass, I went into the cloisters, and he suddenly appeared, and we just looked at each other and literally flung ourselves at each other in front of all these people. He said to me, right in my ear, 'I love you.' I said, 'So do I.' And we stuck to each other for the rest of the evening.

He hadn't told me he was coming back because he said he wanted to give me a surprise. Apparently, he'd told his superiors that he wanted to come back and improve his English. So I ended up getting the shock of my life. It was very romantic.

He wasn't what I'd call a typical Spaniard. You know, extrovert and full of life and jolly and laughing and frightfully passionate and all the rest of it. He wasn't like that at all. He was quite quiet and deep and introspective, which I am as well, but we just always seemed to have a lot to talk about. He didn't even look Spanish – he's the only Spaniard I've ever met with blue eyes and fairish hair. He had a lovely face, a very gentle face. Apart from the chemistry factor, I just felt I'd come home with him. That's all I can say. We just felt we were made for each other.

Because it was his second visit, and I didn't know the people he was with, it was much easier for us to segregate ourselves and go off on our own. So we finally realised there was a lot more to this than deep friendship and we acknowledged that we loved each other. He would skive off lessons and come over, and we'd either stay in or go out for the day. I suppose over the eight weeks we must have spent half the days together. Nights were impossible, obviously, because of the children, but yes, we were often together in the daytime.

We would spend the first few hours just totally enjoying each other's company but, as the time came for him to go, we would start discussing everything again and it became more and more fraught, because I could see no way out. It was quite simple to him – well, not simple, but it was a clear-cut choice. He could leave the priesthood and marry me, or stay in the priesthood. Whereas to me, there were a lot of other things involved – or so it seemed at the time.

He was quite determined that I was what he wanted and that, if necessary, he'd give up everything for me. He was about eight years younger than me – I'd have been about forty – and this was one of the things that frightened me. There were so many things that frightened me, not least the fact that I'd been so badly let down the first time. And we loved each other so much, I couldn't bear the thought that, if he gave up the priesthood and married me, later on he might regret it and begin to hate me. To me, this was unbearable.

I don't think it had got as far as, 'Oh, you can come back to Spain with me.' It was, 'If you want me, I will give up everything. I'll give up my priesthood and we can get together and when we've made this decision then we can discuss what we're going to do later, what sort of job I can have, maybe a teaching job in England or in Spain, or in a university somewhere. But first, let's sort ourselves out.'

But there were so many complications. I was divorced. I had four children. It seemed an impossible load for a celibate priest to take on. He didn't see it that way at all. He was quite willing to take on everything – my family and the whole caboodle. But we'd have had to have lived in Spain and, much as I love Spain, I wasn't at all sure I could live there. If it had been me on my own it would have been a different story altogether, but I had to think of my family as well.

The children liked him – he was a very likeable person – but I don't think they realised he was anyone special. When I told them, years later, they were absolutely flabbergasted. They were so used to thinking of me as old Mum who was always there, who never got up to anything terrible, didn't have men in the house and wasn't jumping in and out of bed with different men all the time like some of their friends were – quite moral in a sense. So I think it was a shock to them – after all that time, to have had an affair with a priest!

We did feel guilty – oh, yes. I don't think I ever tried to justify myself in the sense that I would sit there and say, 'Oh, well, I've been so good all this time, why shouldn't I have an affair with someone and, after all, he's perfectly willing?' He felt guilty, too, but he was quite liberal – I never once saw him dressed in priest's clothes except when he said Mass, and he was fully aware that even a priest can fall down every day and sin, and get up again and carry on the next day. But he always said, 'God understands how we feel. And the way we love each other nobody, least of all God, can condemn it.' That's what he felt. I did, too, but then he'd go off at the end of the day and all the guilt would come back. 'What am I doing? It's a terrible sin.'

One Sunday, he said Mass, and I thought, 'This is appalling. There we are, in and out of bed . . .' I couldn't bring myself to go up to Communion, because of the fear of mortal sin. In the end, I did confess it to one of the brothers. He said, 'I can't give you absolution unless you make up your mind not to do it again.' I couldn't give that promise. So he gave me conditional absolution. He said, 'He's going to go back to Spain, you know, but God loves you, God forgives you, and I'm going to give you absolution whether you want it or not, so kneel down!' I don't think Carlo ever confessed it. I asked him if he would, and he said, although he felt guilty, he didn't feel it was anything terribly wrong. He had fulfilled himself as a man. It was a meaningful relationship, not just lust. So I stopped feeling guilty for a while. But when you've been conditioned to it since childhood . . .

The whole thing was so incredibly fraught. We were deliriously happy, desperately in love with each other, but at the same time it was so cloak-and-dagger, which made it feel very sordid. It was an agonising time. The whole eight weeks were swings from being deliriously happy to desperately unhappy. I don't think I've ever been so happy, yet so unhappy at the same time. I had it at the back of my mind that this couldn't go on, I couldn't let it ruin his life. Because he was an incredibly good priest, and he loved being a priest, he'd always wanted to be a priest. So, on the one hand, I thought, 'How can I do this to him? How can I ask him to give up his vocation for me?' But, at the same time, I was swept along in all this high romance, and it was hard to be logical. In the end, sheer fright and terror made me finish it. And, if you were to ask me if I regret that, yes I do, I regret it bitterly.

His idea was that he would go back and see his superior and say that he wanted to leave the priesthood and why and, depending on what he said, he'd come back and see me and we'd talk it all through together.

I was friendly with one of the brothers, the one who heard my confession, and Carlo liked him very much, too. So we both decided we would tell him, just to have someone else to talk to. We both independently saw him and, of course, he went through the 'Are you sure?' business. He didn't sit down and say, 'Look, this is against the rules of the Church. You can't do this, you can't do that.' He seemed far more concerned about what we might be doing to ourselves and to each other. It did help a bit having somebody fairly objective to talk to. But it wasn't until two days before they all left that I decided I just couldn't go through with it. Not for particularly noble reasons, but because I was so scared he'd get to hate me later on.

He was absolutely devastated. He begged me and begged me and begged me; he said, 'I won't push you, I won't rush you, I'll wait.' And I thought, 'How can he wait? How can he go back to being a priest with all this on his mind?' I thought the best thing would be to say no there and then, and finish it. To have a clean cut, never write or anything again.

Maybe if I'd not been through four years of depression, it wouldn't have happened. But I was so unsure of myself. And, after bringing up five children . . . well, you can imagine: not having time for men, because the kids took up all my energy and time. Not wanting another relationship, anyway, because my marriage had been so traumatic. It was difficult to trust anyone else, and I was so afraid of being hurt again. Then along comes this marvellous person with whom I had so much in common, who lifted me up. And then it was so dreadfully painful.

I wasn't being strong, I was just being frightened and taking what I thought was the easy way out. I feel very sad about that even now, because he suffered, and watching his suffering was part of my suffering.

On the last day he told me he would never, ever regret it, because he now knew what real love was, what it was really like to love a woman, so he could understand a lot more what people were going through, how traumatic it was. He said all the time he was with me, he felt like another person; he'd always felt something was lacking before. We were like kindred spirits, and he felt he could go and do his work on a deeper level because he had a much better understanding of human nature and what it is to feel love for someone, temptation, everything. It did make a great deal of difference to him.

When he left, I just completely broke down. I collapsed. I now know what it means to be mad with grief. I think he would have coped a lot better. I heard he went to Guatemala, to preach and live among the poor in their shanty towns. I'm sure he would have thrown himself into his work.

You ask me whether I think I did the right thing. Sometimes I'm quite clear that I didn't do the right thing for me. I wish I'd said yes, let him go ahead. But I was so terrified. Because things had gone so badly for me always, I just couldn't believe they were going to go right for me then. The ironic thing was – I didn't know it then – that my husband had died quite shortly before Carlo and I met.

So he went back to Spain, and the priest we'd talked to left, too. That was terrible, because when you love someone, you want to talk about them, don't you? There was no one I could talk to about it.

It was the most painful time of my life. Far more painful than my husband going because I realise now that I didn't really love him. I never felt able to love anyone – I don't think I'll ever love anyone again like that.

It took months and months to get over the initial agony – years, really. In fact, I think there's a part of me that's never recovered and I don't think it ever will. Sometimes even now, when I think about it, I cry. Loving him as I do, it's still distressing to go into it in depth, even though I have written reams about it. I used to go to bed and wake up about three in the morning and just cry the night away. And I had this excruciating pain all over. I had terrible nightmares which went on for months and months. I used to spend all my free time going on the walks we used to go on together. I was just so thankful that the children weren't young and dependent on me, so I could indulge in my grief. It was as though someone had died, as though he'd died in a way. I'd lost him completely and it was as though I'd cut out my own heart. That's the only way I can describe it.

As far as my religion was concerned, I still poddled along to church in a moronic kind of fashion. I went through the motions, put it that way. I couldn't pray, I couldn't do anything. Then I decided I couldn't carry on living where I was. There was too much unhappiness. I thought, 'I've got to pick myself up and start something new, a completely new phase to my life.' So I moved to another city, started going to the local cathedral and made some new friends.

After a while, though, I started questioning all sorts of things. This went on for months and months and then, one particular Sunday, I went to Mass and we were all standing up mumbling the Creed, and I remember looking at all these middle-class university types and thinking, 'How can they believe all this rubbish? How can I go on believing all this rubbish?' I made a conscious decision then that I wouldn't go to Mass the following Sunday. It was a beautiful sunny day, so I took a bus and found a seat on the downs and sat there reading, expecting a thunderbolt to hit me. And, of course, nothing happened.

Gradually I began to rethink my spiritual life. I'd done a short theology course some time before, but I decided there were so many things in the Catholic Church I could no longer countenance and that it wasn't doing me or the Church any good to go on being part of it, so I opted out. I evolved out of it into something else. The odd thing is I feel no guilt, no regret, nothing, absolutely nothing at all.

For the first couple of years, I thought of myself as a lapsed Catholic. Now I'm an ex-Catholic, definitely. If somebody said to me, 'Would you go back?' I'd say no. The way I feel at the moment I wouldn't. It's like a millstone falling from my neck. I'm not bitter about it at all, it's just not me any more, not my way.

So now my spiritual life is completely different from what it was. I do transcendental meditation, I don't follow any particular path, I just do my own thing. I'm far more together now. As far as Carlo is concerned, I'm a completely different person to the one I was then. And, of course, I'm fifty now and he'd be in his early forties, so I don't know if he'd be attracted to me as I am now.

I'm completely free, though. My husband is dead, the children live away. If he suddenly appeared out of the blue, I'd say yes. But I'm quite sure he wouldn't want to go through all that again at this stage in his life. I don't know. There's no way I would attempt to contact him. I do ask people if they ever hear from him, but no one ever has. Some years ago, I met someone who married a priest from his order, so I told her about Carlo. She said, 'Why don't you write to him? You really ought to. He might still be longing for you.' I went home, sat down, and wrote this long, long letter. I even went out to post it. But I couldn't put it in the letterbox. I tore it up, and I've never tried again.

Elizabeth

My first contact with Elizabeth was an anonymous phone call during the day. She wouldn't give me her name or telephone number before she had asked numerous questions about the nature of my research and the uses to which it would be put. Even then, she insisted on a pseudonym. To this day, I don't know her real name. I had to use her pseudonym even when sending her story – via a friend – for checking. She insisted on coming to me – 'I don't live that far away,' she said – because she simply couldn't risk having me visit her. Yet, despite great nervousness, she obviously wanted and needed to talk to somebody. When she arrived, she was almost visibly shaking. It took half an hour before she could even begin to relax. In appearance, she is fair, slightly plump, 'ordinary'. A very far cry from the popular image of a priest's 'mistress'.

How far back do you want me to go? Well, I was brought up as a very traditional Catholic. Irish Catholic parents, a lot of statues in the house, a lot of Sacred Hearts and saints. My father was in the St Vincent de Paul Society, my mother helped arrange the flowers in the church. They always had priests round at the weekend – it was always 'Father this' and 'Father that'. Oh, yes, they were pillars of the community.

The fact that they had a really bad marriage seemed to be neither here nor there. What was important was that they appeared to be good Catholics – the ideal Catholic family. But I felt rejected from a very early age. I'm the eldest, and my mother used to say to me, 'If I hadn't had you, I wouldn't have had to stay with your father.' It got so bad that they stopped speaking to each other for a long time. So it was an awful atmosphere to be growing up in, especially as they were such staunch churchgoers. There was always that hypocrisy which I found hard to cope with, and it led to schizophrenic feelings towards the Church. Oh, no, no one else knew about it. Ever.

I went to a Catholic primary school, Catholic secondary school, was a good Catholic girl. As the eldest, I was kept very much under lock and key. I couldn't wait to leave home so, as soon as I was eighteen, I got myself a place in a Catholic teacher-training college. I was still a practising Catholic because I knew no different. All my friends and family were Catholic, and it was always a case of it's Sunday, you go to Mass; it's a holy day of obligation, you go to Mass; it's Friday, you don't eat meat. There were never any two ways about it. That was just what you did.

So I was very rigid and blind in my obedience to the Church. And, funnily enough, it was at this Catholic college that I first started to question it. Because, although some of the same things applied, there were people there who were flouting the rules, who were hopping in and out of bed with each other under the eyes of the nuns. It was quite a shock to the system when you'd come from a family like mine to suddenly come across all this promiscuous behaviour, which is how I saw it.

The effect it had on me was that the very first man who kissed me, I felt I should marry. He was at the same college, so we met when I was eighteen and knew each other for a while just as friends – he was in the year above. I suppose, because he came from the same Catholic background, he understood the way I felt. We actually had quite a lot in common at that stage – the Church and teaching and folk music – so we got married, just after I graduated. He'd been teaching for a year and I was twenty-one.

No, I wasn't a virgin. We had slept together before we married. That really clinched it for me. I always remembered my mother saying, when I went away to college, 'You behave yourself, now. Don't forget, I'll be watching you. If you get up to anything, I'll know about it straight away.' I really and truly believed her. So when we first slept together, I was convinced she'd know about it. I couldn't go home for weeks. When I did, I could hardly look her in the eye. But, of course, she didn't notice a thing. It just meant that, until the day we married, I couldn't enjoy sex. Even then it wasn't so great. He hadn't had many other girlfriends, either, and none he'd had full intercourse with, so we were both very naive and fumbling about the whole thing.

When I look back now, I can see that I didn't love him in the way that you should love a husband, but it was inevitable. We got pushed along into it, there was just an acceptance. It was a big Catholic wedding, with both sides of the family, full nuptials.

I got myself a job at another school in the same town. We had two children – we had Francis just a year after we got married. I knew nothing about contraception. My knowledge of the facts of life came from a book written by nuns. It was only when I had him so quickly and then, afterwards, got pregnant very quickly again, that we started thinking about contraception. Otherwise I could see myself being just like all those other Catholic women of my parents' generation, getting pregnant year after year. I didn't want that, because I did want to teach as well.

So, because we were good Catholics, we went off and found out about the Catholic birth control method. Of course, that meant there wasn't a lot of spontaneity to what we were doing. But when Maire was born, I had a bad time with her, anyway, and went off sex for quite a while afterwards. That gave us time to think about the type of birth control method we wanted. So we went along to the Catholic Marriage Advisory Council and learned about this method, which really stood us in pretty good stead. I mean, maybe I wasn't very fertile – or maybe my husband wasn't – but whatever the case it certainly seemed to work for us.

Then my husband moved jobs, to a different town. Because the children were still little, I brought them up while he was teaching, planning to work as soon as they were old enough.

We'd always been very active, like our parents were, in the Church, because you just were. We weren't as bad as them – I didn't have a picture of the Sacred Heart in the house – but we did think it was important to bring the children up as Catholics. They were baptised, and right from the word go we took them to Mass, every Sunday. Everyone used to say what a nice little family.

The parish priest was a much older man – he was in his early fifties then – and he'd been there a long time. We were welcomed into the active Catholic community and, because we were interested in folk music, my husband started playing the guitar in Mass. I'd help out as well. I did a bit of cleaning in the church, and the flowers. I enjoyed it. It was part of my identity, the culture I'd been brought up in. The community were our friends as well. That's one of the things I've always liked about the Catholic Church – it's as much a social activity as a religious one.

It went along like that for some time, until Francis started at the little Catholic school attached to the church. A year later, Maire joined him. We'd got quite friendly, my husband and I, with Paddy, the priest, and he used to come back sometimes to the house. My husband would offer him a whisky or, if it was just me there, it would be a coffee. He has got something of a drink problem, though I didn't know that at the time. A lot of priests have drink problems, haven't they?

Sometimes we'd have meetings in the house, Bible study and prayer groups, and sometimes Paddy would come along as well, though at this stage it was still 'Father'. That's how he wanted it, being Irish and a lot older. He is very traditionally Irish, not a go-ahead English priest at all. He's imbued with Irish Catholicism and that includes to some extent the social side of being in the Irish club, being a presence there, people buying him drinks, asking him to pick the raffle tickets, all that sort of stuff.

At some point, we'd been talking about me going back to work and he said there might be a job at the little school and he'd have a word with the head teacher about it. Now, because he's the priest, Paddy does have influence. I don't know to this day whether he used some of that influence to get me the job, but I did get it. So it worked out really well. It also meant that Paddy and I had something else in common.

By this stage, my husband was starting to lose, not his faith, but his interest in the Church. He had a bit of a breakdown, basically, all tied up with his background and the influence of his mother, which was still very strong. He felt the pressures, as well, of having a newish job which had more responsibilities attached to it, and in which he wasn't so happy, plus two children. There wasn't any financial pressure because I was back at work. But he started to drink as well. I think he was finding the community he didn't have at school down at the club. So he started going down there quite a lot. He'd never been much of a drinker before. Maybe he was catching up, a late adolescent. He just wasn't very happy.

There was one occasion when it all got too much for him. It was to do with the birth control method we were using and the fact that some of his mates used condoms, and some of their wives were on the Pill. He couldn't understand why I didn't want to go on the Pill. I just didn't, not then. Looking back, I was a bit of a prude. I didn't think it was right to muck about with your body like that – which is ironic, really, considering – but also I'd been brought up to think the Pill was wrong. He didn't fancy condoms because he thought they denied him pleasure, so we couldn't reach a happy conclusion on that one. So we carried on with the natural method.

But we did have this very bad row one evening when he wanted sex and I didn't and . . . basically, he forced me. I'd made it perfectly clear I didn't want to do it, and that it wasn't safe and, while I didn't mind the idea of having another child, I'd only been back in work a year, I liked teaching and I didn't want to give it up. But he insisted and said it was ludicrous that we had to live our lives according to this temperature chart and so on, so that was that. Then I found I was pregnant.

I was distraught. I didn't know which way to turn. I mean, my parents wouldn't have seen a problem – 'Oh, marvellous, another soldier for Christ' – and his parents would have said the same. To give him his due, he was very ashamed of what had happened; he couldn't really look me in the face for a while after that. When I told him I was pregnant, he tried to make up for it, but I wasn't interested. Part of me wondered whether he wanted me to have a career. His mother hadn't, so it was almost as if he wanted me to be like his mother. I started to resent her a lot as a result. And I resented him.

I hadn't been at the school long enough for maternity leave. But, again, Paddy swung it. When I found out I was pregnant, I told my husband first and Paddy second, because I was so distressed and he *was* our priest. I went round to the presbytery and, as soon as I saw him, I just burst into tears. His immediate response was the one my mother's would have been, but then he could see that I was actually very upset and he tried to understand. When I look back, I think, 'What was I doing, telling him?' But he was the priest, and you told your troubles to the priest.

From then on, he seemed to feel a responsibility towards me. He certainly helped smooth my way back into work after I had Nicky, and when I was off on maternity leave he'd come round and see me. He started to unwind with me, that's what happened, to relax. In a lot of the homes he went into, everybody saw him as Father and would look up to him and never treat him like a human being. With me, he started to reveal himself as a human being, to talk about his own difficulties. So, without really knowing it, we did start to grow close.

When Nicky was six months old, I went back to school and he went to the childminder. My husband was drinking more and spending more time in the club, and we started growing apart. We still had sex, but only very occasionally and, when we did, he used condoms. Paddy would see him in the club but he never let on what he knew. My husband never found anything unusual about Paddy coming round here so often, because he was used to it.

What I'd told Paddy served as a bond between us. After that, I found it easy to go and talk to him. I wouldn't just go and give him my confession. It was also seeing him in a one-to-one situation. He would come round for coffee or whatever and I talked to him not just as a parishioner but as a person. I think I saw it for a long time as just Father coming round, and me being a good Catholic woman offering him tea and sympathy.

When Nicky was about eighteen months old, there was a trip coming up at the school to Lourdes, and Paddy asked if I wanted to go on it. The children were both going. I couldn't really afford it, but he said, not to worry, the school would cover some of the cost if I went along to help out. So I went, with Paddy and another teacher. I think he did it out of the kindness of his heart – he knew I needed a break and although Francis and Maire were there, my mother looked after Nicky so it was a break from him, and from my husband, which was the most important thing. Paddy knew things weren't well between us, but not the full extent of it.

So we went to Lourdes and had a very nice time. It was hard work but it was a really good experience, and a break. And, basically, what happened was that after we came back Paddy sent me a message via one of the other teachers to go round to the presbytery after school because he'd got something for me. I assumed it was something to do with

Lourdes, so I put the kids in the car and went to the presbytery. I left them in the car while I popped in. He let me in and he looked in a real state. I didn't know what was the matter. We went into the visitors' room and sat down and he said, 'I'm very glad you've come because I've got something to tell you.' I had no idea what it was. And he just said, 'I love you, and I don't know what the hell to do about it.'

I couldn't speak, I was so shocked. It was so unexpected. I hadn't made the shift from Father to Paddy. I remember saying, 'What do you mean? You're a priest.' And he said, 'I know. That's why I don't know what to do.' Then he got up, came across to where I was sitting, took my hand and said, 'I've just got to kiss you.' So he did.

I couldn't think straight at all. He was asking me to see him in a completely different light. I'd gone to him for help, for advice, because he was my priest, he knew my husband and my family, and it really hadn't occurred to me there was anything else to it. It wasn't even as if there was anything going on in Lourdes. He never indicated in any way that he felt differently about me than he did about the other teacher, who's a friend of mine. But here he was, telling me he'd been in agony all week because of seeing me so often and not being able to do anything about it. Apparently, that's when it all came to a head for him.

I suppose what I felt was a real conflict of emotions. On the one hand, I was thinking, 'This is wrong, this is Father So-and-So kissing me in the presbytery, and what happens if the housekeeper comes in, and my children are outside in the car'. That was fear, total shock. But it had been a while since my husband had kissed me like that, so there was also a bit of me responding. He asked me how I felt, and I had to say, 'I don't know, this is all too sudden.' And he said, 'I need you and I want you, and this has never happened to me before and I don't know what we're going to do about it, but that's the way I feel.'

I was up and down, up and down – 'I've got to go' – and he was saying, 'But you can't go until we've talked about it,' and I was saying, 'I can't talk about it now, I must go, otherwise people are going to talk. How am I going to face them? What shall I say?' And he said, 'Don't say anything, just say you had to pick something up about Lourdes. And can I come and see you later?' It happened to be an evening when my husband had a scout group meeting, so I knew he wouldn't be back till late. I said yes, he could.

I don't know how I got through the rest of the evening, to be honest. I took the children home, gave them their tea, sent them out to play, couldn't believe what was going on. By eight o'clock they were all upstairs and I had to have a stiff drink. Then he came round and it all came pouring out: how he'd felt about me for months, how it had all crystallised in Lourdes, that I was the only person he could talk to, because neither of us was happy. With him it had a lot to do with the priesthood, not being seen as an ordinary human being but as someone different and apart. Loneliness was very big. What was left of his family was back in Ireland; he hadn't got a curate, just the housekeeper, and she went home at nights. I think he felt totally trapped by the image people had of him and I was one of the few people who had seen beneath that image and been able to talk to him as a man. He'd responded to that.

At first it was kissing and hugging and lots of talks. Then one day I was ill and I didn't go to school. He was taking Mass there that morning, so he asked where I was and came straight round. I was feeling awful. He said he'd come back and see me later on. I'd got this awful migraine. I felt a lot better after lunch but I was still wandering around in my nightie. And he came back and that was the first time we made love.

It didn't bother me at all that it was in our bed, not at all. My husband should never have forced himself upon me that time. That's not to say I didn't feel awful about the whole thing, because I did – and I still do, to some extent. So does Paddy. Because, although I was active in the Church and so people expected us to be friendly, once the relationship shifted into this other gear I became very aware of how we talked to each other, how we looked at each other. The whole thing suddenly became a lot more secretive and pressurised and difficult to cope with.

Once we'd started being physically involved it was even worse, because there was so much at stake. It was all the practical difficulties as well, the fact that he lived in the presbytery, where there were always people coming and going. Most of the active parishioners would recognise him or his car. So for us to get involved was extremely foolhardy, and I don't know how we've managed to keep it secret. But we have. I think some people suspect or gossip, but they can do nothing about it, really. Not without proof.

I don't think either of us had any idea of where it would lead us. We just felt there was nothing wrong about it because, although initially I was totally shocked, and although he's a lot older than me, he can give me a lot of things my husband can't. I don't just mean sex, but companionship, a bit of attention. For all his faults, Paddy is very understanding. He likes the children and they like him – he spends more time now with them than their father does. But he's very confused, and that's getting worse and worse.

We've been having this relationship now for four years. It's been a terrible strain for both of us. Let's face it, he's approaching sixty, he's only ever been a priest, he comes from an Irish Catholic family, born and brought up in Ireland, has never done anything else, can't do anything else – he's not qualified for anything else. So, if he left the priesthood, he wouldn't get a job, he'd sacrifice his pension, there'd be a big scandal inside and outside the parish, and what could he do? Nothing.

At the moment, he's still Father and, wherever he goes – out visiting the sick or out with the school or in the social club or wherever – he has that position. If he was to leave all that behind, and come to me, he'd have nothing. I'm saying all this now quite frankly, but it's been very difficult for me to accept it. Because he has filled a gap in my life and has helped to fulfil me in some ways. My relationship with my husband isn't good but I think, without Paddy, it would have deteriorated to the point of divorce because of the anger. I've been able to work through some of that anger with Paddy, and now I tolerate my husband for the sake of my children and because it's a cover for this other relationship. So why should I leave him?

Not long after we started sleeping together . . . this is the bit that's really difficult . . . I got pregnant. Because he'd never slept with a woman before, he knew nothing about contraception, for all he might have talked about it from the pulpit. He knew nothing about condoms. The whole idea would have been anathema to him. And I still had this thing about the Pill. But when we first started making love, the whole idea of the safe period was shot to hell. It was the last thing on our minds. Looking back, I can't believe we were so stupid. But we both got totally carried away, so within two months, I was pregnant. It was just the most awful, awful, awful time. I was a Catholic teacher, in a Catholic school where the parish priest had made me pregnant.

Now maybe you know why I'm so scared. You can imagine the scandal it would have caused, can't you? We were at the start of a relationship, getting close, realising what we meant to each other and then – poof! – God's bolt of lightning. I remember telling him. He came round for coffee and I just blurted it out. He literally seemed to age before my eyes.

I was beside myself. But, at the same time, I felt we had to go along with what had happened. I'd got pregnant, I should have the baby, even if it meant passing it off as my husband's. That would have been difficult, because we were hardly ever having sex, and Paddy knew that, but I could have done it and passed the child off as his. I thought quite seriously about that – and about leaving my husband and going off with Paddy and the children. It's ludicrous when I look back – what would we have lived on? How could I have explained it to the children, to my parents? But at the time, I felt my husband didn't need me any more but the children did, and so did Paddy. You might say he was a father substitute, and maybe he was, but there comes a point where you can't really analyse it any more. When it just is.

I liked the fact that he's a caring person, that he's spent all his life in parishes, that he's involved in the community and the parish. He's not always the easiest person to talk to and some people find him much too conservative. He's a product of his time and culture. The last person in the world to whom this should have happened.

Hell on Earth is how I'd describe the next few weeks. Our lives just fell apart. We couldn't tell anybody, and there's something terrible – terrible – about keeping that kind of secret to yourself. The longer we left it, the worse the situation was getting. I'm surprised he didn't have a nervous breakdown, I really am. I don't know how he managed to carry on, doing his duties, saying Mass, when we'd got this to think about as well.

He'd come round and sit at the kitchen table, put his head in his hands and just cry. That was very distressing for me. But whenever I said, 'Look, we could do this, go away together,' it was always, 'No, I can't face it.' I don't think he could ever face it for one minute because of what he had to lose. He couldn't confess it. He said to me once, 'This is between me, you and God and only the three of us will ever, ever know.'

So we had a few weeks of awful nights and days just talking about it and in the end we agreed I should have an abortion. I was so tired of thinking about it. It still upsets me. I rang the clinic, made an appointment, told my husband I'd got awful period pains and asked him to take the children to school, and Paddy drove me to the clinic. I took a bus part of the way, then he picked me up. I could have gone the whole way on the bus, but he said no, he had to take me there. He also gave me some money towards the operation.

I can't begin to . . . I felt like I was in some kind of nightmare. Everything else had seemed so normal, the kids going off to school, my husband going off to school, and there we were going to this clinic. The last thing Paddy said to me was, 'God will forgive us,' which wasn't a lot of comfort to me at the time. I think he did genuinely feel that God would forgive us, but I couldn't see how, because we were committing a mortal sin. I still can't reconcile what we did, not at all. Because it's wrong.

They were very nice in the clinic, very understanding, and the thing itself wasn't half as bad as I'd thought. I was in and out in a few hours, because it was still in the very early stages. But you can imagine how difficult it was to come out and pretend everything was normal again. Paddy was waiting in the car, and he did try to be understanding about it. But I just cried all the way back home.

Luckily, there was no one else there, so I went straight to bed and stayed there until the next morning. I told my husband I was still feeling awful, and just needed to be left alone – they were used to my period pains. I had the most awful night. You know that phrase, the dark night of the soul? That's what it felt like. I even thought about suicide. I'd even worked out how many pills I'd need. But then I thought there really would be no hope for me at all if I killed myself. I've got to pay for what I've done.

It's taken its toll on me as it would on any woman. It was my baby, my body. It's taken its toll on him because he's had to carry on standing up in the pulpit preaching about love, marriage, the sanctity of life, even after what has happened. I did say to him once, 'How can you do that, talk about the sanctity of life, when you took me to the clinic and helped pay for the abortion?' He just said, 'We didn't have a choice. Life *is* sacred. But we didn't have a choice.'

I think to this day that he sees what we did as different from the theory of abortion. If someone else had an abortion, he would think it was a grievous sin. He'd try and dissuade people, he'd call it murder. But when he was caught in that same situation, he had no hesitation in doing something he knows is very wrong. I can't explain it and I don't think he could explain it. In the end, we stopped talking about it. It was too painful. It still is painful. I mean, we've come through it, it's over, and it's best left alone now.

I've never confessed it, no, never. What would I say? That's not to say I don't regret it. I do. But I think the guilt I feel and the pain is my punishment, not just a few Hail Marys and Our Fathers.

The funny thing, though, is that, whereas having Nicky more or less drove my husband and me apart, having the abortion brought Paddy and me closer together. It's our shared secret and we rely on each other to keep it. I suppose suffering is what's drawn us together, because we have both suffered over it. We can't ever be the same again.

We still see each other. We're a lot more careful now when it comes to sex, though we don't have sex so often. After that, I did go on the Pill because it seemed to me that going on the Pill was nothing compared to an abortion. My husband still doesn't suspect anything.

I don't know what will happen. It's a status quo, really. Maybe it'll change when the children get older and more independent. It's not a happy situation; it's not the one I would have chosen, but I don't see any way out. At least this way we're still together, because I do rely on him. He's there whenever I want him. I don't abuse that. I don't make his life difficult. It's like a joint need that keeps us together. But we have to be very, very careful and that's a big strain.

Someone said to me a few months ago, 'You're not looking too well.' And I was having a look at a photograph from five or six years ago, and they're right. I don't look as well as I did. I look quite a bit older.

It has affected my faith, yes, because I can't reconcile what we did with the teachings of the Church, so I try to put it to the back of my mind and hope that God has forgiven me. The other week, I even went to a Quaker service with a friend who's a Quaker. I don't know whether I could cope with that. It's very plain compared to what the Catholic

Church has to offer. But I do find it hard now to pray. Maybe that'll come back in time.

You can't blame the Church, but I do to an extent, because if they hadn't imposed the celibacy rule, all this pain and suffering wouldn't be happening. I know we're paying for our actions, but when I was younger I thought life was black and white; now I see it as shades of grey. It doesn't seem so straightforward any more.

I always used to think that people who had abortions were beyond the pale. Now I'm one of them. I find that very hard to cope with. That's why I don't think about it very much. I'm thinking about it now, but I don't usually. I think the Church puts us in some impossible situations by condemning abortion, by refusing to accept sensible contraception, for refusing to allow priests to marry. It's crazy.

There was a time nine months after I conceived that I got very depressed because that's when the baby would have been born. Again, Paddy was the only one I could share that with. For a while, I couldn't stop thinking about it, and looking at my other children and feeling . . . terrible. But there's no point thinking that way, is there? What's done is done.

I've had some periods of real anger, like I've never, ever had before. I didn't know I had such anger in me. It's frightened me at times. I don't know whether I'll carry on with the Catholic Church or not. I've really started questioning it in recent years. But at the moment, I'm just carrying on. And I don't think there's any point in leaving my husband now. There was a point where I should and could have left him. But not now. Maybe when the children have left home . . .

Now, three years later, I think I understand why it happened. I was asking too much of Paddy, much too much. I was asking him, a man in his fifties, to leave his job and his home and everything that went with that for me, when I would have lost my job and home as well, and had four children into the bargain. Where would we have gone? What would we have done? What would we have lived on? We would have lost family and friends and upset so many people. I can see all that now, but at the time it was very difficult to accept. I do think it's now between him and me and God and we have to live with that on our conscience for the rest of our lives.

Louise

Louise is an attractive, dark-haired woman in her early fifties. A widow with two grown-up children, she is an English Catholic of the Brompton Oratory school. Devout and active within her parish, she is obviously perplexed at the situation in which she finds herself: that of being very much in love with a priest, who returns her feelings, but who, when she and I met, was in an agony of indecision about whether to stay in the priesthood and sacrifice his relationship, or to sacrifice his calling for the possibility of marriage. 'At some time in the future,' she told me, 'he'd like to talk to you about his feelings and all the terrible conflicts he's having to face.' A rare invitation to hear the other side of the story. Early on in our conversation, Louise's poise deserted her and she began to cry. 'I'm afraid there'll be rather a lot of this,' she apologised. In her elegant living room, she then poured out her heart for six hours.

I met James first in the Charismatic Renewal about five years ago. He was newly appointed to the parish, and I'd got an unflattering picture in my mind's eye of what this new priest was going to be like. Then this gorgeous creature turned up and I thought, 'This is so unlike my mental picture, how extraordinary! What an attractive person.' There was an immediate attraction, not just a physical one but something very profound, much deeper than that, which I grasped hold of. I told myself not to be so silly, and wasn't it nice to have a jolly nice person in that position, and I had no business to let my thoughts go any further than that.

We met once or twice at various functions and then the parish put on a Life and Spirit seminar and I was part of that. We found ourselves as a team praying for people, and the rapport we had in prayer was quite beautiful, and very noticeable to the people we were praying with. Many months later, he said, 'Do you remember those days when we used to pray together? I used to feel the most tremendous empathy with you.' So it wasn't just on my part.

After some time, I found myself becoming more and more attracted to him, but we didn't talk privately or anything like that. I had to be very firm and tell myself not to be so stupid, that a man like him must have had women falling at his feet ever since he started in the priesthood. So he was just somebody I enjoyed being with and found easy to talk to.

Then I had a bereavement, which was the catalyst which caused me to review the whole of my life. I just knew James was the person to go to, as he has a great gift for listening. I told him more about myself, my feelings and my life story than anybody else in the world, even my late husband. It was as if I could stand naked before him and yet not be ashamed, because he wasn't going to put me down or make me feel embarrassed or awkward. He was there to help put me back together again.

Over this period of time, our friendship really grew. He found that he could share with me quite a lot too and this became meaningful for him because we did have this tremendous rapport and he found that he could also unburden things to me that he'd never talked about to other people.

For one reason or another, we didn't see each other for a few months. It was a traumatic time for me, and I needed to talk to him again about the things that had happened during those months, so he came over to see me. I found myself giving him a big hug and telling him how much I'd missed him, and I knew there was a response. He said something like, 'Me, too.' I thought, 'What am I hearing behind all this? Does he feel something, too?'

I really was confused. I was so attracted to this man, but I tried to keep my own feelings and emotions unexpressed to him as I didn't want to spoil our friendship. I just felt that he meant so much to me, I would be content to see him occasionally rather than not at all. Being with him was like an injection of something I really needed, a topping-up of my batteries. I couldn't explain it to myself. But I do know, each time I see him, it's the same for him. I only have to put my arms around him and I can feel him relax.

He shared more and more of himself and we got close physically, so our hugging turned to kissing, and the closeness and the attraction was just overwhelming. It was such a beautiful growth of our friendship, because it started on a spiritual level – we still pray together when we meet and we're very much at one at these times. It went from friendship to emotional reciprocation and, when the physical part came, it was just the natural climax to a very deep and slowly built-up friendship.

About this time, I had been reading some books and trying to understand the position I felt I was getting into, and I read a book called *Touching the Face of God*, all about celibacy and intimacy, which said how it's essential for everyone to have intimate relationships, whether sexual or not, and how the psychology of relationships is so much better understood these days. It really set me free by saying that deep friendships and feelings were both OK and permitted, because that is what you feel; it's what you do with those feelings that you have to think about.

But I was still experiencing some guilt about the feelings I had for James, and I remember reflecting, 'I've got to be fair to this man. Ours is a lovely friendship. I have to tell him what I feel about him and give him the chance to back away completely'. So I did. I said, 'You must know by now that I love you, and I feel it's only fair to tell you that if our friendship is to continue.' To my utter amazement, he answered. 'Me, too. I love you.'

I could hardly believe my ears, because up to then he'd given no indication. Yes, we'd been friendly, we'd been close, but as to that depth . . . Then we started sharing with even greater freedom, and it was like a barrier coming down, like a piece of glass that had been between us just disappeared, and we suddenly relaxed in a new way with each other and looked back over our friendship and how it had built up. He said the first time he saw me, it was like a bolt of electricity going through him. I said, 'What did you think about that, then?' and he replied, 'I said to myself, "This is what they warned me about in seminary!"'

I told him I felt the same way too, the first time I saw him, but how there had been no way I was ever going to admit it to myself or to anybody else at that stage. It seemed incredible that it had taken so long for us to share that. So the rock and foundation of our relationship is very deep.

I had come to terms with a loving relationship without sex and I was prepared to accept that, because the rest was forbidden. But I also knew that, given the invitation, I probably wouldn't be able to refuse. One day we were talking about life and compulsory celibacy and the fact that James had never really come to terms with it, and he told me that he felt he wouldn't be a fully integrated person unless he had a complete sexual relationship with someone. I was taken aback. I thought, 'Is this an invitation?' I asked him later whether he realised the implications of what he'd said. He replied, 'Yes.' He said he was secure in the love we had for each other that he wouldn't be rejected. So it was not a seduction, it was a mutual decision.

After that, it didn't take long before we had a full relationship.It just happened. I remember asking him, 'Have you thought about this, because it's possibly going to change the rest of your life?' Here I made a misjudgement. Knowing him as a thinking, caring person, I presumed if he was going to take this next step, he'd have thought it through. He hadn't. He hadn't thought through the implications at all. He didn't realise the power of falling in love, and of physical intimacy; the impact it has on emotions. He hadn't even bargained for falling in love. Not that we would go back or that we regret it in any way, but where I'd thought we would talk and discuss and come to terms with it first, we've had to do that afterwards.

He'd never been in a close relationship like this before. I think many women have fallen for him because he relates so well to them, but he'd never responded. He has said he didn't think when he was young that he was mature enough to have handled anything anyway, so his shyness was then his defence. Then I came in with two great feet, and now we're in this terrible dilemma. Where do we go from here? We're right in the midst of a period of evaluation, which is beautiful in one way, as we share deeply, but it's traumatic and painful as well.

It's about a year and a half since that conversation. Sometimes it seems that we've known each other for ever, but it is a short time, short but precious and very concentrated. And we really have got closer and closer. It's like finding the other half of oneself, and this is why it's so painful to face that we may have to separate, because it feels like we're being torn, literally, physically.

I do have some guilt feelings, but not so much before God – I am open with Him. It's more the discretion or deception required to meet and be together. We'd like the freedom to share our lives with our friends, to be open and honest with people, but of course we can't. It's the double life that really gets to James – he finds it very stressful. The fact that we have an intimate relationship he seems to be able to handle better. He says, 'At least it's more natural and healthy than living a fantasy.'

We're both very committed to the Lord, and I just have to say to Him, 'If I could, I would like to make this right. I look through my journal and see how I've tried to pray through every stage of our relationship and, yes, I'm sorry, but this is how it is, in my weakness and humanity this is where I am, Lord. Can you put it right somehow? If you've got to tear me apart and that's the right thing, then you've got to tear me apart.' James says the same.

To begin with, he was overwhelmed by the whole experience and we were both on a joyful 'high'. Now it's more difficult, trying to take time out of a busy parish life. He's extremely caring and sensitive to other people. So often I feel I'm put at the bottom of the list, because, like a wife, I should be tolerant and understanding if duty is calling. I understand this, but it can hurt. I'm sure, as well, that he thinks, 'This is what I really want, but I shouldn't be seeing Louise, so I'll do everything else first and put that last, to satisfy myself that I've done everything possible before I actually do the thing I want to do.' We all do that with treats, and sometimes there isn't even any time left over for the treat.

We usually meet once or twice a week. Often it's late, usually after a meeting, and, although we find a tremendous rejuvenation when we see each other, it is the end of the day and it can be hard as we're both tired. We might have deep things to talk about and he's often here until very late, then the next day we're like wet rags, even when he stays over, which came later, and was quite a big step.

We occasionally share one of his days off together, and then we have time to relax and just 'be' with each other. Once, we managed a few days away, which was very special, but took an awful lot of organising.

Our relationship has grown tremendously since then. It's so valuable and precious to both of us. I said to him the other day, 'Do you really think we can part? Do you really think we can live without each other somewhere in our lives? That we can just walk away from each other?'

He said, 'Up to a few months ago, if I'd really wanted to, I could have probably broken it off, but I don't think I could now, you're too much part of my life.'

We speak on the phone most days. Usually he'll ring me at night, and that's a high spot of my day. I feel very disappointed if I'm expecting a call and I don't get one. I have to be careful how often I ring him because there's a fifty-fifty chance someone else may answer. That can be very frustrating at times, and humiliating. Two adults in love, and unable to contact each other when they want to.

Really, the whole thing started to become very stressful during the spring. He was under a tremendous lot of pressure, flying around everywhere, and I was frightened that he was going to have a total breakdown or end up wrapped round a tree or something. In the end, he went to see his Bishop and said he needed some counselling because he was questioning his priesthood, his celibacy, and his ability to cope generally. He didn't tell him about me, because he said all these problems were there before I came along, I'd just been the catalyst. He said, 'If I tell the Bishop that there's a woman in my life, he'll probably say, "Cut the woman out and your problems will go away."' The women tend to get blamed for everything.

He's now seeing a counsellor, and that's very helpful, as the counsellor sees me as very much a part of the situation and not a shadowy figure to be left outside. He wanted to meet me, so we had a shared appointment with him, and he was most understanding. He wanted to see the sort of person I was, and hear what I had to say. He was interested in helping James find peace in his life, whether in or out of the priesthood.

James is a wonderful priest and pastor. He knows he's called to the priesthood to be a reconciler, a healer, a listener. If he left, he would really miss the sacramental side of his priesthood, the saying of the Eucharist – he finds that a spiritually feeding time. Yet, as we've got closer, he also says, 'I don't know how I can live without you, because you give me so much, you give me the love, the affection, that I've craved since I was a child.' This is true – for both of us. It's like water on a desert when we're together, we just soak each other up and feel alive. And, because we're both soft people and loving people, neither of us has the strength to get up and walk away.

It's such a bitter-sweet thing. I used to find the partings and 'When am I going to see you again?' so stressful, but we've almost got beyond that now to the depths of the pain, the depths of the love. They are so enormous that, although it's important to know when we're going to see each other again, the longing almost pales into insignificance when we look at what's going to happen overall. Sometimes it seems like a double crucifixion of parting is the only way out, the only way we can both cope with it, because it's too painful otherwise. We just don't know how to go from here.

We were discussing it the other night, because we'd both been away for a week, separately, and he came back and said, 'I really believe God is calling me to stay in the priesthood.' I just fell apart. We'd been together the night before we went away and we'd had such a loving, affirming time that I was really looking forward to coming together again. Then I was hearing something I had been dreading all week, dreading ever since we started. I went down into a black hole, totally into a black hole.

When I finally managed to start thinking again and we were talking it through, he said, 'I'm not saying we can't have a relationship of some sort.' I asked, 'What do you envisage?' And he replied, 'I haven't really thought out how it's going to be.' I said, 'Are we still going to be able to talk? Are we still going to be able to meet?' 'Yes.' 'Is it the sex you're talking about?' 'Well,' he said, 'do you think we could continue without the sexual side?' I found myself saying, 'We could try, as there's so much more we share. But, knowing us, I don't know how we'd manage.'

I was so distraught, I couldn't face a night on my own. So he stayed and we continued talking most of the night, by which time he'd done an about-turn. It was such a night of tears and agony. In the end, we both agreed we just couldn't leave each other.

So gradually we clawed back to where we were before. What's hard for me is that one minute I feel it's all going to end and I'm facing the pain of that, and the next minute my hope is kept alive again that this relationship can continue in some way as yet to be lived out. That's really where we are now, but there's still this terrible decision to be made. James is now going through the official channels and discussing it with the Bishop, who now knows of my existence, but not who I am.

After meeting him, James said, 'He was very gentle, very kind, very concerned about you as well as me, and that you should have what help you need.' Not every couple would get that consideration, and I am grateful.

How he would manage if we had to break completely, how I would manage, I just don't know. I have no idea of what it would do to him, to his ministry, or how broken he would be by it. I think men are actually stronger in a lot of ways, as they don't invest their whole emotions in a relationship in the same way as women do. They seem able to compartmentalise their lives much more. That isn't to say their feelings are any less, but they seem to be able to box them up and say, 'These two or three hours are priestly business, an hour tonight is Louise and the two don't overlap,' while for a woman her relationship permeates the whole of her thinking and her life.

God knows our weaknesses but, because of the way things are at present in the Church, people would be very upset if they knew. We have to be sensitive to what they used to call 'causing scandal'. In my bolder moments, I say, 'Well, that's their problem. We're trying to work out our lives as privately as possible.' But I do understand the shock and hurt people would feel.

James says that breaking up is the last thing he wants to do, and that's where the anger comes in. I think, 'Who has made these rules that are causing us so much pain? What is detrimental to his priesthood about us being together? What is impure about the sort of love we have for each other that it somehow sullies this cock-eyed version of what it is to be a priest?'

I understand that celibacy is meant to keep them free to love all people equally, but if they're not free within themselves, it's limiting. If they're living a fantasy life on one level, which gets them away from thinking about their need for a personal relationship, personal fulfilment, I don't think that's healthy. I don't think God asks them to do that. God saw man and said, 'It's not good for man to be alone, we'd better give him someone.' And He gave him woman, to complement his being, for mutual love and support.

Also, I think of St Paul, when he says it's better to marry than to burn. Some priests *are* burning – their unresolved sexuality is burning them out. If that were to be satisfied, they could then go out with that loving and that sense of fulfilment to give even more to their ministry.

This doesn't denigrate in any way the calling to celibacy, which is the real calling for some, but not all. Where it's a gift, it is beautiful and gives great strength, but enforced celibacy is an imposition and a burden to many who know they are called to serve. And it makes for a choice which I don't feel should be called for between the vocation to priesthood and to marriage. I just don't see why they can't be compatible.

We've tried to be honest with each other. In any relationship, but especially in a relationship like this where there is no formal commitment, you have to be totally honest. If you start hiding things and the other one finds out, where's the trust? And in relationships like this, you've got to be able to trust. The only right you have over each other is the trust and love you can give each other. You've got no marriage lines to hit each other over the head with, no promise to each other, no hold over the other person. So you are very vulnerable.

That leaves me feeling very insecure, especially as he's honest enough to keep saying, 'I don't know what to do next, I don't know how we're going to end up. It tears me apart so much. I can't leave you, yet I feel I am also called to be a priest.' I never know quite where I am and I'm somebody who likes to have a goal, something to work towards. I find it very difficult living from day to day not knowing what each day is going to bring, let alone the future.

What would I like to happen? Well, the ideal is the impossible: that we would be allowed to marry and he would be allowed to continue in priesthood. I've had enough ups and downs and hurts in this life to feel I could be a good 'Mrs Priest'. In no way am I aspiring to that role myself, but I know I could support him in his ministry and, because we can pray together and have that spiritual empathy, I believe we could be used by the Lord in many ways.

Initially, I didn't think marriage was an option. I'm not going to ask him to make a choice, that wouldn't be right. Once, the counsellor asked him straight out if he'd ever told me marriage was not on the books. He said, 'No, I've never said that.' So the counsellor asked if it was a possibility, and I heard James saying, 'Yes.' I said to the counsellor when I saw him on my own afterwards, 'Having had this possibility of marriage, this jewel, held out to me, I don't know whether I can put my hand out towards it in the knowledge that I might be very hurt, or whether to reject it as a possibility in order to protect myself.'

Obviously, for me marriage would be absolutely wonderful, but until that point it hadn't been in my thought patterns. Now that it is, I can't help but look at it as the best outcome for me. We've both talked about it a lot and, as he said, 'If I came to you not having sorted myself out, what sort of basis for marriage would that be?' I agree with that, and therefore I've bent over backwards never to manipulate or put pressure on him in any way at all because, if he was put in those circumstances, he could turn round and say, 'I'm miserable, you forced me into this', and that's not the foundation for a good married relationship.

So, for the first time in my life, I'm having to be patient, to think about what I'm saying and not to put on any pressure to get a decision. Not that I'm a desperately manipulative person, but we all have this ability in us and I'm having to recognise it and stop it at source. Yet I've got to say what I feel, to tell him how good I think marriage could be, while recognising that there would also be times of regret, terrible pain and sorrow at what he's left behind, trying to keep a balance. Whatever decision is made, there will be a bereavement for him; we are both aware of this.

Some friends I've talked to say, 'Why don't you just get out now, before it gets too hard?' But I can't. I love this man, I can't just leave him in a limbo-land. If I left him there, he would be in a pointless position, and what's that going to do to him? Is he just going to sink back into the mire again? Other friends say what we have is precious and worth holding on to until we've worked something out. That's what I feel. I shall be there to love and support him as long as he needs me.

The few people who know about James are generally supportive and understanding, although they're also anxious for him, and concerned that he makes the best decision for his future and peace of mind. It's good he has a few people he can talk with, but we have to be so careful. Sometimes, the talking and the tears are too much and we need to share with someone else, someone who can stand back and just listen. I have some very good friends – mostly not too close to home – who are most supportive.

Then, of course, there are all the practical implications to be considered: the loss of his job, status, salary and home. At fifty, what do you do for a job? So many priests have no formal qualification to offer. If they're real pastors, where do they fulfil themselves?

Ecumenically, there may be openings, but the doors seem to be closed in the Catholic Church when one of their priests leaves. Instead of being employed in some way to use their experience, they are barred.

Another thing I feel is that the Church establishment seems to point the finger at those who leave, for whatever reason. They seem to think these men lack commitment. I would pose this question to the Church: 'What are we doing that is causing these people to discontinue their calling, when so many of them are patently still called by the Lord and still want to serve Him? What is this burden we're putting on them that they can't carry?' Because this isn't a burden the Lord's put on them: compulsory celibacy is a man-made law.

As one friend said to me, 'The spirit of the Pharisees is alive and well in the Vatican, putting burdens on people that are not really necessary for their calling to love God and to serve Him.' It's only by standing up and being counted, by voicing their views, and maybe by leaving the active priesthood, that those concerned will get the Church to take the issue seriously. Rome seems to wear blinkers, denying that there is a problem, closing ranks. One day, if they don't listen and take note, there will be no more ranks to close.

My faith as I understand faith is my relationship with the Lord and that is as firm as ever. He is my God, He is my rock, He's my salvation, He's the one I go to, the one I talk to, the one who's going to sort out this mess, the one who carries me in the black times and in the light times. As for the Roman Church, I said to James the other night, 'I don't know how I'm going to stay in this Church that can cause such anguish, that seems to be to me no longer a loving mother but a spinster aunt.' She doesn't seem to give the love and support to her most favourite sons; she puts impositions on them which, in this day and age, I don't think are necessary to their priesthood.

I think priesthood has to be looked at again. I've got a lot of radical ideas about that. I think priests should come up from the community in which they live, called by the Holy Spirit. They could be married or not, that isn't the question; it's on their suitability to be the presider of that community, not necessarily for ever, maybe for a time.

I don't think parish priests necessarily have to be deep theologians or canon lawyers; they need to be loving, caring pastors who want to serve God and serve God's people, without restraints and with the option of the support of a wife and family. Maybe it wouldn't even need to be a full-time job. They could have a job of work, because economics do come into it. The Church has to change its whole idea of priestly life. The community should support their priest – and his wife and family – more directly, as other churches do.

Sometimes, if I look at the whole of the Roman Catholic Church, I despair. It seems so fossilised. So I have to lower my sights to my own community where we are a loving, serving family, worshipping God together. That's 'church' to me. I find the institutional Church top-heavy, too clerical. Loving God and having a personal relationship with Him is what it's all about, whether you call it Methodist or Catholic or Anglican; to me, we are all one body in the Holy Spirit. But I would find it difficult to find my spiritual home somewhere else, and so would James.

One question I want to put to him – and it's a bit hard of me, I suppose – is: 'You don't agree with the imposition of compulsory celibacy in the priesthood, yet you're still in that priesthood. You're searching to be an integrated person, yet what sort of integrity is that going to be if you stay there? Serving a church you have such a fundamental disagreement with?'

This morning I was getting angry in bed and having this mental conversation saying, 'Isn't it time for people like you to stand up and be counted? How many of you are living this disintegrated life because you are putting yourself under the jurisdiction of something that you're not living out? Something you can't give your whole heart and mind to. Isn't this making a compromise within yourself?'

It's so hard for many priests because they have this great calling by God and they also happen to have been brought up with this Catholic tradition of priesthood. They're forced to compromise their right to marry because of a law that says that's the only way they can answer and live their call to priesthood. But the more this view is discussed, and the more people vote with their feet, the more difficult it will be for Rome to shut their eyes and say it isn't happening.

If James does leave, it's going to hurt a lot, and I don't know if he'll be able to take it. But maybe he has to make that sacrifice for those in the future. If he left the priesthood, I think there would be a grey time. We'd want to be married but we couldn't be married in the Catholic

Church. In the giving of ourselves one to the other, I would feel married before God, but we would both like the blessing of a Christian community, and to belong to one, as well.

That's where we've got to. In my bolshiness, I say, 'Why should we move? This is where all our friends are, so if we move it will be very hard.' OK, there's also the other side of it, that he is parish priest here, which means we might be forced out by social pressure, not wanting to scandalise those who can't accept us. Then we'd have to go and find another parish where we could belong and take an active part.

I believe there's no sin involved in getting married – we're both free – but there is this 'grey time' between register office and official laicisation where technically we're not married in the eyes of the Church. I don't know how we'd cope with that. I mean, to me, in my heart, I've made a commitment, I can't give any more. Before God I've given all I can. He hasn't; he can't at the moment. We've discussed this often. I shall be faithful to him and committed to him until he tells me to go.

He can't make a similar commitment, because he hasn't made his decision. He knows he has a commitment, a responsibility, of sorts, but he's scared of the implication of 'I love you', because that means he's got to do something; it involves decisions. Fear of the unknown, as far as he's concerned, must not be discounted, and I have to face the fear of losing him. If we don't look those fears in the face and share them, it will harm our relationship.

I do fear that loss when I think of all the things that he is in my life. If he wasn't here, it would go into black and white. He's the one person I can talk to about my family, about my children, about the big things and little things that happen in life, without holding back. He's my dearest friend. He's given me the affection and the love, the understanding, the spiritual and emotional support I need. He has taken away the loneliness of being on my own, he makes me feel alive and of worth, he fulfils so much in my life. The thought of not having him there is like looking at a great black hole.

So we both have a huge fear. My fear is losing him; his fear is 'What happens if I leave? What happens if it doesn't work out? This could be the biggest mistake of my life.' But we mustn't let those fears overtake us.

The relationship has given him a tremendous affirmation. He's always been a 'love', but I think he's always been seeking to be liked. He's very gentle, very kind and always drawing a response from people. It's given him an awareness of himself, a freedom to express love and to come to terms with it and to be a more loving person because he is giving his love to me and I am giving my love to him. This gives him security, because he knows where his heart is and where he's loved. It's given him inner strength, and an understanding of a relationship he'd never dreamed of experiencing.

He says, 'I used to see these youngsters snogging down the street and I used to get terribly sniffy about it, but now I look at them and think, "Be happy, children, just be happy."' He says, 'It's given me much more understanding of the power, the physical attraction and the beauty of love.' Before, I think he was afraid of it, because it was such a powerful thing in his life, and now he's been able to come to terms with it much more, with his sexuality and with his emotions. And it has given him courage to look at other issues in his life, like his questioning of the Church, his other day-to-day relationships.

I have said to him, 'I feel inadequate in what I can offer you.' He said, 'You've no idea what you've done for me. You've helped my spiritual life, you've helped in all areas, it's been so fruitful.' I think it has been fruitful but, of course, stress and pressure can destroy that if we're not careful. Guilt could destroy that but, thank the Lord, we're not in that position. He doesn't like the deception and nor do I, though it doesn't impinge on my life so much.

We're both basically honest people, and this is what has made us go forward to resolve what is an unsatisfactory way of living, neither one thing nor the other. Some people manage it for years, but we know we can't. It's a hard place for me to be, this particular crossroads, waiting and wondering if we will take the same road forward or if we'll go our separate ways. I feel angry that we have to make a choice – any other two people who fall in love and are unmarried would be able to work out their relationship in a normal way. We can't. We have put this whole thing in God's hands. And we trust that He will eventually lead us to sort it out His way, whatever that way might be. He won't let us go down the wrong road for too long. We just have to trust. If we don't trust God, who do we trust?

Patricia

I first heard about Patricia through a mutual acquaintance who asked for the number of the Seven-Eleven support group. 'I've got a friend who really needs someone to talk to,' she said. 'She's having a relationship with a priest, but she's married as well, so it's making her ill.' It was some time later that Patricia herself rang and invited me to go and see her. Having a relationship with a priest at all is a strain, but having one when you're married is even worse. So it's not surprising that Patricia – a small, plump woman with long, jet-black hair – chain-smoked, twisted her fingers as she talked, and jumped if the phone rang. Not surprising, either, to learn she's on anti-depressants. I had to send the first draft of her story to another friend's house, where she could pick it up. Later, when I had to ring to check something, she whispered, 'I can't talk. Gordon's just come home.'

I was brought up C of E – Sunday School and church three times a day on Sunday – but when I got to about twenty-four, I'd got children and I sort of dropped off and didn't go for ages and ages, not until I started going to the Roman Catholic church about eighteen months ago. I'd kicked against it when I was old enough to make up my own mind, because I was made to go so much when I was a child.

I was married to my first husband for ten years, and I've got two daughters and a son and a little granddaughter. They're not religious at all. That ended in divorce, then I lived by myself for a while till I met Gordon, to whom I'm married now. He's divorced as well, and he's quite a bit older than me. He came to live with me eight years ago and we eventually got married.

Of course, him being Catholic, he was convinced he'd never be able to go into a Catholic church again, with us both being divorced. It was all right us living together, though – they always seem able to justify themselves. He's an old-fashioned Catholic, but he'd lapsed, and he was thinking that things were like they used to be. But they're not. They have changed. That was really my first introduction to Catholicism.

I met Kevin, this priest, on my first day at work at the newsagent's. It sounds a bit corny, but there was sort of a click. He's not a Roger Moore or a Pierce Brosnan, but he is attractive. Of course, I didn't know what he was, who he was. He just said hello and walked away. I said, 'Oh, he was nice,' and they were all laughing. I said, 'Why are you laughing?' 'Well, he's a Roman Catholic priest.' That didn't mean much to me, not being Catholic, but I gradually got talking to him week after week.

Then, when I was getting married again, Gordon said they wouldn't let us do it in church, so I said, 'I'll have a word with the priest who comes in the shop.' So I did, and he said he would bless the marriage for us. 'You know,' he said, 'we've got to give in now because people get divorced all the time. If we said you can't come to church because you're divorced, we'd have half the congregation missing.'

So he blessed the marriage after the register office, and I stood in church afterwards and thought, 'I've got the wrong one here,' but I knew I couldn't do anything about it. Everybody thought so much of Gordon, including my dad, who's eighty, and I thought, 'If I don't go through with this, it's going to kill him.' So, I suppose it was a bit silly getting married but, on the other hand, if I hadn't got married, I'd still be in the same boat, because Kevin would still be in the priesthood. It was just a friendship, though, then. It wasn't a sexual relationship, not until a couple of months afterwards.

Then Kevin started getting friendly with Gordon as well. They share a love of football. Kevin eats, drinks, thinks, sleeps football. The other priests' rooms at the church are covered in crucifixes and his is covered in pictures of the team he supports, not a space on the wall. He manages a local team as well, and has lots of trophies. So I've got all this to contend with, too!

Twelve months last November, I was really ill and they couldn't find out what was the matter with me. They thought it was multiple sclerosis. They still don't know what it is, but I'm a lot better now, and back at work part-time. All this business doesn't help, but Kevin can't understand that. Anyway, when I was off work he missed me, so he started to come to see me.

At first he used to bob in for ten minutes, and gradually the ten minutes got to half an hour, and then he'd ring up, 'Are you in this morning because I'll come down?' So it started from that. He'd come round once a week for the whole morning or the whole afternoon and he'd ring up every day. Then I'd see him at church, and he'd say, 'Come early and I'll come out and have a natter to you.' I thought it was a bit pointless, but he said, 'At least I can see you that way and I'll know you're all right.'

I'd started going to church with Gordon after we got married. The priests there were really nice to me. So I said to Gordon one day, 'I don't know if to change religion.' He said, 'It's up to you, please yourself.' So one day when Kevin came down, I said, 'I'm thinking of swapping.' He said, 'It takes about six months normally because you have to go to classes, but you used to be a practising Anglican, you know what it's all about. So really it's going to be a waste of time. I'll teach you privately.'

That made life easier for him visiting, because I was ill. After a few months, he came down one day with his oil and crosses and whatnot and converted me – 'Right, that's it!' Then he kissed me. And it was the real thing. It wasn't just a peck.

Up to then, when he was going he used to give me a kiss, just a little peck on the forehead, but gradually the kiss got longer and I thought, 'This guy isn't just giving you a peck like he would everybody else.' So this day, I asked, 'What are you doing? Why me?' You know, after thirty-two years in the priesthood. I mean, he went in when he was eighteen and he's fifty now. 'After all the sort of women you meet? Because there's nothing special about me,' I said. He told me: 'There is to me. But then, there always has been.' And I said, 'Oh, you make a habit of this, do you?' He replied, 'No, I've never been out with a woman,' and I believe him. No matter what he's done, he's never lied.

I was pleased, because I did really like him and I was attracted to him. In fact, I think I knew from the beginning, right at the back of my mind, that I'd end up in bed with him. I didn't realise the difficulties it would entail. He said afterwards, 'You know, I liked you for a long time. I fought against it long, long before I gave in to it.' He said he wasn't looking for a relationship. 'I just couldn't believe it,' he said. 'I never, ever thought it would happen to me. I know we're not infallible, but it just never entered my head.'

We didn't actually sleep together for a while, but we got very, very close. It was some weeks afterwards, when he came to see me here, that we slept together. I knew then that it was inevitable. He was just shaking. He said, 'I know it'll happen, but I'm shaking because when you think of the length of time it is since I've been out with women ...' I said, 'When you were eighteen to twenty-four, you must have gone out with them, because you were allowed to then.' 'No,' he replied. 'I never bothered. I was too interested in football.'

I say to him sometimes, 'Are you sure you're a priest?' I mean, I find it amazing how priests, who have not had any sort of sexual relationship with anybody, are when they're in bed with you. He's not shy, not after the first time. They learn quickly! I used to wonder whether he'd done it before, but he always said no. I'd say, 'How do you know what to do?' And he'd say, 'Well, everybody knows, don't they?'

I've not had to worry about contraception because I've been sterilised. He didn't know this at first, obviously. I didn't tell him. After that first time, I said, 'You fancy being a dad, do you?' And he said, 'What do you mean?' 'Well, you never bothered with anything – you're a good Catholic, you are!' He asked me, 'You'll be all right, won't you?' I said, 'I hope for your sake I am.' I kept that up for quite a while, and then I had to tell him, I couldn't let him go on suffering.

It did cross my mind that I shouldn't be having a relationship with a priest. At first I thought it was my fault, then I used to sit and think, 'No, it's not all my fault.' A lot of people might say, 'Look what you've dragged this poor man into.' But he didn't need any dragging. He will say that himself. He says, 'I don't blame you for any of it, really. It was me that did all the running.'

We both knew what we were doing. I knew what he was, and so did he, so there's no excuse, really. They know when they come out of seminary that it's a black and white issue, and all this running to the Pope isn't going to make one scrap of difference. John Paul's not going to think, 'That poor woman wants to marry a priest. We'd better let them all get married.' I don't think it'll make any difference at all, especially not with the present Pope.

I have asked him why he became a priest and he says he doesn't know any more. He says, 'I like people.' I asked him why he didn't become a social worker or something. But he says he's never regretted being a priest. He's got the best of both worlds now, of course. I once asked him, 'In black and white, would you miss the sex now?' And he said, 'Yes, I would, but if I had to go back to being what I was then, like the perfect priest, I think I could do it.'

He says it's not making him a worse priest. 'I'm still as good as I was and I do a lot of good and you do a lot of good, and the fact that we've got each other is one of the bad bits from the religious point of view, but you've got to weigh one up against the other.' You see, they can always justify themselves. He says that himself, though I don't think he'd justify himself if the Bishop had a go at him.

I told one of my closest friends about it and she said, 'I don't doubt that he loves you. He must do.' And I said, 'But he loves God more.' She replied, 'Well, he can't do, really, because he's breaking every rule in the book.'

Jonathan, the C of E vicar, knows. I met him in town one day when I wasn't feeling too good and he said, 'What's the matter with you?' 'I'm a bit cheesed off.' 'Come on, get the kettle on, I'll come home with you.' So he came down and he asked, 'What's the problem?' For ages I kept saying there wasn't a problem, then eventually I told him it was a fellow I'd met and he said, 'I thought it might be.' I was crying by this stage. 'Well, it's no good getting in this state. You've got three options. You either stay as you are, finish it, or you leave home and go and live with him.' So I said, 'Well, I can't do that. He's a Roman Catholic priest.' 'Bloody hell!' said the vicar. 'I know who it is.' And he told me, because, of course, they know each other. 'He's changed so much during the last few months and I've been wondering what's changed him. He's more outgoing, more chatty, and I know why now. He must love you an awful lot because he's very, very level-headed.'

Kevin doesn't know that Jonathan knows. He doesn't know anyone knows. He thinks you shouldn't tell anybody, not even your closest friend, because he's so afraid that if you tell one person they will tell another, no matter how good a friend they are. And he says if his parents knew about us, it would kill them – they're very traditional Catholics. No, he hasn't confessed it. I haven't confessed it, either. I'd have to take a flask and sandwiches if I went!

So you do feel guilty. He feels guilty because he's cheating the system and getting away with it. Still, it's better than cheating the system and getting caught. I don't feel guilty because I've got him, I feel guilty because of the Catholic Church. Apart from Kevin, it was one of the best moves I've ever made in my life, because they are so kind at that church. I mean, the parish priest came the other week and he said, 'Are you all right? You looked a bit fed up yesterday. You're very special to us up there, you know.' So I feel guilty about that, about how disappointed in me they'd be if they knew.

I don't think Kevin has ever felt guilty about me being married. No, he's never mentioned it. He and Gordon are always in touch. Gordon will ring him up. Just before Kevin went away a fortnight ago, it was, 'I'd better give Kevin a ring 'cos he's going away tomorrow.' They'll have a laugh and a joke together, talk about the match. I know I should feel guilty about that, but I don't. And if Kevin does, he's never mentioned it. Gordon doesn't suspect a thing. He thinks Catholic priests don't do that. I don't always say when Kevin's been and after about a week, Gordon'll say, 'You'd better give Kevin a ring. You've not seen him for ages, he's deserted you.' It's horrible, really, but it makes life easier.

At first I'd see him some part of every day. Don't get me wrong, I wouldn't be in bed with him some part of every day, but I would see him. And he'd come down one or two days a week, until it got to the point where the lady over the road asked, 'Who's that man who keeps calling in the red car?' Of course, his car was parked outside here for six or seven hours. I don't think they'd recognise the car but, by the same token, if he'd left his car in the next street and walked round he'd have bumped into somebody, so it's swings and roundabouts. I just said it was my brother's car because they don't know him, he doesn't live here.

If anyone had told Gordon, I'd just have told him who it was. He knew Kevin used to come down to see me. He reckons we're good for each other, that Kevin cheers me up and that he can treat this place like a home from home. I mean, he used to float in here – 'Have you got the paper?' and he'd be sprawled along the settee, 'Brew up, then.' It was just like going home, somehow. I don't know if that's what started it. He's fairly quiet and shy and he found he could talk to me and tell me about things that had gone wrong, and I'd feel sorry for him.

We both worry that he may be moved soon, because he's been in this parish for four years. I suppose in a way it might be better, because he might be on his own. At the moment, there are two of them, so I never know who's going to answer the phone. But I wouldn't see him as often, which would be awful.

He's more bothered about being found out than I am. So far, we've been lucky. We don't usually go out together. We usually meet here, or at church and church events. If you saw us there, you'd think he was Gordon's friend, not mine. They always have lots to say to each other. If he rings and Gordon answers, they're on the phone for hours. If he rings to speak to me and Gordon's here, I'll just say, 'Oh, hello. How are you?' Then he knows someone else is here.

But he can be so inconsistent. I saw him the other Tuesday and that's quite a busy day for him, with visiting the sick and everything. We went out for a bite to eat, then he said, 'I've got to go into town and do some shopping. Get your face on and we'll go.' He was quite prepared to walk through town with me.

When he comes here, I just tell my mates I'm going out for the day so not to come round. That's the only way we get any peace. All the kids have left home, so they don't know anything about it. He still comes to see me on his day off, and Gordon'll come home from work and say, 'Kevin been up to see you today?' 'Yes, just had a bit of lunch then he went.' Sometimes Kevin will say, 'Are we saying I've been here today? Because if so, I can have a cigarette.'

But thereby hangs a tale. God's honest truth, Kevin came here one Wednesday morning and we were in bed. Gordon came home that night and said, 'I had to come back to town today. I came down the street but your car wasn't parked up so I didn't bother coming in.' Now, my car had been parked outside all morning, and Kevin's was parked behind it. Gordon wouldn't recognise his car, but he must have driven straight past mine and not noticed – it was parked a few doors up. That was sheer luck, just sheer good luck. I'd hate to get found out, but on the other hand if you play with fire it's no good crying when you get burned, is it?

Gordon's a long-distance lorry driver, so he's away quite a lot. In fact, I see so little of him that I think I've got to get on with my life. If he comes home and I'm not in, that's his bad luck if I don't know he's coming home.

No, I don't love him any more. Until I met Kevin, I was quite happy with him. But now, I'm in bed sometimes at night and I think, 'I wish it wasn't you.' But I wouldn't get a divorce. It's very selfish, but financially it would just be hopeless. I couldn't keep myself on the money I earn at the shop and, at my age, I couldn't get a better paid job, especially not after being ill.

It is a strain. I'm only like I am because they pour anti-depressants down me as though they're going out of fashion. The minute I stop taking them, I'm back to square one, crying all day. That's all down to the relationship. I wasn't depressed at all before that.

What happened was that I lost weight and I was just crying all day. Gordon was saying, 'What's the matter?' 'I'm just depressed.' 'You'd better get to the doctor's.' So I went to the doctor, said I was depressed, but didn't tell him why. This went on for a while and in the end I thought it wasn't really fair so I told him what the set-up was. I didn't say who Kevin was or where he was from. So, of course, they put me on these anti-depressants and I took them and things got better, and then I stopped taking them and I was back to square one again. The doctor keeps saying, 'You can't take them for the rest of your life, you know. You're going to have to come to terms with it some time.'

It's a strain for Kevin as well. He admits it's a strain, but he doesn't go on about it. His attitude is, it's no use regretting it, it's done now. He does have some very down days, though. I rang him one Sunday and he said, 'I've been sitting here thinking about you all day and there's nobody to talk to.' I think in that way I've helped him. He's always had me to talk to, and there's always someone there who can say, 'Cheer up, it'll get better.'

I'll say, 'Do you wish you'd never got into this?' And he'll say, 'No, I don't ever wish that, but it is very difficult.' I've given him two or three chances to get out. I've said I wouldn't betray him or anything. But he says, 'No, that's not what I want. I want what I've got.' At first, he said to me, 'If this relationship goes on, do you realise how hard it's going to be for you? I'll always be there to help you but you'll always come second. I'll tell you I'm coming over at ten o'clock in the morning and then I'll have to go and christen a dying baby. You can't make an excuse like a husband can to a wife. I've got to go, there are no two ways about it.' I don't mind coming second to the job, but I do mind coming second to his football!

I had no idea when I got into the relationship how difficult it was going to be. He knew what his life was like, but I didn't. But then, I didn't think it'd become as involved. I suppose being C of E all my life didn't help, because I didn't realise the demands that the Church made on Catholic priests. He's so conscientious. You have to laugh sometimes: we were in bed one day and he said, 'What time is it?' 'Quarter to twelve.' 'Bloody hell! I've got a bloke to bury, I'll have to go!'

I don't think he sees any contradiction. I suppose I've got more time to think about things but he seems to put them to the back of his mind. So it's like two separate lives, his life with me and his life at church. I have this argument with God sometimes: 'Why have you got him all to yourself? Why can't you share him? You've had him all his life.'

Now he's away on a course for three weeks. If I wasn't taking the anti-depressants, I'd just be in a heap because he won't ring up from there. Oh, no, he can't do that. If it were me, I would find a way to ring him somehow, even if I just said, 'Are you all right? I can't speak.' But he says, 'I'll think about you a lot.' I say, 'Phone, don't just think.'

He did phone from the station, actually, when he got there, but that's all, and he's been gone a week. I even asked him to come back a few days earlier, said I could get away for a few days, but he said, 'It's when you start telling outright lies like that that you get caught.' I mean, he's out enjoying himself all day.

To be fair, he doesn't know I'm depressed. I haven't told him. I suppose I think he's got enough to think about. Also, he'd probably only say, 'Why? I can't do more than I do.' Which is true. And he'll ring up every other day, or I'll ring him.

I hope I'll get rid of the depression, because you'd think by now I'd have accepted it for what it is. But I don't want to get addicted to the tablets, even though the doctor says they're not addictive. They don't make you high or anything like that, you just don't worry as much.

I sometimes think, 'Do I ever wish I'd never met him?' And the answer's no. I'm glad I met him. It's coming to terms with the fact that you love somebody that you can never really have that's hard. Because I do love him, yes. I care more about him than I do for my husband and I have much more patience with him. I used to give into him all the time at first because I thought, 'Well, he isn't used to women,' but now I think after eighteen months he should be getting used to it. Why do I love him? It's his personality. He's kind, he's thoughtful, he's a good listener. It's their job, isn't it, being nice? And he was never a challenge, let's put it that way. He says there are so many women who really will have a go at you, mainly because you're a Roman Catholic priest and you're a challenge to them. He said, 'I never felt I was a challenge to you and that was why I liked you.' Sometimes he'll be talking to someone else from church and I'll say afterwards, 'Why did you spend so long talking to her when you tell me not to speak to you?' And he'll say, 'I haven't got a guilty conscience with her so it doesn't matter. I can stand and talk to her for an hour but I'm involved with you so I think everybody else will notice.'

He says there was a spark there initially and he says, 'You've just got such a fabulous personality. You've got a lot to offer.' I'll say to him, 'Do you love me?' He'll say, 'I think an awful lot of you.' I say, 'That wasn't what I asked.' He won't commit himself. Once, I was crying and he asked me why and I said, 'Because you don't love me.' And he said, 'Yes, I do, but I find it hard to tell you things like that. But you know I do, I wouldn't be here if I didn't. I'm not going to risk everything just for a one-off.'

But if it did ever come to light and we did ever get found out, and they gave him another chance, I still think he'd take that chance. I don't think he'd come out of the priesthood. In some ways I resent that, but it depends what mood I'm in. It really does. Some days I think, 'It's your own fault. You knew what he was.' Sometimes I think if it did come to the push he ought to give up the priesthood. But I don't think he will, not in the near future. If we get away with it for another ten years or so, then it might be different.

I'd never ask him to leave, but I do ask him sometimes what will happen eventually, when he's done all the things he wants to do. And he says, 'If you still love me, I'll come back for you and come out of the priesthood.' But I don't know if that would ever happen or not. I can only hope that he will do what he says and that we will end up together eventually. I'm prepared to wait. It's just a question of whether you can get away with it for so many years.

My biggest fear is that he's going to change his mind and say, 'I'm sorry it happened, it should have never happened, I don't want to see you again.' Even though he says he never will, that he'll never hurt me, you can't guarantee that. So now he's away for three weeks I think, 'He's had a week already to reflect on everything. Is he going to come back and say we'd better call it a day?' He always says if that ever happened it'd be me who did it. He says, 'I've got to go by what you want because I'm not in a position to offer you anything better. So you'll be the one who gets fed up because I can't offer you anything more than you're getting now.'

But I don't think I will get fed up. Frustrated and angry sometimes, and bitter that I've found something I think the absolute world of and I can't have it. I mean, sometimes I'll have a go at him if he's not rung for a couple of days and he'll say, 'You don't know what it's like.' He comes back from his course in a fortnight, but he's already told me I won't see him for ages because he's got family coming to stay for a month, then Confirmation. Then I get, not angry, but I think, 'Can't he just make two or three hours for me? He can make it for football.' 'But football's my life.' So it does cause a few rows.

You always feel they're there for somebody else but quite a lot of the time they're too busy to be there for you. They're there if you've got a problem, like when my friend's eighteen-year-old daughter got pregnant and she was desperate. I was talking to him about it and he said, 'Can't her mother get her an abortion?' It's then that you say, 'Are you really a Catholic priest?' But he says if it's the only way out . . . He says it's like birth control, it's just a waste of time, nobody wants dozens of kids running round. He says, 'You've got to be realistic about these things. You can't let religion rule your whole life.'

When I tell him he's not really practising what he preaches if he thinks it's all right for people to have abortions and birth control, he says, 'That's life.' I don't think he'd stand up and preach against abortion. He'd just avoid it. They're expert at avoiding things, aren't they?

I really don't know what to think about celibacy. Sometimes I think that when people go to them with marital problems and they've never experienced it themselves they're not in a position to criticise or offer advice. But if priests were allowed to get married, it would be an enormous expense for the Catholic Church. I mean, when you think of the four of them up there, if they were all married, all had families, they'd want four houses. So it's a way of keeping costs down!

All he ever says about it is, 'I'm not the only one, there have been loads before me, there'll be loads after me, so celibacy doesn't really work.' The other priests go out at night and I ask him where they go. 'I don't know,' he says. 'I don't ask them, it's nothing to do with me. Even if they have got a bit on the side, I don't want to know.'

If he did finish with me, I'd be devastated. I just don't know how I'd get by. I guess I want someone to wave a magic wand and make everything all right, but that doesn't happen. There's just not an answer. There's no way out of it. No easy answer to it at all.

Pauline

Pauline is one of the first women I met when starting to research this subject three and a half years ago. A researcher for a charity, she possesses an attractively husky voice that is the legacy of cigarettes, as I've since discovered during half a dozen evenings spent in bars, pizzerias and over nightcaps at her flat. When I first met her, she was involved with a priest who had left the formal ministry after having two relationships. He subsequently returned to the priesthood. But the big love of Pauline's life, Dermot, has never left the priesthood.

To go right back to the beginning, I was adopted when I was eleven months old. It's only very, very recently that I've traced my real family, none of whom are Catholics. I wasn't brought up a Catholic, either. My adoptive parents were very good to me, but I guess that sense of initial rejection has never left me. So you could say I'm looking for a father figure, but maybe it's more to do with forming relationships that have a built-in rejection, that are open-ended, that can't go anywhere. Only the rejection isn't to do with me, but with something greater than me – God. Maybe it's also a fear of commitment – on my side as much as on the priest's.

My parents sent me to church as a small child, but didn't attend themselves. At about nine, I stopped going as well. After school, I went to university. I was an atheist at this time. My courses included the sociology of religion, which fascinated me, though it never occurred to me to look for its spiritual dimension. I ended up getting married to one of the other students, a strong atheist. It was a fairly brief marriage, just a couple of years, and when it finished, I decided to do VSO work in India. While I was there, I had a long relationship with an Indian and

185

ended up staying ten years, but in the end I realised I had to come home. He didn't want me to go.

Also while I was in India, I became involved with Catholic missionaries. We used to have long discussions about religion and belief. I'd started becoming religious, anyway, and found myself being drawn to the Catholic Church because it seemed more universal, though I had, and still have, enormous reservations. Those reservations have actually increased with the passage of time, but from the start I was quite rebellious. I didn't agree with a lot of the rules and regulations, but those didn't seem to me to be the essence of faith, not even Catholic faith.

Anyway, in the months running up to me leaving India, I'd been having religious instruction from a priest. And suddenly, on the plane home, I realised I was in love with him. It was such a shock – 'I'm in love with the guy!' So when I got home, I bombarded him with letters telling him how I felt. He did reply, but non-committally; he never talks about his feelings, he doesn't understand them. But now, I'd say it's a very deep friendship. We've met up several times since 1988.

Thinking about it, I suppose it does have something to do with the myth of the untouchable: 'safe' relationships. I've had a couple of what I suppose you could call crushes, relationships that were aspiring rather than consummated. With the priest in India, it was all tied in with my conversion and with moving country after so long. There's certainly a pattern there. I can see that. I'm now hoping to break that pattern.

My most important relationship was with another priest I met after I came back from India. We met, in a perfectly normal way, through voluntary work, because of our shared interest in India. There was an immediate attraction on both sides, which was quite obvious. We got on very well and he said, 'Let's go for a drink.' I'm quite used to that, with other priests or other friends. It doesn't have any implications for me.

Some weeks passed and – it sounds like a cliché, but I was given tickets to a concert of religious music, Stabat Mater, and it came to me I'd like to go with him, so I invited him. I didn't even think about what that meant. He accepted extremely readily and we went to the concert together, then for a drink and a meal afterwards. And it went on like any normal – if you like – relationship, like any date that moves forward. We started being in touch quite a lot, talking a lot on the telephone, meeting frequently. It developed into an average, ordinary relationship. We went to very ordinary places: to the pub, to the cinema, for walks, sometimes to the countryside or just around the town, to church. In many ways it was very normal – I keep using that word. We visited my friends. Their main fear was that I would get hurt, which, of course, I did. I was grateful to them for that. Otherwise, they just accepted him.

At one level I suppose it did seem odd, asking out a priest. But as I was a convert, I didn't have the deeply engrained reservations that cradle Catholics might have. Politically, I didn't really accept the sort of situation that says priests should be different in that way.

Was I attracted to the man or the priest? That's a very difficult question. Initially, a lot of it was that he was a priest, because of my conversion, my need for security. But if I stayed with him, it was because he was a man.

A lot of priests can definitely send out vibrations that they are open to a relationship – though it's by no means true of all priests – so it's actually quite easy to form an understanding perhaps at a slightly deeper level than would happen in normal circumstances. And when it first happened, I was very much seeking an answer to problems, without actually realising what it was I was looking for. So those things got mixed up. Partly there was the thought of the man as salvation, the traditional woman's problem. It didn't stay like that, but a priest can seem very much like a guru, somebody who has the wisdom that one is looking for and doesn't easily find.

One of the things that attracted me was his great honesty and his willingness to show gentle qualities, which you don't find so easily among non-priests. A priest is more willing to express those qualities, what you might call the feminine side. I was also attracted by his spiritual side, and by his concern about social matters.

Why do you get involved with anybody? It's a very human thing. It's as if you shut a door in your mind that asks the questions. I didn't ask about the rights or wrongs, the pain of it or where it would lead. It was a very worthwhile relationship in itself. It's also very exciting falling in love – that was mutual. We just very much enjoyed being together, talking and doing things together. It just seemed right. Oh, yes, it was a full sexual relationship, and one that we both saw as potentially lasting. He made it very clear that, even if he left me, it was something that would last. That's one of the great pains of it, that he made it clear how important it was to him, but he was still going to leave. Which he did.

On his side, there was no premeditation. Thinking about it now, he'd spent many years on a remote mission station, so maybe for him it was about attachment to an idea: an idea of perfection and God. He'd had one major relationship before, which lasted two years, and he'd had several ladies who had a strong romantic interest in him which he hadn't followed through. He denied they were really that interested in him. He would rationalise it and see them just as friendly people, when it was obvious to me that it was quite a different situation.

He didn't dress as a priest. He wasn't a parish priest, he belonged to a community which doesn't wear a uniform. So he looked just like any other person. I've met women who've had a relationship with a priest who was very frightened of being found out. That, for me, would put an intolerable strain on the relationship. There was great honesty in Dermot's behaviour. He wasn't prepared to hide it that much. He acted as though he wasn't worried. We'd walk down the street hand in hand or he'd put his arm around me. I never felt the pressure of watching eyes, and that's one thing I liked very much about him. I respected him for that courage. Though, I wondered if, subconsciously, he was almost hoping to be found out. As for me, I wasn't at all bothered about being found out except for his sake and how it would affect the relationship.

On the other hand, as far as his religious order was concerned, it had to be clandestine. We were always away from his world: I couldn't visit his friends or colleagues, some of whom I knew independently, because there was 'something to hide.' If we'd just been friends, even special friends, that wouldn't have been a problem. So I felt very cut off because I couldn't see his family or be acknowledged. Those are the sort of things that hurt and make you realise you're not having an ordinary relationship.

We talked about the relationship incessantly at first and that's one of the problems with this kind of relationship. It can get distorted. You're always talking about The Problem. At first, I saw his situation very much as The Problem, and I would storm and rage about the system. Then *he* became The Problem, with me contributing to it. It was a way of avoiding the central issue.

Dermot himself would quite simply pretend it wasn't happening, despite all the evidence to the contrary, and that's a way of not acknowledging that it's serious, and that love has implications, particularly among mature, middle-aged people. It's quite a common syndrome. It makes you realise quite sharply and painfully how many contradictions people can live with. They can actually deny that something is happening when any neutral observer can immediately see that it is.

People would talk about hypocrisy but it's not that simple. It's not hypocrisy so much as denial. I've heard some extreme examples of that, like a priest who denied he was having a relationship with someone who'd just had his child. He was still referring to it as a spiritual relationship, and refusing to call it romantic.

Really, you need trained counsellors to talk to, and they're not easily available, especially for the women. I recently read an article in a Jesuit journal, 'Advice to the Priest Who Wants to Stay Active.' It was all about how to deal with a 'particular' friendship, and all about how the priest can cope. Not any word of compassion for the woman's situation. It's very difficult for the woman to find someone to talk to, though groups such as Advent have been a great help to me. Other people don't really understand and say you only have yourself to blame. Yet if you went to a friend with another kind of relationship problem, they'd see it as natural. So you do have to take responsibility for that – you both do, it's not the woman's responsibility to decide what's right for the priest – and that can be a great stress.

Some people might deal with it by putting off making a decision, or by leaving the situation. Priests sometimes leave the priesthood precipitately, though they're more likely to leave the relationship. In my case, it meant he didn't take full responsibility, according to my lights, for the relationship. He tried to just enjoy it for what it was that day. You can't just live for the day. A relationship has to be worked at and built on. It's almost like a teenager who has dates and doesn't want to think it might become more serious, even though he might recognise he's in love. He doesn't want to think about it ending or going on. They don't have to make those kinds of decisions,

Dermot had to acknowledge his previous serious relationship, which had very much upset him afterwards, and he hadn't come to terms with it. He really tried to deny that just as he tried to deny our relationship.

He never denied the fact of it, never tried to make it a hidden thing, but he would deny that it meant something important about himself – that he needed or wanted a loving relationship, which for an average person is normal. He denied the fact that deep within him was a need for a relationship, not just a sexual one but a much deeper and broader relationship, and that, without it, an important part of his character was being denied. He would acknowledge that our relationship existed, but not that something should follow on from that. For him it was forbidden, so he would act as though it was an exception, an aberration, something not really about him.

He found the moral contradiction hard to take, though he was against compulsory celibacy for priests. He nevertheless saw it as a deeper contradiction, that we couldn't have a normal relationship as a couple while he remained a priest. So we tried to avoid the issue. We both saw it in terms of him making a choice ultimately. We tried to put off the moment but, every so often, when the pressure got too great, he would leave me. But he returned several times.

For me, the implications were that we should build something together. For him – he felt a sense of vocation, of calling. I felt that same feeling of calling and mine was just as valid as his, though I couldn't be a priest. I was angry that I couldn't be. I saw it largely as a male-dominated system in the Church which I don't support, so it seemed logical to me that we should break out of this prison together. It wasn't a feeling of taking him away from his vocation but rather of deepening it and expanding it. And I felt, if he was expressing himself fully, all that part of him that needed love and needed to love, then he would actually be a better priest, a more fulfilled person, more committed, a person with more understanding of other people. I certainly don't see it as a weakness that he was an ordinary man who wanted a girlfriend. In fact, I see it as a strength that someone can love in that way and give love in that way, because he's a very giving person.

In the early stages, I didn't ask him to make a decision, because I didn't want the relationship to end. I was hoping he would come to the conclusion that this was meant to be and, because I grew up as a lay person, I grew up with the idea that love is the most important value. Because it was acknowledged as love on both sides, I thought love would win through. To me, it was a real relationship that in any other circumstances would have led to marriage or living together, and happily so, I believe.

So I was hoping he would leave the priesthood, since that's what you have to do if you want an ordinary relationship. We were both always aware that it was a temporary state, and that went on for four years with a long interruption in the middle. We became aware that we couldn't carry on having a secret relationship, so it became focused on the question of whether or not he'd leave. The moment that became the focus, it affected everything we did. And I believe he panicked. It was too much pressure and he went again, which was the last time I saw him. That's two years ago. We had no quarrels, no rows, no fundamental problems between ourselves apart from his situation, which is obviously a fundamental problem in itself.

I've thought a lot about it over the past few years and I now think that, although he didn't admit to being afraid, he was. He saw his order as a great womb that he clung to. He's been with the community over twenty-five years, and it's hard for those of us not in a community to understand that sort of attachment. It's his life. And most of that life he'd lived with just one other priest, an older father figure, in a remote mission. They had a nice little life, warm and secure. He hated leaving that to go back to the community. Then he tells me that the community is everything and he can't bear to leave that.

The idea of getting a job is very difficult, too. But he was never explicit about that. He'd just talk about what God wanted him to do. You can call anything what God wants. So then he'd be obsessed with the concept of letting go, not being attached to things, and he'd leave. The next week he'd be back with me again. When it was on, it was very, very on. We even went on holiday together. Then the day we came back he said we'd better end it. It was dreadful. It was too much like reality. He said, 'It's very difficult to become ordinary.'

It's not just fear of the College of Cardinals, but of having gone into the seminary at eighteen, having weathered the most difficult period of your life sexually, and then having relationships in your forties. It's tribalism, really. The necessity of finding within the community what you can't find outside. It's so nice helping people and being liked by them and belonging to them.

His colleagues made a big thing of not being intimate, because of the problems intimacy could bring. Yet they were very institutionalised. As an outsider, I was always struck by the fact that they weren't close friends in the way I consider friends are, men and women I'd talk to much more intimately than he would talk to them. He couldn't acknowledge that – it's not easy to say, 'I'm not a free person.' Instead, he would justify it in the name of his vocation. But it wasn't the call of God or the caring for people, because the nature of his work was fairly administrative and I thought, 'He could be doing that in the outside world.'

He wasn't to my mind the symbol of Jesus that he thought he was, because he wasn't symbolising that to a lot of people as he didn't know many people who weren't priests. And, as I say, he wasn't on terms of intimate friendship with them. He didn't have a parish, he had little contact with the outside world. I used to talk about the 'real world' and he'd get terribly upset. In one way, he stayed because he couldn't say no to the authority at work. In another, it was like he was married to someone else, so I felt a sense of emotional betrayal.

I've worked through a lot of the problems I had then. I've been going to a counsellor for the past couple of years. I can see now that I've tended to turn to a priest as a guru. Yet Dermot didn't like giving advice to people. He just behaved like an ordinary person, and one of the things I've learned from this is that priests *are* ordinary people. They're not the sort of demi-gods which, traditionally, they've been made out to be. They're ordinary people with all their strengths and weaknesses and good qualities – just like anybody else. I find that a strength now when talking to priests.

On the other hand, I look at the priest performing the rituals, and I see a normal, fallible human being. Which is fine in one way, but it does rather destroy the magic that takes so many people into church. I'll stay with it, but in my way, following my conscience. The Church as it is no longer meets my needs.

What did the relationship do for him? Oh, it gave many things. It helped him know how people lived beyond the narrow confines of the community to which he belongs. And it brought him closeness and intimacy and sharing of the sort that was also denied except in an institutionalised way. It allowed spontaneity. It opened up his life to the outside world. To me, it gave love.

One of my friends said, 'If you'd got him, what would you have done with him?' The purpose seemed to be the quest, initially for the unattainable, but then it became very serious. But she was right – if he'd been free, he might not have been the man I'd have wanted to settle down with. So I think I'm glad it ended. But that might be just part of my coping mechanisms.

For me, it pointed to a lot of the problems in the Church – that the priesthood is this closed élite hierarchy of chosen people. Maybe they feel more called by God than the average person, know more about scripture or theology, but someone else may be an expert on engineering or bird-watching. That whole idea of a man or a woman being up on a stage is all wrong. It's actually what Jesus criticised about the Pharisees. Truth is a mystery to be explored, not something we possess. So I'd like to see quite a different kind of priesthood.

The Church would be much stronger if it didn't have this focus on a male-dominated, authoritarian hierarchy with hidebound traditions, which are good in terms of continuity and maintaining moral and spiritual values, but also mean you've got a fairly ossified system. It's not just a question of rules, but of the whole structure. I'd like to see women priests. I'd like to see the whole system changed so that priests are no longer seen as little gods who appear at the altar at a great distance from the congregation. Many priests try hard to break that system. I would like to see compulsory celibacy abolished, because very few people are natural celibates. And the whole emphasis on celibacy is part of that much wider culture.

If you're asking why I wouldn't go to his superior, I could not betray him, I could never do that. That's why I wouldn't speak in a very obvious public way now. I have no right to trample on his position now. That's up to him to do. It's not easy. Most people wouldn't want to parade their private lives. Only in moments of greatest anger has it passed my mind, and then not seriously. And if I did go to his superior and tell him, he'd probably say, 'Yes, I know. So what? A lot of people have done this. I'll talk to him.'

I know of a lot of serious relationships with priests which in other circumstances would lead to marriage. There are a lot of people out there, really. And in one way we should speak out, but in a sense it has to be the priests, the people who are caught up in the system. Or nuns who are involved with priests. It has to be the people *in* the system who speak out. If Dermot did that, I'd have no doubts about helping him in whatever way I could.

It's very difficult to live with the idea that he might come back again. I don't know what I'd do, because the last time he seemed very serious about it – he *was* very serious about it. I know he's still trying to sort it out, but at the same time he's trying to get on with his ordinary life, which means putting a lid on it. He feels hypocritical and guilt-ridden.

I don't know whether I'd risk it again, because each time the pain has got worse. I feel stronger with coping with it, but each time he's gone, because the relationship has deepened, it's been more difficult. We didn't just repeat what we'd done before, we went into ourselves and each other much more deeply. And I still find it hard to believe it could be over, because I still believe in it.

It's left me feeling, first of all, very loving, but also very angry, and I've had a lot of difficulty admitting that anger. At first, I blamed myself for getting into that situation, for doing something that was wrong and stupid, for obviously having hang-ups that got me involved with a priest. I still sometimes wake up in the night feeling angry: with myself, with the system – while not blaming it for what we did – and with him for not having the courage, as I see it, to carry it through. Was it worth it? Oh, yes, yes, because I feel very lucky to have had that relationship. I feel unlucky that it ended, but I don't regret the relationship at all.

Lorraine

Lorraine is a slender, elegant woman in her early forties, who lives in the top-floor flat of a handsome old house in a southern university town. There's an attractive continental lilt to her voice, and she has an impressive, idiosyncratic command of English: the quintessential sophisticated European. So it's odd to hear her, in a living room awash with plants, telling a story so at variance with her appearance – a story of frustrated love and sublimated sexuality.

I was brought up in a warmly practising Catholic family in Belgium. My mother especially was very involved. To her, the religious quest was very important. She used to read a lot, and she had quite a lot of priest friends, so priests were familiar to us. She didn't want us to be exposed to the ghastly pre-Vatican II Church, so she did everything she could to personalise the contact. Thanks to that, I've got no memory of that earlier Church. I never went to those Masses in Latin which made no sense to children. Where we went to church, there were lots of friendly happenings, lovely singing, nice liturgy. I don't remember having been bored stiff throughout long Sunday Masses and sermons. So that made the Church look very positive to me.

I left this quite lively set-up after school to come to England, as an *assistante* at a Catholic private school where, again, there was a lot of intelligent thinking. This was twenty-one years ago, when I was twenty-one. It took me about ten years to realise that Vatican II was gone and that the Church was moving backward. To me priests were nice, friendly people whom you could speak to so, with Vatican II having just happened and things changing all over the place, when I met this priest I thought it was only a matter of years before marriage for the clergy

195

would happen. It seemed so powerful and worth waiting for, it was like a vocation, you know, like being a priest's wife was something worthwhile to do. What a fool I was!

He was chaplain to the school, so he used to come in to say daily Mass and take various liturgical activities and participate in the social life of the convent and school generally. He was only a few years older than me and he'd only been ordained a year, which I didn't realise at the time. I think it was quite nice for him to meet people around his own age.

One thing that struck me fairly quickly was what a natural kind of strong man he seemed to be. He didn't fit at all my normal expectation of what a priest was like, which was fairly sedate, a bit middle-class and proper. He was from the country and it showed – he was physically strong, involved in sports, and said what he thought, even if it wasn't always what you were supposed to be hearing, which appealed to me, though I think it shocked some people. I very much admired the gift he'd made of his life. I thought, 'My goodness! Here is somebody who is an ordinary, lively human being who is also generous enough to have taken on this rather awesome life. Why has he done this?'

I also found him attractive physically, sexually. I'd had boyfriends and he seemed more mature than any of the others, and kind, and dedicated, and hard-working. But, looking back on it now, I also think the fact that he was a priest mattered. I don't know that I would have noticed him had he not been a priest, and that worries me in a way, because I think there was something of the father figure about it. You know, by the time I was twenty-one I had learned that priests were good news. I had had older priests in my life who were friends of my family and entirely trustworthy, and this was me picking my own man from among them.

It wasn't the choice an adolescent should make, which is to go right outside your family and choose somebody who is all your own. In a way, I was playing safe, perhaps all the more so because I was in a foreign country and I needed some safety. Other men felt more dangerous to me. Being abroad is not like being at home; it's more difficult to pick up subtle social clues. This matters a lot when you are dealing with the opposite sex. So I went for a man with whom I was familiar, and I think now that was a mistake. If he had left the priesthood, would my love for him have persisted? How much of the priesthood was tied up with it? I really don't know. Probably quite a lot.

The way priests wear this clerical collar everywhere means they're constantly in a professional position where people see them as superior and safe. You're never his equal. It's powerful stuff. There are infinite possibilities for closeness and distance, for control. What they wear gives them special rights and status, yet they can shed it whenever they want, which is dangerous.

It took a while to get to know him, because initially my English wasn't very good. I used to have breakfast after morning Mass and would go and speak to him as best I could, bringing some of the girls in with me. We used to have discussions and laughs, but it was fairly superficial because my ability to communicate at that stage was very limited. It grew better, and the relationship grew deeper, as time went on.

I was very interested in him. I just wanted to understand. I felt I could trust him, it was interesting male company and, because the school was miles away from anywhere, I was quite cut off. It took me three or four months to realise I was falling in love with him – I was really naive. Then I was worried. I actually tried to leave because I thought, 'I mustn't hang around here, this is getting dangerous.' I went to see one of the nuns, explained what I thought was happening, and said maybe I'd better go. She supported me. She suggested I had a word with the other chaplain and he said, 'I don't think you should run away, it's something you should be able to handle.'

Once he'd said that, it sounded right. He said, 'Priests can have friends, why not persevere with this?' So I decided to stay. The idea was that I could always be friends with him. This went on for another few months, but I noticed that he was growing uncomfortable with me and giving me ambiguous messages, being trusting and talkative sometimes, and at other times keeping me at a distance. So I got very confused and wondered what was happening.

That's when I told him how I felt. He kind of ignored it, pretended it hadn't happened, and then asked me, had I got over it? Was it all right now? I was horrified! I thought, 'What does he mean "got over it?"' By that time the other chaplain wouldn't speak to me. The one time I managed to get him to see me, he took me out into the courtyard with everybody around. I felt very put down and humiliated by that and I didn't try to speak to him again. I distinctly felt he had two tracks: one was official, the other unofficial, and he didn't want to be cornered into saying things that he might think but didn't want to say publicly. Now, I suspect he was involved in a relationship himself and was trying to give me leads not to lose heart, but he couldn't do that openly.

When I had told Stephen, and he'd reacted in the way he did, I accepted that I had to put it to the side. He obviously didn't want to deal with it, but he was equally obviously wanting to be friends. He was always very affectionate and I always felt loved, but he would never say anything, and I knew that if I tried to corner him saying anything, I would just get pushed away. So I just accepted what was going on for what it was, a friendship with different undertones of tenderness and sexuality. I felt very attached to him and I felt he was very attached to me.

Then I had to go back to Belgium, because I was at the end of my year. So I went back home and stayed with my parents for a bit and told them what was happening, that I had a priest friend and I was in love with him. They were absolutely horrified. I don't know why I told them – it was stupid, really, but again I just thought it was the truth and they would deal with it for what it was. But they didn't. They were advising me what to do and I thought, 'No. I'm old enough to make my own decisions. And I want to follow this relationship through.' Then the situation at home became uncomfortable because they were frightened for me, very anxious and disapproving.

So I came back to England to work as a French teacher in another boarding school. I had kept in touch with Stephen – I'd written to him and said I was missing him and I was very fond of him. When I came back here, he thanked me for the letter and said he was really pleased to have got it and he was sorry he hadn't replied but he had been thinking about it. I eased his conscience by saying it was a difficult letter to reply to. I was always making things easy for him.

I visited him a few times. I remember the first time he let me into his territory, his flat inside the parish house, and he showed me old photographs of his childhood. It was strange – we'd known each other for about a year by the time he did that. We saw each other two or three times a month at that point. He knew I was trying to stay over here. And yes, he was in love with me, I have no doubt about that. But he wasn't very good at detecting his feelings, and he was confused about the emotions of it all. He was schooled in thinking that these things weren't important, that being in love was something to be fought and discarded, not to be treasured, so it was devalued.

When I decided to do teacher training, that was the beginning of a new phase, because I was about 50 miles away from him. In one way it was a miserable time, because I would go to see him and he would be friendly, but there were times when he was meant to come over and he let me down. I was doing well in teaching and I was enjoying it, so I started to draw boundaries in my personal life, developing one of my own as well as seeing him.

I still thought we would share a bit of life, that things might change in the Church. I really did believe, stupidly enough, that Vatican II would carry on progressing. There had been some spectacular leavings over the celibacy issue, so I thought things would change and he would be able to marry me as a priest. I never thought of him leaving the priesthood to marry me.

I remember speaking about that to my mother and she said, 'I think you're unrealistic about that.' That did alarm me, because I think I was getting close to realising that this was the case and she made me face it, very gently. I said I knew there had been some married priests in Germany, but she said, 'As far as I can see, this is not going to be on the cards for a long time. Certainly not with this Pope.' That was Paul VI.

So I began to realise that I had a much more long-term life to deal with, and I went to parties with my teaching friends and went out with a couple of other men, but he was always in the background. We still saw each other now and again, maybe every couple of months or so, but it was still terribly significant inside me. And he never said, 'This can't go on.' Nor did he say, 'I don't feel like that about you.' He never said that. So there was this kind of bumping along, especially in terms of mixed messages of tenderness and affection and doing things together, but 'It's OK as long as we don't talk about it.'

He is absolutely hopeless at emotional talk. More recently, I've tried to make him talk about things and he just won't. He'll have a one-word answer or a joke, and you really have to persevere. I don't like this very much, especially when it's a painful subject. Also, he's not a thinker, he's a man of action.

Around this time, I started thinking that maybe I could work with him in another way – by proxy, as it were. I wanted to understand what priests and their lives were really about and, funnily enough, the local parish was very forward-looking and decided to invite lay people to share the priests' lives, to have a life of prayer and also to share the domestic arrangements like cooking and buying food and eating together. I thought that would give me a chance to see what they were like and also to get involved and have support in my prayer life. So I moved out of my rented flat. I was one of four women in the house and I made some really good friends there and learned a lot. It lasted five years altogether, during which time I'd learned everything I needed to learn about how priests function!

It was a parish house, so we really took part in the life of the parish. Also there were regular prayer times like morning prayer and evening prayer together, organised like a mixed community. It was a large house and they needed the income, so they thought it would be best to have people living there who cared about their way of life and were willing to share it for a short while.

Stephen came down to visit that house a few times. It was easier in that context, of course, with other priests about. At that point, I'd say our relationship was a special friendship. I always had the feeling that he cared for me and was involved and wanted me to be around, but he was also ambiguous about how much he was going to give me. I thought, by working on it, I would get him to be less ambiguous and more open about it, because I didn't think we were doing any harm. We weren't sleeping together, so I thought, 'What's the fuss? Can't we just be friends like ordinary people?'

That was the goal I had in mind, just to have a special friendship. I wouldn't try to have any sexual contact, but I expected him to be fair to me and to treat me like a friend. Yet sometimes he was really closed and other times he wasn't, sometimes he would talk and sometimes he wouldn't. Not so long ago, he told me he had always felt very close to me and that he didn't know how to handle it. He wanted to be close, he didn't want to lose touch, but he didn't know how to do it, and that it had been confusing for him as well. I suppose he was quite young and immature due to his training and his lack of experience of life.

But, then, he said the same thing two years ago and he's behaved no different since. So how am I supposed to interpret all this when it still hasn't changed any of his behaviour, not significantly?

The women in the parish house were accepting of our friendship, and how serious it had been, but I never told any of the men because there was a disapproval of things like that. The relationships in the house became very ambiguous as well because, although we were sharing food and a roof and prayers, we knew that there were some aspects of the priests' lives where we were not welcome. When they were going about their clerical business, they didn't want anything much to do with us: we were just four women among many, even though we felt we had the special status of house-mates. I realised then how priests deal with women generally and with relationships.

Over the years I was there, two or three of the women got involved with priests in the house, and the other priests tried to pretend it wasn't happening for quite some time. One of them became very involved, and the woman became pregnant – I think they had sex only the once. There were some incredible things said by the other priests like, 'She did it on purpose,' as though she'd done it to destroy his life. These were nice men, people I thought I knew and trusted, saying things like, 'He doesn't need to marry her.' But he did. He left his order and married her, even though his order had recommended that he didn't do so, and had said they would post him out in the missions somewhere. I heard the other men saying such things as, 'These things happen in a moment of weakness. So what? You don't want to let your whole life be blighted by it.' I found it terribly confusing because these were people I respected and was fond of, and yet they thought I would approve of what they were saying. It never crossed their minds that I might be shocked.

Another of the girls became close friends with one of the men and, at the beginning, he was spontaneous and open about it. Then he got frightened and it was emotionally painful for both of them. He wanted to stay a priest and she didn't want to get in the way of that – she was a very religious girl. They decided not to see each other very much. Then he phoned her one day and said, 'I can't stand this. It's over. I'll never see you again.' She nearly had a nervous breakdown. It was terrible. Her studies went to pot, she used to cry and didn't sleep well at night. It was the suddenness of it, the cruelty of it.

That's when I moved out. I thought it was just hopeless. It taught me how incredibly important it is to them to be priests and to have this image of the perfect man, and how powerful the structure of the Church is. These were very intelligent men, yet they never really thought very far away from what the Church thinking was. It was terribly important for their identity that they were priests according to the mould that was given them.

OK, fair enough, perhaps they felt that was what they had promised their lives to, but it also entailed being unfair to other human beings, and that's wrong. It could make them ruthless, including saying things about women or about other priests that were uncharitable, and not realising there is a lot of double-think there, because you preach about Christian love all the time and about relationships and you try to give yourself to all these people, but you can betray the people closest to you at any time. Which means you can't have friends, actually, and many don't. I've come to the conclusion that many priests don't have real friends because they can't – and not just friends of the opposite sex. I wonder if it doesn't damage their ability to have friends, full stop. Because committing yourself to a real friend does mean loyalty to an individual in a way that I think they have lost touch with. Perhaps some of them would even go as far as to say that they must not give their loyalty to any individual. But isn't this inhuman?

Everything is for the job. If they live in one parish, they give themselves to the hundred people who are parishioners, then they go to the next parish and they love those people whom the Bishop has ordered them to love. They'll be up all times of the day and night answering the phone and seeing these people, giving Masses and doing all the things which they feel are their duty, yet what about the last hundred who loved them and had become involved with them? They might never see them again and they're not really bothered; it doesn't matter, it's not personal, it's a job.

So I moved out, and shared a flat with some other women. By that time, I had been working as a teacher for three or four years and I was getting responsibilities. I really enjoyed all that. For a while, Stephen took the opportunity to come more often. He'd come for the evening, and once he even stayed the night, when the others were away. I'm pretty sure, looking back, that he might have slept with me that night. But I was blind to this, and anyway I would have thought it was morally wrong. I had put a lot of energy into this celibacy business and I couldn't think any other way. Also, I'm not an impulsive person. I need to make a decision before I carry it out and, as far as I knew, we were still on the celibate track. No one had said otherwise.

Also, I'd been quite hurt, so I'm not sure I would have been able to allow it to happen. All this 'I'm coming,' then 'I'm not coming,' and 'Yes, I love you,' 'No, I don't.' I had become emotionally cautious by then, and I don't know that I would have wanted to get physically involved. It would have reopened the wound completely and I would have had to deal with that again. There was a part of me that wasn't available to him any more and that didn't particularly *want* to be available to him any more. But I do think when he came that night, he was quite vulnerable and open and willing – and I put him in the guest room!

By that point, I wasn't saying I loved him any more, and I wasn't really feeling it, either; we were just friends. But why was he still coming down and still inviting me up and still taking the trouble to go places with me when, for a priest, that was quite a big deal? There was no need for him to do that. Also, the non-verbal messages were positive. If I had tried to push him to more commitment to me, perhaps we could have gone further, I don't know. But I was waiting for something mutual to happen, or else for the Church to become more understanding. I never tried to force anything.

In the event, I'm glad I didn't do that, because if I had forced things what would have terrified me was that he would have regretted it, then thrown it back at me, saying if it wasn't for me he'd still be a priest. I wasn't having that. I couldn't face the responsibility of causing his life to change, perhaps for the worse. You probably need to be quite assertive in a relationship like this; you say what you want and then go for it. Then, if it doesn't work, you get out. Whereas I just sort of hang about and wait for things to happen, which means that little things happened but big things never did.

For instance, because of him, I've never had an intimate, sexual relationship with a man. I found it embarrassing in my twenties; I felt ashamed of not having a boyfriend – I wanted one. And I couldn't tell people I had somebody but he was a priest. I felt a bit like a non-person. Then I grew more confident about it, and found I could be accepted for what I was. I didn't have to say what kind of relationship I was or wasn't having. Also, the more you learn about people's lives, the less straightforward they appear. Sometimes people have sexual relationships and are deeply unhappy, other times partnerships don't work out, and there are actually quite a lot of women on their own who have learned to enjoy life. So, in my thirties, it stopped bothering me. I decided being single was just as good and I began to enjoy it. There was a kind of unfairness, though, which I shouldn't have put up with; I became a self-appointed custodian of Stephen's celibacy. For all I know, he might have broken his vow.

If I discovered now that he had had sexual relationships, it's difficult to know how I'd feel. At the moment, I can think about it and laugh. It would add another twist to the whole absurdity of the situation – it would make a good novel, if nothing else! But I actually might feel hurt and betrayed.

As I see it, the strongest grounds for not having a sexual relationship with a priest is because they promise publicly not to. They're old enough to know what they're promising, so they have to realise they're betraying a promise. Whether they should all promise this or not is another matter. And then, what happens when – if – they love a woman and are loved by her? The Church doesn't want to know about that.

As for me, I went out with two people but I had to finish it each time because I just couldn't get involved. Either I was still too involved with Stephen or I was too hurt, I don't know, but there was something in me that wasn't responding any more. I felt bad about that, because one of them was a lovely man and I liked him a lot. I could see intellectually that he would have been a good person to marry if I was going to marry anyone, but I wasn't responding in every way, emotionally and physically. There was something turned off. I think to a certain extent it's still there. I don't know that I'm capable of responding on that level any more. Something's locked in.

It's so complex. The vision I had was of a non-sexual relationship that would be intimate and special, but not exclusive; the best you can imagine of a Christian love relationship, which would respect individuality but at the same time maybe make the sacrifice of sex. I know some people still hold that vision quite dear. I think it's the only healthy notion you can have of a celibate commitment. But is it healthy? Perhaps if you are mature, it is. My own experience is that what I was trying to do was to jump about six stages of human development all at once. And what I did was to overlook my sexuality, which is the last thing you should do in that kind of setting. What you want is to have a healthy, strong sense of your own sexuality, so that even when you're not living it out genitally, you know where it is and you can still be sexual. But I ended up being inhibited and making myself into a non-sexual person. So, sexually, it is quite dangerous. Emotionally, it's very dangerous, because I don't think you can make up for those missed stages of growth – at least, the majority of people can't.

Initially, I thought I had been very mature sexually, by being able to control myself. Now, I think I also did myself a lot of harm. I became too controlled, tight. I hadn't been during my adolescence – I wasn't particularly sexually timid then. OK, perhaps there was a root of puritanism around in my Catholicism, but it wasn't prominent. There was a lot of freedom around during my adolescence in the late sixties. Then I muzzled myself terribly, because I loved Stephen so much. I think my emotional and sexual development were interrupted. The oppressive aspect of the relationship was emotionally damaging, and the commitment to celibacy, which wasn't really my own, became a dead end.

I remember that first year, a few months after I realised I was in love with him, sitting down one evening and thinking, 'I've got to decide what I want out of this relationship.' Feeling I had to decide whether I wanted it to be sexual or not, even though the choice wasn't exclusively mine. Had I wanted it to be sexual, I would have found opportunities to indicate to him that I wanted it to be. But I gave a lot of moral thought to it and felt I was making a big moral decision in my best-informed way. It took me ages. I looked at the pros and cons, the will of God, everything – I was only twenty-one! – and I thought, 'No. I shall work within the rules. I shall be celibate with him.' It was a big decision and for many years I thought it was a good one. Many years later, when I became low and quite exhausted with all these deprivations, I went to a counsellor. That's when I began to look at it in a different way. I'm not saying it was completely negative. The moral intention was there, but in human terms I wasn't ready to make a decision like that.

I haven't avoided sexual pleasure; I've learned to enjoy it. From that point of view, I suppose I haven't obeyed the Church, which seems to view celibacy as people never having an erotic thought, never having any erotic pleasure. I haven't missed out in that way, but I would have liked to have slept with a man. For years, I had erotic fantasies and sexual dreams, daydreams even, so in my imagination I would enjoy sex and sexuality. What I didn't realise until I went into counselling was how dangerous that was, because I was choosing sexual fulfilment in my dreams and celibacy in reality. The imagination was strong, yet it was second best in terms of fulfilment. In a way, those daydreams fuelled the relationship because they were so good, but they were only happening in my head. I didn't realise until much, much later that I mustn't indulge in that any more. So now I don't. I think it also shows that I was in two minds about the celibacy business; I undermined my own commitment in my fantasies.

I've known a few priests and I think I can see what happens to some of them. Their emotional development goes into a fridge – the sixty going on twenty kind of idea. Many have never known a woman, they don't know what a naked woman looks like except maybe in a film, they've never touched a woman, never been kissed. OK, maybe you don't need that, but it also means a human woman has never spoken to them about herself, so they don't know how a woman thinks or feels, and *they've* never spoken about themselves in an intimate way, so they don't know themselves very well, either. You need to be intimate with somebody to find out about yourself. The Church is stuffed full of men who have not grown through adolescence, who are frozen in a state of late childhood. These deprivations are sad. Most of the priests I have known have been emotionally deprived to the nth degree.

Stephen could never be openly affectionate with me. It was always in secret, which can be so destructive. Once, for instance, I drove him somewhere, dropped him off and made to kiss him as I usually do, and he stretched out his hand instead. Another time, we went to Medjugorje together, which was Church territory, i.e. his territory, his people. And he never acknowledged that I was in any way a special friend of his. I

206

felt really hurt, especially as he'd invited me to come, though in a way you get used to that sort of treatment.

I don't think anybody who knows him knows that I exist, even now. In Medjugorje, I went with a group of handicapped children and I got on very well with them and their leaders and, you know, from the public point of view, it looked like I had been recruited to do this particular job, not that I had come because I was his friend. He just treated me like he treated everybody else. He didn't even say goodbye to me. He was the leader, he was the big boss. How I tolerated all this rubbish!

Is he a good priest? I don't know. Perhaps it depends what you call a good priest. According to the traditional model, he probably says all the Masses he's supposed to say and is there when you call him. I know on this Medjugorje trip, though, I was a bit taken aback to see how frustrated the women became with him. They were women with whom I had things in common, women who expected their judgement to be taken into account, who felt they should have a say, and he was quite autocratic. He and the other two priests made all the decisions, even if they were wrong ones. When the women rebelled, he was furious. They were very impatient with what they felt was his narrow-minded dogmatism. I don't know if he'd still be like that – it was a few years ago now. We never talked about it, because he never took the trouble to find out what I thought.

He probably would have said that the trip was his responsibility, but to me it looked like he had power that he did not want to share, certainly not with women. He was completely blind to that. The idea that he might discriminate against women would horrify him. He would probably have a good rational explanation for it. I'm too used to the way priests think! I know they all say it's not the power that attracts them, it's the service. I spend far too much time anticipating what people like Stephen would think. Sometimes it stops me thinking for myself. They answer in my head before I do.

I was highly aware all the time that there hadn't been any promises to me, there hadn't been any commitment and, being a good Catholic, I accepted all the system's values. I thought, 'I've got this special friend who's a priest and that's as good as I can get. It's both a privilege and a trial.' I did think it should get better and I did feel hurt every time he let me down, so there was something in me that didn't accept it, and I did get angry. I became hardened as well, and gradually realised it was a dangerous business and there was no guarantee that it was going to get any better.

I do think now that I should have pushed him to have a proper relationship. That would have meant both of us taking responsibility and would have meant a better chance of growing than standing by the side of the path waiting for something to come along. It would have meant not feeling deprived. It might have meant lots of difficulties, but at least they would have been real, instead of all this pussy-footing around when actually there was nothing very real going on. Or maybe I should have stopped much earlier and realised that I owed it to myself to get out of a self-destructive relationship. Then I could have had counselling earlier, which might have unlocked my energies again to have a real relationship with someone else. There's been an awful lot of wasting time.

I haven't missed having children. That's not one of my great regrets. I've missed the day-to-day intimacy of a real partnership much more. My main regret is in getting involved in the first place, though I don't regret for an instant moving to England. I like living here, I enjoy my job, I've got good friends, there's lots of good things. I had to fight hard to survive and probably that was good for me.

Why maintain a relationship which is so hopeless? Perhaps this is going to sound crazy, but I really thought there was God's plan of some kind in it. I thought I just had to stay where I was, do my best in it and that things would work out; that I would be betraying myself and all my life had been about if I didn't do that. I had invested an enormous amount in moving over here. I don't think I could acknowledge that I'd made a mistake in that respect. Losing Stephen would have meant losing a big part of my life which was still mysterious to me.

Now, it's different. I feel more stable. I wonder what's going to happen. It doesn't matter enough to hurt me any more, and I haven't got much more to lose. I've got my own life, my own friends. The relationship seems such a waste. He's as unreliable as ever and I don't want to put up with this any more. I think he may have some genuine feelings for me, but that puzzles me. He told me not that long ago that I had been very special to him and still was, and that he would like to see me more often. I'd like to see if something better will happen – but I won't hold my breath! There's still some part of me that thinks surely life can't be that crazy.

It was about eighteen years into the relationship before he admitted he cared. It was one of those special moments. I'd gone to see him and it took an age to get rid of all the phone calls and all the people at the door, but eventually we had a nice meal together, and we cuddled up on the settee and chatted. He loves talking about the past and it was all coming out, all these things that we did together and the people that we knew, and I made him talk about himself a bit. It was a lovely summer evening, so we went out for a walk, and in the dark we just hugged each other. Afterwards, when we came back into the house, there was an atmosphere of intimacy, and it was much easier to talk. That's when it tumbled out about how much he loved having me around, what it had felt like. I was very moved because I thought maybe I could have tried to create an atmosphere like that before. I asked him why he hadn't said any of this before and told him how it had been really hurtful not knowing. He said he was very confused and he hadn't meant to be hurtful. Then he said, 'Why don't we keep in touch more often?'

I clarified it the next morning, in the cold light of day, and he said, yes, he did want to keep in touch more often. For a while he did. He phoned once a month, and he came down to see me again very quickly, he even said 'I love you' on the phone. But it's tailed off again now, I don't know why. Maybe partly because he's very busy – the diocese is short of priests, so he doesn't have a curate. He's phoned me two or three times to say that life is rather miserable and it's difficult to get over to see me. I take it with a pinch of salt. I've little sympathy – his last visit was ten months ago! If he wanted to get another priest to take his calls for an evening he could do that. He has a deacon working with him. I don't think not taking even a day off is at all a sensible way of leading your life. If they ordained married priests and women, they would have plenty of priests, so it's their problem. I don't go up to see him, because I don't feel welcome there.

Stephen leaving the priesthood is a scenario I play in my head less and less often. One of the reasons I haven't been too outspoken with him is because I don't know what I would say if he said, 'OK, let's make a go of it.' I don't think I want to now. We're even more different now than we were twenty years ago. We have very different lifestyles.

Then, I was willing to compromise on many things. Now, it's different.

For a long time, we had the Catholic world in common, and we could talk about our parishes and the friends we had in common. But now I have joined very radical groups in the Church: feminism, women's ordination – a sort of resistance – working with the oppressed in the Church, women and others. Stephen is part of the Establishment. He would feel attacked by this sort of action. So it does worry me a bit: what would we talk about? Maybe I'd just plonk a few home truths in his lap – and ask for a few answers as well. I feel much more capable of doing this now. And if I lose him, then I lose him.

As far as he's concerned, I think he still sees our relationship as in rivalry with his priesthood. Sometimes one wins, sometimes the other. Perhaps I will always be in his mind, fighting an unequal battle with his priesthood. But what if he came to realise his priesthood had become barren, or he wanted to investigate a relationship and turned to me? I'd want to say you can't keep a woman hanging on twenty years and suddenly decide you're ready for her. Because I haven't been waiting on the shelf for him to take me down. I've carried on living. He's welcome to share parts of my life, but I'm not handing it all over just because he's decided it's what he wants.

It makes me wild when people say a relationship makes a man a better priest. It's true, they do become better priests out of closeness with us, and they use it ruthlessly. They don't even realise what they're doing. I saw it in the parish house, having us around, nice, friendly, well-intentioned girls, who did a lot of practical things but were also very caring and had a lot of affection to give. They thrived on it. They looked so much better and they enjoyed it; they said so. But they couldn't be bothered to keep in touch when we left. Presumably other women are doing that for them now. It enrages me. I can see it – when they get closer to you, they blossom, they have more to say in their sermons; bless them, they start putting their shirt collars right, the whole thing is so much better. But would they give you an ounce of credit? My foot!

I think Stephen has grown more tolerant and accepting of people during our friendship, but I don't think a priest can change substantially and stay in the priesthood. I think a priest who grows to adult stature has to come into confrontation with the system. Some of them solve it in creative ways which allow them to remain in the Church, at some cost to themselves. They're the good ones. But many of them don't want to face that, so they grow so far, then stop.

He'd probably say the relationship has given him a few headaches and some guilt. He did say it mattered in a positive way to him, but I can't help feeling I must have given him trouble, too, inside his head if nowhere else, wondering whether it was OK to love a woman or not.

For me, no, it's not a good thing for a woman to love a priest. It's too self-destructive and damaging. Of course, it's not something you plan to do; it happens. And the Catholic Church simply has no space for that. It won't consider that it happens to quite a number of women and priests in spite of the celibacy dictate. For me, it has been self-destructive, and I'm not prepared to pay that price any more. I've already paid twenty-one years, you know? Ideally, I'd like to find a creative, non-destructive solution to the problem, but I can't think of one. Very few priests could love a woman in a way that wouldn't be damaging to her. In the main, they are bad news for women, and will be as long as they are brought up the way they are.

As for whether I still love him, I don't know. I still have a genuine fondness for him. He's somebody I've spent a lot of time and energy on and there's something about him I'm really fond of. He really is a nice man. I don't know – how do you feel about a husband or a partner after twenty or twenty-five years, especially if he hasn't been very considerate to you? I certainly don't feel in love with him any more, don't feel any of the great excitements of the beginning. The way he is at the moment, I wouldn't want to live with him because who would do all the giving? Whose territory would it be on? I'm not sure we even know each other well enough now. He doesn't have any idea of how much I've changed, and maybe he has changed a lot, too, who knows?

But we've been through a lot together, and we've seen each other a few times a year for twenty years, so I wouldn't want to write him off. I do feel great warmth for him in some ways and a great deal of anger as well.

I'm angry primarily with the Church as an institution and the people who support that institution, because it's irresponsible to keep an archaic state of affairs which causes an awful lot of human suffering. They haven't kept up with what is going on in the outside world, in terms of human knowledge, like psychology. Science is bad news, you know, so meanwhile they still live as if this were the Middle Ages, creating naive little girls the way I was at twenty and well-meaning young priests like Stephen was, without giving them a chance to grow and develop and go through ordinary human experiences. By going through the inevitable stage of being exclusive with a woman, being head over heels in love, being sexual, that's how ordinary human beings grow. My friends' husbands have grown a lot through marriage. I'd like to think my priest friends have grown as much, not only spiritually but in every way. I don't think spirituality is a detachable part of a human being. It doesn't grow independently of the rest of the person.

But I've covered a lot of ground in the last six or seven years, because of counselling, and also because I have become much more of a feminist. I've distanced myself from the Church and started re-evaluating all this for myself. So now I feel like I'm in a very different place.

Thinking about it now, unbeknown to myself there was a self-damaging aspect to my life. I had been brought up in a patriarchal society where men and women complemented each other and were fond of each other, but where the women had their place, and they weren't equal with men. I was allowed to do an arts degree, for instance, which was useless in everybody's mind, because I was a woman and I would get married, so it didn't matter. My brothers, on the other hand, became engineers.

It was easy to slip into that way of relating because I didn't think for myself enough. I didn't think my own thoughts could be right. The Church was bound to be right. I adopted that system quite blindly. I did accept that probably I was a sexual object, a temptress, and I had to be careful otherwise I could destroy the priest's priesthood, which would be very damaging. I accepted all these compromises and hurtful rejections and ambiguous relationships, because I didn't think I was entitled to anything else.

It's a story of oppression, the whole thing, and there are no people more oppressive than those who are themselves oppressed, because you treat people like you're being treated. That's where a lot of these priests are. Certainly, Stephen was an oppressed man when I met him. He grew up in an oppressive, working-class Catholic setting, and he did the honourable thing by the Church, which was to become a priest. So now he's a good boy, but I don't think he feels free to re-evaluate things very much.

It's taken me a lot of time and hard work to realise that I do have a voice and I can re-evaluate things. Then I found that what I was beginning to think more and more strongly was exactly what Christian feminists believe, and I became involved with them. Women realise now that they have been standing for things in the Church that they don't need to stand for.

It's only been in the last year or so that I've started talking about my relationship with Stephen. Before then, it was such a secret world that it was split off from the rest of my life. It would have been too unbearable earlier on to explain all the ins and outs, and non-Catholic friends wouldn't have understood very readily. They would have been willing to help and understand, but it would have taken a lot of explaining because this celibacy thing makes no sense to ordinary people. Then I joined a Catholic women's group and realised there were other women in my position. And, of course, the more you speak, the more your perspective of your story changes. Then, realising you were writing a book, I began thinking, 'What do I have to say? Who am I?' It's changing all the time, and it's still changing. I don't know where I'm going to end up – I don't know if it's a can of worms, but I've opened something and something's coming out.

I don't know what stage my faith is at now. I just can't accept the dictatorial, exacting God who had been hiding inside me. I feel very angry with Him, yet I do believe in a God of love, vulnerable, deliberately powerless out of love. And I've learned to like myself a lot better.

Having distanced myself from the Church, there is little support for a faith. I used to value going to Mass. I still do, but I can only go now and again. I find the liturgical set-up so painfully rejecting and so horribly patriarchal. I feel very sensitive to the double standards. Some of the priests I see are people I've known for years and I still don't know whether I'm a friend or not. They still treat me, sometimes, as if they had met me yesterday for the first time. It's their problem, but I witness this ambiguity all the time and I just feel so angry about it, and so hurt.

I'm also a bit frightened of all this development in me, because I see that it could lead to a radical break with the past twenty-one years, which could include a break with Stephen and with a number of Catholic friends and other priests I know who still have these unfortunate, if well-meant, ways of thinking. I'm less tolerant of that now.

I'd like to think, as I grow more comfortable with myself and my life, that I would be around for him if he needed me. If he had a crisis in his life, I might be helpful to him. I might not be able to offer him partnership, sexual or otherwise, but I could still offer the kind of things old friends can offer each other when they live fifty miles apart. At the moment, I'm staying on the sidelines, and it might stay like that until one of us dies. That would be sad, but it wouldn't be any different to what it's been over the last twenty-odd years.

I'd like to change the relationship rather than cut it off, but I don't know if I'll be able to do that. I'll have to see. It feels like I would be cutting off twenty-one years of my life and seeing them drift away. I'd rather see it transform itself. But, whatever happens, if we stay together, it's certainly going to be different.

Margaret Ulloa

Margaret and Luis Ulloa live in a first-floor housing association flat in Southall, Middlesex. It's a bustling, multi-ethnic area, and a bustling, multi-ethnic household. Margaret is a no-nonsense English woman, a teacher in a primary school. Luis is a warm, gentle man from Ecuador. Their children are bilingual in English and Spanish, so conversations tend to be a mixture of both languages – more, if there are French or Italian visitors. Theirs tends to be open house: I've been there when a French boy was staying, when they've had other visitors, and when two women popped in to talk about the best place to buy Hindu phallic symbols. The Ulloas are extremely hospitable, active within the Catholic community which Margaret has known since she was a child; knowledgeable, not just about movements within the Church to which they still belong but also about international efforts to improve the status of married priests and their wives. Ex-secretary of the Advent Group, Margaret is now on the executive committee of the International Federation of Married Priests.

I come from a strongly practising Catholic family. Both my grandfathers were converts from Cornish Methodism, and one grandmother was a Spanish Catholic and the other Irish Catholic, so there were two sides of a very strong, very committed Catholic tradition. We were all brought up in the same way. As soon as you were big enough to do something in the parish, then the parish – this parish, where we are now – was the community to which you committed your energies. So my brothers and sisters and I were catechists, parish councillors, we ran youth choirs, youth groups that did odd jobs for old people. The parish took up the bulk of our free time, because most of our social life

215

revolved around it. It wasn't only a religious thing, because the community here was so vibrant and interesting that you could have a social life which revolved around it. One brother married someone from the youth choir, another went out with someone from the same choir.

So that was the background in which I grew up, in which you gave your time and energies to the Church. As my father was something of a linguist and the parish frequently received visiting priests from other countries, quite a few of them gravitated to our house. So we grew up with little fear or awe of priests because they were always lying round on our carpets eating my mother's cooking.

I went to train as a teacher in a Catholic college, partly because I was told, by my good Catholic grammar school, that I wouldn't be given a reference if I didn't apply to one. But I was quite happy to apply to this one – Christ College, Liverpool, where I trained between 1966 and 1969.

I had the usual run of boyfriends during this time, but I had the feeling that nothing was quite enough. I wanted something more complete, more total. I had a very strong desire to somehow live out the sense of commitment which I'd picked up from my parents. So the obvious thing for me seemed to be the religious life. I hunted about and looked at various congregations, and the one that attracted me was the Franciscans, because of the spirit of poverty. Also the congregation, the Franciscan Missionaries of the Divine Motherhood, sang the Divine Office, which had a powerful pull on me and still does. Of all the things I miss in the religious life, oddly, it's that loss I feel most acutely.

So that was the clincher. I entered the novitiate in September 1969, was clothed in April 1970, and had a two-year novitiate during which I worked on a farm, learned to mend shoes, worked in a maternity hospital – that was a revelation to me. We were sent in to watch lots of births, which was very unusual in most religious novitiates, but normal in ours and very, very interesting. I learned a lot from it.

When I was professed, I was told I was going to teach in Australia. You didn't have any choice. Australia was the last place I would have chosen. I fancied going off to Africa or somewhere. I was sent to North Victoria, to a high school, where I worked *incredibly* hard for four years. We did everything ourselves: cleaning, maintenance of the grounds, of the building, teaching to A-Level on a full timetable. If a child expressed a strong desire to do a particular subject, one of the sisters would swot it up. So you taught things you didn't know you were capable of teaching. I taught Indonesian to A-Level because I replaced the Indonesian teacher. They said, 'You can speak Spanish, French and Italian, learn Indonesian.' So I got a tape-recorder and learnt it. In four years, I taught that, English lit. – which is my subject – art, Australian history, eighteenth-century English history, all to A-Level. It was very challenging. I loved it. I loved the teaching, the farming community, the community life.

I was sent home on leave just before I was due to make my final profession. Being away from the intense workload, I was able to think, and I went and asked for a year out. My Superior General wouldn't give me a year out. She said, 'You must get a dispensation from the last three months of your vows and leave.' I said, 'I don't want a dispensation, I'm prepared to live out my vows, but I'd like a year to think about it.' She said, 'No – go.' So I went.

That left me in England, high and dry in January, the worst time to look for a teaching post. I found the first post I could, teaching English and drama in a local high school, where it transpired the person I was replacing had just had a nervous breakdown. I soon understood why. It wasn't a happy place. In the space of the first two terms, I received two other offers: a Scale 2 post teaching English at a good high school; and one from Michael Hollings of St Anselm's Church here in Southall, who said he needed someone to take over from Sister Madeline, the director of catechetics. He said: 'I can offer you a room and £20 a month – do you want it?' I thought, 'I've got no commitments, this is really interesting, I'll have a go.' So I came to live in the parish, for a pittance, and I worked very hard for two years, training catechists. At one stage I had almost fifty catechists, some just sixteen or seventeen years old. It was a fulfilling, satisfying, demanding couple of years. It also involved things like big-scale art work with the children. The parish was open to anybody at that time, so you got involved in all sorts of things.

In the August, Michael was moved to another parish, Notting Hill, where he is now. I stayed on. In the meantime, Luís, my husband-to-be, had arrived in England from Chile, via Italy, and was working with the Missionaries of Charity in Kilburn. He was not very happy. He was finding it difficult, had little command of English – he's Ecuadorean – and the only name he knew of someone who might help him was Michael Hollings. So he turned up on his doorstep saying he wanted to earn the money to go back to Chile – he'd left there after the coup. He actually belonged to an Italian order, the Josephites, who had sent him to teach in Chile, but he left the order after some years to become a secular priest because he felt it was so protective and separated from the ordinary people that he couldn't bear it.

Michael said, 'I can't offer you anything, but if you go to Southall, my old parish, they could do with an extra pair of hands.' So he turned up in Southall with hardly a word of English, and as I could speak Spanish, I started helping him.

We fell for each other without telling each other. We each decided to say nothing and do nothing, because each of us thought you couldn't pull somebody out of a role that was obviously made for them. People all knew he was a wonderful priest, and I was happy in my work. But one night it simply came out how we felt and it took us half an hour to decide to marry. That was after three months: I hadn't held his hand, I hadn't gone out with him, he hadn't given me a kiss. It took us thirty minutes. It was completely insane, actually – there's nothing to recommend it. He had a suitcase with some pyjamas and a breviary and some sheets in it, and that was about it. I had the residue of what I'd saved from £20 a month – which wasn't much! So it was completely crazy to get married.

The thing that really put the fear of God into us wasn't the bishops or anything, it was telling my mother. She was in hospital at the time, having an operation, so I went home and told my father, brothers and sisters, all of whom were astonished but completely accepting. They all knew Luís and liked him a lot. My mother also knew him and liked him a lot, and in principle she was also in favour of married priests, but the law said no. So I said to Dad, 'You tell Mum.' He told her the day she came out of hospital. That night, we walked round there – in fear and trembling, I can tell you. I've *never* been so nervous of anything in my life. We went to be confronted by my mother, and all she could do was cry.

She was terribly – indescribably – grief-stricken, because she knew we would have to marry outside the Church. There was no other reason

– not Luís, not the fact I was marrying a priest in itself; she could have reconciled herself to that if he had got a dispensation. But we wrote and wrote and wrote to Rome, and other people wrote, and we never heard a single syllable from them. Nothing. Not even no. We said, 'Tell us how long we have to wait. Shall we come to Rome? Is there anything you'd like us to do?' In the end, we wrote and said, 'If we hear nothing from you, we intend to marry in Acton Register Office at 11 o'clock on 8 June.' And we heard nothing, so we carried on.

Afterwards, we had a concelebrated Mass in my mother's front room with three priests and much rejoicing. That was something my mother had to be persuaded very hard to accept because at first she said that if she condoned a Mass in her house, she'd be condoning our wrong decision. But the great thing about it was that she said, 'I will never accept that what you have done is the right thing, but I will accept that what you have done is what you think is the right thing, and therefore I won't reject you.'

She has never accepted it. No, never. She thinks the Church should change, she's in favour of change, but she would never break the Church's law in any circumstances. The thing she couldn't come to terms with was that we went outside the law to marry – we were unmarried in the eyes of the Church and we were living in sin.

I must say that we didn't lightly decide to marry outside the law. From Luís's point of view, he'd been in a seminary since the age of ten and had always been within the Church. He was forty-eight – he's almost eighteen years older than me – he'd been ordained for nearly twenty years and he'd been a religious even longer, since before his ordination.

From my point of view, I came from a family which was actively committed to the Church and I was working for the Church when I decided to get married. It was not a light decision to say, 'I will not have a Mass for my wedding,' because that was the first thing that occurred to me. Not that a Mass makes a wedding, but I like that sense of community that you have in Church, and it was the community I'd grown up in for thirty-one years. It gives me a sense of support, all sorts of things. So it was a great grief to me to say, 'I will not have my friends at my wedding.' I would rather have had a dispensation, though, with hindsight, seeing what you had to do to get a dispensation, it was disgraceful and I wouldn't have wanted it. But then, what I wanted was to marry within the Church.

I didn't have a problem with marrying a priest. I already thought celibacy should be optional. About six months before I met Luís, Michael Hollings had deliberately invited one of the convert ex-Anglican parish priests from Australia to say Mass in his parish. At the end of the Mass, he said to the congregation, 'I hope you like our visiting priest – and that's his wife in the front row. You see, they're just the same as us when they're married, aren't they?' So I saw nothing wrong with it.

As for Luís, all his life he had been convinced of the need for a married priesthood, and of his own need to marry. He didn't want to stop being a priest – there are a great number who leave because they reject things about the clerical system and marriage is merely a trigger factor. In our case, Luís consciously wanted to get married. He'd always thought, 'I must at some stage marry,' but he hadn't found the right partner.

Eventually, after eleven years, a dispensation fell through the door. We'd just moved into this flat. It said, first of all, 'You may never live where anyone knows that you've been a priest; you may not teach religion; you may not teach in a Catholic school without the Bishop's permission; you may not preach; you may not take any pastoral role in the parish . . .' It forbade everything any layman can do. And at the end it said, 'You must be a most loving son of the Church.'

Personally, I would not have acted on receipt of such a document. But we thought of my mother and of my husband's brother, who was in much the same situation, and we had a small official stamp put on our marriage. So we're now officially married. We exchanged vows in a ceremony that lasted approximately thirty seconds. We wouldn't give it any more – we weren't going to be any more married. My mother was absolutely thrilled to bits. We'd had both children by then and she'd come to both their baptisms and she loves Luís, absolutely loves him. She just couldn't get past the law.

Luís was also held back by the fact that we were truly impoverished. If one of my children wanted to get married like that, I'd die of worry. We had nothing. We had enough to buy a ring each, a suit for him, a dress for me, and return tickets to Cornwall, and that was it. He worried about not having money, but I said, 'I've always been poor, why are we arguing about money? Let's get married.' Poverty has been a continuum in my life – it's what took me into the Franciscans, it's what took me to work for Michael Hollings. It was through no sense of nobility or self-sacrifice. But I've always been poor, so why not be poor and married?

Luís wrote to his Bishop and said he was getting married, and he needed his possessions – as a secular priest he had £5,000 to £6,000 worth of furniture, clothing, books. The Bishop sent back a note for $50 with a little note attached: 'With my blessing.' Luís wrote back and said, 'If you won't send me anything, could I please have my photo albums?' We never got them.

He came in September, we decided to marry on 8 December and we got married on 8 June. Luís left the parish just before Christmas because we felt it wasn't fair on the parish priest here – who was very supportive of us, as was the curate – to have people saying, 'Oh, those two are living in the house together.' It was his responsibility.

So Luís went to Michael Hollings' house and I went home to my parents. We decided that I should stay in the parish until I had personally told, not only my family but all the people who had known me since I was a little girl, what I was doing and why. We'd both been in a public position in the parish and we felt we owed it them. We had the most amazing amount of support. Only one person really refused to accept us at all. When I'd been round them all, I told the youth choir and the parish council. I said I'd have to resign because I was marrying outside the Church. Someone stood up and proposed a vote of thanks and I was given a vote of thanks. Everyone gave us so much time, love and support. They were remarkable, really.

Very few people said, 'You're taking him away from God, you're taking him away from the Church.' I wasn't taking him anywhere. He could have said if he hadn't wanted to come. He's a big boy! When people said things like that, it gave me cause for anger. The thing that made me really angry was the reaction of my previous order. I had a good relationship with them so I wrote and said, 'I would like to bring my priest husband-to-be to meet you.' I got a letter back saying, 'A priest's fiancée would not be welcome.' I wrote back a long letter which I asked the Superior General to show to the community. I heard she pinned it up on the noticeboard.

It just seemed the right thing to do, you see. I probably wouldn't have got married otherwise – I was thirty-one. I wasn't looking to get married for the sake of it. I knew I wouldn't be satisfied with just anybody, someone with a semi-detached and a nice job. I wasn't interested in that. That's why I went for the job with Michael. And Providence – whatever that means – must have had a hand somewhere, because I was offered three different jobs while I worked with Michael, three really interesting jobs: working for a team catechising the deaf, with travellers, and in the catechetics team in the diocese. I turned all of them down because they didn't seem right. I can't rationalise it but some things just feel right here [*touching her stomach*] and something else that looks on the face of it much more sensible and secure does not feel right here.

Someone back in Chile did suggest to us, 'Why don't you come back here, work as a parish priest, and she can be your secretary and common-law wife?' I just wouldn't have considered it for a single moment. I couldn't bear to live in that sort of dishonesty, to live clandestinely. We'd have given each other up first. Which, mentally, we had done. We'd both made a conscious internal decision to give each other up. How could he get up there and preach to his congregation about keeping up their marriage vows while people were thinking he was celibate when he was not? What we did consider was becoming Anglican, but we thought, 'No, this is really silly.' Culturally, it was too far for Luís, besides which, it wouldn't have been strictly honest for me, because the Catholic Church is my church, warts and all, however cross I get with it, or however much I disagree with it. It's my family. Your dad might get cross with you for coming in late at night, but he's still your dad, isn't he?

I've always felt that it was part of our job to be part of that group of people who give up the exercise of the ministry in order to permit other people later to exercise the ministry as they see fit. There was a story someone told me about the Japanese in Burma. They were fording rivers and didn't have time to put up even a temporary bridge, so a line of tanks would go down and sacrifice themselves so that the next line could get across. One set of tank commanders would give up their lives to permit the others to pass. That makes it sound terribly magnificent, but when you're living it, it's not magnificent – it's uncomfortable and nasty. Yet one of the things that sustains you is the sense that you're doing what you do for others.

We did initially intend to go back to Chile. Fortunately, we didn't. This was 1979, six years after the coup. So Luís was stuck here, which gave us a difficult start to our marriage. First of all, somebody found him a job as a linen porter in a psychiatric hospital in Southall. This was not funny. Luís had been Vicar General of his diocese, with many large parishes. He had five degrees. Now he was working for an immediate boss who was a seventeen-year-old who'd left school with no qualifications and who thought all foreigners were shirkers, and he was pushing a trolley around all day.

Then we got married and we had lots of interrogation by the police. That was hard. We were interrogated in separate rooms. 'How long have you been married? Do you intend to buy a house?' All sorts of questions to trap you.

I got the first job I could that paid more than £20 a month, which happened to be as a clerical assistant with the DHSS. I did that for three months. It was a horrible experience. We were still not sure whether we were going back to Chile or not, so I didn't want to take a teaching post. Instead I got a job as a careers assistant in the Careers Service. We got a flat in Ealing, then Luís had three months' unemployment. That was very hard for him. He had a new culture, new language, new weather, new food – and no work. Plus a wife who was working. I had to do things like fill out the forms. Can you imagine – anything that would be his role normally. He'd lost much more than most priests who leave, much more. He was left with nothing.

We had all the normal stresses of the early days of marriage, plus all the other things, plus three months' unemployment. We got to the point of saying, 'If we put this pen down on the table, it will stand up and write its own application form.'

Luís was turned down for jobs for the most stupid reasons. He was turned down for a job as an occupational therapist with elderly people, which he'd have been very good at – he made our furniture, that bookcase, yes, he's very good with his hands – because they said, 'You'd want to hear their confessions.' His English wasn't good enough for him to say, 'Don't be so absolutely stupid.' He just sat there and looked helpless. He applied for a job as a social work assistant and he was told, 'You've had high position, you will not be willing to put yourself under people who are so much junior to you in experience.' We offered ourselves as houseparents to National Children's Homes, saying we would bring up difficult children along with our own. They didn't even give us an excuse. I can see why – people look at ex-priests and think, 'There must be something wrong,' even if they're not Catholic.

By the time we found we couldn't go to Chile – our entry permit was refused – I was expecting Miguel. He was called Juan Miguel after John, the curate in my parish, and Michael Hollings. I became pregnant very quickly – we married in June and Miguel was born in August the following year. We became homeless about six months before. We were in a flat that was not suitable for babies. The landlady was nice to us, but we'd made other arrangements to look after a house for someone for a year. We were all fixed and then this other woman backed out. The landlady had already got someone to move into our flat, so we camped out at my mother's. My two sisters moved out of their room and we had it while they slept downstairs.

By great good fortune, we were found a two-bedroomed flat in Acton by the housing association. It was so tiny you could spit from the front door to the other end of the bedroom, but it looked like Buckingham Palace to us. I remember standing in the flat and crying with relief, because it was only a month before Miguel was born. I was very large and tired.

Luís then got a job in a big chain store in Ealing, selling electrical goods. He used to come home with a big grin all over his face – 'This lady asked me about such and such a washing-machine, and I was going, "Oh, yes, oh, yes" – and I hadn't a clue what she was asking about!' Fortunately, we both have a sense of humour. That's really what got us through that time.

Some people may think that your problems are over when the priest decides to leave the active ministry and marry you. It's simply not true. In some ways, the problems are only just beginning. It's not easy being involved with a man who has been brought up to believe he is holy, who has been put on a pedestal, and who may lack social and practical skills. He needs a lot of support, because the very clear role has been taken away from him and he has to fall back on himself completely, find a new role. To give up all that, all the status and the power, and go into ordinary relationships can be very difficult.

He's not accustomed to coming to a relationship just as himself. The seminary training can lead him to believe he has what others haven't. And quite often people who become priests do have a lot of personal charism. They also have an image and a personal introduction to people – they can always be Father. What they don't have is relationships unprotected by their status. Yet, by its very nature, a relationship between a man and a woman is saying, 'This is me in relationship to you.' That's one of the great problems which comes from the separate nature of the priesthood. You have to live with somebody who doesn't yet know who he is, and who can take any amount of time to make that discovery. So we had a hard time at first.

Before you marry, while the priest is still sure of himself and what he's doing, however intimate your relationship, he's still in control of that side of his life. When you marry, all the things that are most important to him are suddenly out of his control. I know one man who was adored as a priest and when he got married he couldn't do anything. Not anything. That's really hard to live with. Because you, the wife, can't do anything about it. You can't supply a cure.

There's all the practical side as well, because it can be hard for the man to find work, unemployment can be stressful, especially in this situation where the man has lost the job at which he's competent and finds he's being turned down for jobs which are very much beneath his competence. Restoring someone's self-confidence in that kind of situation is a lost cause, really. It's taken years for Luís, and in some respects there are things he lost when he married me that he will never regain, because he's never been in a position where he's been able to exercise much of his skill and the things he is best at. And he was *very* good at them.

It's like asking a wonderful concert pianist to wash up in a restaurant or work in a laboratory: 'We won't treat you badly, we just won't let you play the piano any more.' In Luís's case, it's been a great deprivation. That's not always true – you get some priests, like Adrian Hastings, in an academic role, and they don't change the role when they marry, so the work side never impinges upon them. Some people can get jobs which allow for their sense of service – as social workers, teachers, prison officers. But for someone not working as an academic who isn't able to get a job with an outlet for his sense of service, there can be a tremendous feeling of deprivation.

The great thing for us was discovering people who had the same experience and been through the same mixture of kindness and unkindness. When a man leaves the priesthood, people see it as him having a problem with celibacy. That's a travesty. In reality, some men leave *to* marry, some men leave *and* marry. The majority leave because they disagree with other aspects of the Church. They're rejecting not only compulsory celibacy but a whole form of clericalism which they find unacceptable and of which celibacy is simply one element. Most of us would say that celibacy is a rich and valuable gift of God which can serve the Church in a profound way. But celibacy is a gift which is not given to everybody, and compulsory celibacy is one part of a whole clerical set-up which many of these men find unacceptable. They no longer wish to live that pattern of ministry, that structure of authority, of superiority. They don't accept that model of the Church any more.

When a woman falls in love with a priest and they are looking at the future of their relationship, they are almost always isolated. They generally don't know about others who have been in this situation, and have little or no support from people who can help them. This difficulty is increased for many women by the fact that the priest's role is seen as precious and special, and his background and training give him a language and a behaviour pattern which is unfamiliar, and about which she is, at least initially, diffident – there's a lot of authority built into priestly training, and it's a very big step to overcome the instinctive deference of the lay Catholic.

But it's too simplistic to write off as cowards those priests who do not choose to marry, and who instead remain in a clandestine relationship. For many, their life is very worthwhile and they don't see a way of doing what they do best outside the official ministry. For others, the recognition of the practical complexities of what lies in wait for them can be very daunting. So not every priest – nor every woman – would feel they were doing the right thing by marrying.

Eventually, what has to happen is a new understanding of ministry. The ones who never acquire that new understanding can feel deprived and always feel they're lacking something. You have to be quite clear-headed as the wife of that person not to take on the guilt for that. There are people who impune that guilt to you, who say, 'You are responsible for this. You dragged him from his path to sanctity.' A small number of people did say that to me – only a few, but they were very hurtful. I was astonished at how offended I felt.

Luís would be the first one to say that if he hadn't married, he might well have gone on another track, away from God, because he couldn't have sustained the work he was doing. He's always said priesthood is like being a fountain – you give out water and give it out and get nothing to feed in. He needed something to feed in, or he'd have dried up and couldn't have given out any more. My understanding of it is, to use the same metaphor, that marriage gave him an input to the fountain, but he couldn't see anyone who wanted to be sprayed. So, at first, he stopped putting out. He was too hurt, too unsure of himself.

I've gone through all kinds of moods – rage, frustration, desperation – but it's got to come from the person himself. You can't say to somebody, 'Have confidence.' It doesn't work. I don't think my husband realises how esteemed he is. I'm certain he doesn't. All my family esteem him, my friends esteem him, the parishioners esteem him – he's a much nicer person than me. He's gentle and thoughtful and very kind, and much more patient than I am. He's the absolute antithesis of me. How he can't see it I don't know, but he cannot see how people admire him, and I've given up trying to tell him.

Luís is a wonderful dad – though it was a bit of a surprise to him, what it entailed! I can remember him turning over at four in the morning when I was getting up to see to Miguel, who was teething. He said, 'If I ever get to write another sermon, it's going to be so different!' He found it a shock to the system in practical ways because, having gone to a minor seminary at the age of ten, he hadn't even seen baby brothers or sisters at any close quarters. He found it hard adjusting to having his sleep disturbed and me being much occupied with the babies, but he just adores them, and it's quite mutual.

What he's finding hard now is seeing a teenage boy behaving normally, because, when he was the age of our son, he was a seminarist, wearing a cassock and getting up at 6.30, praying, having breakfast, having an hour's study, fifteen minutes' football, an hour's study, praying, study . . . And our son is not a seminarist, and this has been a great surprise to him. He thought all little boys behaved like seminarists.

So he's had to do some capacious readjusting at each stage of the children's lives.

Many of the priests who marry are at least in their late thirties, so they're settled in their ways. It can be a rejuvenation. After Luís had been married a while, people said he looked younger – and he did. Marriage gave him lots of hope and enthusiasm and stuff which he'd run out of. It had many positive sides. I've probably made it sound like it was unmitigated difficulties, but it wasn't at all. We may not have had much money but when he did things, we enjoyed them. Like when he made the bookcase: it was so large, and took so long, that when he'd finished it, we just sat and looked at it and enjoyed it, like the television, for two hours! Because we literally married with nothing, we've had an enormous appreciation for everything we've done. We've enjoyed it enormously.

There are other positive things. Early on, we decided we owed something to people who hadn't been as fortunate as we were in terms of support. In some ways we're atypical, but one way we are typical is in the immense amount of support we've had from people. After two years in Acton, there was a priest who was supportive, and the Bishop, who encouraged us to work on the estate in South Acton. The first baptism in that community, they asked Luís to be godfather. He explained he was a priest who was married and asked whether they still wanted him, and they said, 'Of course.' He was very chuffed by this.

The people I knew in the Careers Service were concerned about Luís's lack of a job, and one in particular took it on herself to look through the vacancies – she put herself out a great deal for him. She found him this job as a biology technician at St Paul's public school in Barnes. He has a biology degree but no technician's qualification and at the time he had little English. They took him on and he retires from there next year. It's a bit of a waste of his talent, but it's been quite interesting and secure and, though I don't worry about money, it's consoling to know he'll have some pension, because he has no pension rights from his previous job as a priest. We've never taken out a mortgage – we'd have been breaking our necks – and we have no hope of one now.

Rosie was born two years after Miguel and, until she was five, I did work at home – I made wooden toys, did freelance art work and private teaching. I was determined that, poverty or not, after all the trouble we'd had, I was at least going to enjoy the kids. They're fourteen and twelve respectively this year. I now work in a primary school. I went for primary after teaching in secondary school because I wanted a job nearby so that I wouldn't have to farm out the children at the end of the day. It's a state school with about 4 per cent of Christians. We live in an area where most people are not Christian, which shows there are other ways to worship, other ways to God and other ways to goodness. I'm delighted that the children have got that experience of knowing other faiths.

We're as active as we can be in the parish. I lead the singing, we're both Communion ministers, we're active in the inter-faith movement and we've brought the children up in the Church – we've never hidden Luís's priesthood from them. We've always gone to the Advent Group meetings and the International Conference. They know more married priests than non-married. But we've had to explain that not everyone likes married priests. I think Luís would say he has ministry in his family, in his work and, in a limited way, in the parish. But you should ask him about that. Regrets? Not one. No, not one. I wouldn't change any of it, even the hard bits, because out of the hard bits has come a great mutual appreciation.

In the first parish where we lived, we felt the priest wouldn't cope with the knowledge, so we simply didn't tell him. We kept a low profile. We've not had much trouble. No one's refused us Communion. One person I know of told my mother, 'They're trying to have jam on both sides by doing what they've done and continuing within the Church.' My mother said, 'That's their business.'

Very few of the women I know who are married to priests are shy, retiring, subservient women. The language in the International Conference at first was all about 'us priests', with women as appendages. Then we women said, 'Oi, why haven't we got a place?' It was a first step. Many married priests have now changed 100 per cent, because they've married forceful women who are mostly well educated, articulate, will stand up for what they think and are willing to take a lead. Luís often says, 'I wouldn't have taken the jump if you hadn't said, "For goodness' sake, stop worrying. If you want to marry, let's get married."'

Perhaps it's more common in the couples who do marry that the women, for whatever reason, have an ability to be decisive at that crucial moment, and then, perhaps, have to keep on being decisive. Yes, I have to say, I gave the push.

I suppose, initially, like many priests who marry, Luís thought we'd have a common vocation as a married couple. He was certainly looking for someone whose support would enable him to live his vocation fully. And, of course, I do see husbands and wives as mutually supporting each other's work and personal life. But that doesn't mean that I see myself as Mrs Priest – I have *never* seen myself as a server to his vocation. It's more a question of embracing each other's callings to flourish.

I'm perfectly content, for example, to absent myself from the room if someone comes to our home to ask Luís for help. I'm happy to see him exercise a ministry, and I'd be delighted if it were more extensive. And, depending on the background and interests of the woman who marries a priest, she may well share much or all of any pastoral activity he has. I feel Luís and I have actually been quite fortunate in the opportunities that we've had to work together. But as for being a 'priest's helpmeet' – no, that is *not* how I see myself!

Around the World

Gisela Forster is forty-eight years old, a former teacher and the mother of three children. To all intents and purposes, an ordinary middle-aged, middle-class woman. But there is nothing ordinary about her story. Because all Gisela's children were born out of wedlock, all fathered by the same man, the Benedictine head of the Catholic grammar school where she taught art. When the truth came out, seventeen years after they met, they both lost their jobs, as well as the love and respect of a number of friends, acquaintances and family members.

Sound familiar? It is, except that this story didn't take place in Britain, but in Germany.

Anna, another teacher, has been married for twenty-five years. She has two grown-up sons and is about to become a grandmother. For the last fourteen years, she's also been having a relationship with a priest, though it didn't become fully sexual until she had a hysterectomy. Every six weeks, she sees him for a day under the guise of counselling. One day, she wrote him a letter and left it on the hall table. Her husband opened it. Despite the row that followed, she still sees her priest and her husband begs her not to leave him.

Another familiar story – but this one is taking place in South Africa.

Julie is twenty-seven. Her Bishop lover is fifty-two. They met when she was fifteen and seeking advice about becoming a nun. It didn't take long for them to fall in love. Their meetings have always been brief – they've never even had a meal together – but intense. She follows him everywhere, daren't invite anyone to her flat in case he comes round, waits for him to ring. She even talks about having his child. But already his visits are becoming fewer.

This story is unfolding in France.

231

* * *

When the Seven-Eleven support group tentatively met for the first time in November 1992, each woman there had previously thought she was alone. Far from it. Not only are there scores of women in Britain who are, or have been, involved with a Catholic priest; there are thousands of such women across the world. In addition to Seven-Eleven, there are similar, often longer-established support groups in Germany, France, Holland and America, as well as in Austria, Italy and Spain. The Irish group, Bethany Revisited, has over sixty members, many married to other men, who between them have borne a dozen children to priests and had six abortions. Four of these stories are touched upon by the group's spokesman (*sic*), Father Pat Buckley, in his recent autobiography, *A Thorn in the Flesh*.

Other books have been written exclusively about women in these illicit relationships, though none – apart from Annie Murphy's racy account of her affair with the Bishop of Galway – have been written originally in English. Instead, they are in French, German, Dutch. Apart from one, they have yet to be translated, a source of frustration to those most actively wanting reform because, for the moment at least, it isolates each country from what could be a powerful international network.

Six years ago, a Dutch social worker called Tineke Ferwerda published a book recounting the stories of some of the 200 women – and a handful of priests – who had contacted her after she had put an advertisement in the Dutch press. They told familiar stories of exploitation, resignation, hidden lives. When *Sister Philothea* was translated into English two years ago, it was reviewed only in the religious press.

Anne Lueg's book has yet to be reviewed at all in Britain. *Wenn Frauen Priester Lieben* (When Women Love Priests), published last year, is the result of ten years of research in Germany by a woman who is herself married to a priest. Her support group, the Initiativgrüppe der vom Zölibat betroffenen Frauen (the Movement for Women Affected by Celibacy), started with a newspaper advertisement in 1983 and now has several hundred members.

Another German book, *Sag Keinem, Wer Dein Vater Ist!* (Don't Tell Anyone Who Your Father Is!), by journalist Karin Jäckel, tells of nineteen cases of children born to men who are still working as priests, as well as a few instances where the priest-father insisted on abortion. She draws attention to the difficulties children face when they cannot divulge the name of their father, when financial arrangements for their upkeep are patchy – if they exist at all – and when their fathers face unemployment as a consequence of marrying their mothers.

In 1993, Odette Desfonds, founder of the French support group Claire-Voie (Clear Path), also wrote a book, *Rivales de Dieu* (God's Rivals), which again has yet to be translated into English.

It would be patently wrong, then, to suggest that the situation is peculiar to one country, due to one set of religious and cultural values. All over the world, priests are in relationships with women. Over the last decade, though, these women have been slowly emerging from the shadows, realising that there are others in the same situation, and they are beginning to speak out. Louder and louder and louder.

Their treatment can differ widely. In some countries, women who have married priests have suffered real misery, being called whores and harangued for taking him off his pedestal. In India, where there are an estimated 5,000 married priests, many of them live with their wives in real destitution, some so poor they are forced to sell matches on street corners to earn a living. In Holland, on the other hand, where some estimates claim one in two priests leave to marry, the role of married priests is an important one.

A useful forum for all of them is the International Federation of Married Priests, founded thirteen years ago by an Italian priest whose wife had visions about changing the celibacy laws. Initially, the federation, which holds congresses every three years, aimed to try to change Rome's mind about a married priesthood. Now, its aim is more to move away from the Roman vision of an institutionalised church into a democratic vision of the Church as its people: 'We are the Church.'

Not surprisingly, its activities are not popular with Rome. The third congress, in Madrid in 1993, nearly didn't take place after the Vatican threatened to close down the Dominican fathers' retreat house which was hosting the event. When the fathers asked for the reason in writing, nothing further was heard, and the congress went ahead, with 370 participants, among them fifty children. The delegates came from nearly thirty countries, including Austria, Belgium, Canada, the Czech

Republic, Haiti, Mexico, Portugal, Switzerland and Uruguay, and, for the first time, Japan and India. At the congress, delegates wrote to Pope John Paul II asking for 'equality before the law with priests in the oriental churches who are legitimately allowed to marry'. They have yet to receive a reply.

In Britain, as elsewhere, the whole issue of clerical celibacy is treated in a piecemeal fashion. Whenever a priest is 'found out' in an affair with a woman, there is a flurry of scandal in the media. Then the heat dies down – until the next time. Up to now, there has been little in the way of a systematic approach. With the launch of the Seven-Eleven support group, that is slowly changing.

Given Seven-Eleven's relative newness, I approached the longer-established European and American groups with more expectation of success in finding women willing to share their stories. I was wrong. Everywhere, the story was the same: 'Sorry. This is an issue that needs to be addressed. But the women are so frightened, very few of them will speak out publicly.' As in Britain, the only ones prepared to be identified are married to priests – those who have broken the chains that bind them and their men.

Anne Lueg sent a copy of her book, and other members of her group sent reams of articles, papers and reviews, but very few personal stories. Tineke Ferwerda's publishers sent a copy of her translated book. Odette Desfonds' publishers sent her book, which tells the stories of thirty women, including herself. The organisation itself, Claire-Voie, was suspicious. What was my interest? What would I do with the material? Only three women could afford to speak out without cover of anonymity, anyway, and Claire-Voie wanted payment for their stories. They need the funds. They had to see the work before publication . . .

Around the world, grown women and men are frightened of speaking out against that which oppresses them. People in highly responsible jobs, many with hard-earned middle-class lifestyles, are scared of Mother Church. It is all too easy to underestimate that fear. But it is a very real one. As one woman living in Germany said, 'What we are seeing in Germany today is every bit as repressive as the Nazi regime of terror.' Yet everywhere there is resistance. The following, then, is a brief overview of the situation in Europe.

BELGIUM

The idea of 'priests' lovers' is one of this strictly Catholic country's biggest taboos. However, following the Dutch example, 'hidden women' in Flanders have recently set up a Flemish association called Philotea (lover of God).

As elsewhere, they know all too well the difficulty of contacting those who may be eligible. 'Going public,' as they say, 'in the way that an ordinary group of people sharing a common interest do, is unthinkable.'

A longer-established group is Inspraak (Involvement), with 300 married priests as members. According to them, 1,000 priests have left the active ministry in Belgium in recent years, and obligatory celibacy is a major obstacle to young men's vocations. So Belgium, like many countries around the world, is suffering an acute shortage of priests.

Yet not all those ordained remain celibate. As one girlfriend said, 'If every priest involved in a relationship were forced to abandon his priesthood, in a very short time, there would be no priests left in this diocese.'

Another woman, not yet forty, told Philotea, 'At first, I couldn't bear to see him in his priestly robes. I burst into floods of tears after every Mass.' She met him when he was preparing for the priesthood. Instead of giving up his calling, he maintained his forbidden relationship under the guise of the priesthood.

Counselling programmes exist to help put priests back 'on the right track'. But most advocates for reform believe the situation will change only when the present Pope leaves office.

FRANCE

In France, one in four priests or members of religious orders leave the active ministry in order to marry. As elsewhere, life is not easy for them. Often they can't find work, and they can also face scorn, unkindness and accusations of betrayal.

In 1989, two women met in Lyons. Cécile had been the partner of a priest for ten years until he finally accepted his celibacy vow and ended the relationship, leaving her deeply hurt. Odette had secretly loved and been loved by a priest, Jean Desfonds, for four years and borne his daughter.

When Jean told his Bishop, his attitude was that the relationship – a loving friendship which had developed into something more – could continue as long as both parties were discreet. When their daughter was nine months old, however, Jean couldn't stand the hypocrisy any more, and left the priesthood, after nearly twenty years, to live an 'open' life. After explaining his actions to his parishioners in an open letter, he and Odette married. They received thousands of letters of approval and support.

Having gone public, Odette, now thirty-eight and the mother of three children, was contacted by more and more women in clandestine partnerships. She began to realise the enormity of the problem – of priests, women and children forced to live a life 'in hiding', lives characterised by suspicion and hatred. Talking with Cécile reinforced her conviction that, because of an old-fashioned rule, such useless sufferings exist, but remain shrouded in hypocrisy.

So, in August 1990, she founded Claire-Voie, which now has more than 400 members, including a large number of 'secret companions' in lifelong relationships.

Its aims are twofold: to offer a place where people with similar problems can go for support and talk in complete confidence; and to establish links with other organisations to try to force a re-examination of the ecclesiastical law of celibacy, 'which is contrary to the spirit of the founder of Christianity, and also to the laws of nature'.

As it has grown, other meeting-points have been opened around France. 'We fight,' says Odette's assistant, Noelle Colle, 'for the couples forced to have secret relationships; the women who have to bring up their children alone; the children who will never know who their father is; the children who, in the name of God, have been abandoned or even aborted; the men who are either forced to renounce the priesthood for love of a woman and face hardship, or who continue their double life, often with the connivance of their Bishop; and the women who are rejected by their lovers in favour of a younger woman, and who can't say anything about it.

'We want to affirm the dignity of the women concerned,' she adds, 'and achieve their liberation. We don't want a battle with the Catholic Church, but to change one law which is unnatural; to get the Church to respect human rights.'

During the last three years, Claire-Voie has campaigned vigorously on these points. Members have written letters to bishops with little official response. The bishops have indicated that they will talk only to individuals, not to an organisation – doubtless, say Claire-Voie, to minimise the extent of the problem. Initially, the Church denied this extent, suggesting that such women were few and far between. Even those bishops who recognised the truth of what was being said felt that there was no point in meetings, as there was nothing to be done.

'Their attitude,' says Odette, 'is "There aren't as many cases as you think, so don't think we're going to change the Church for people like you."'

Undeterred, delegates from Claire-Voie have been to Rome three times. 'Each time, we have been treated like stupid women,' says Noelle. 'Twice we have been closely watched by the police, and intimidated. One priest we spoke to laughed at what we had to say.'

The first delegation, of seven women, including the partner (for ten years) of a bishop, went to Rome in August 1993 to ask the Pope, via an open letter, to look at their situation. Monsignor Monduzzi, Prefect of the Casa Pontificale, met them, and Fr Jean Stern, who said he was a specialist on celibacy, told them that 'Priests having known the love of a woman must do penance,' and that the women involved were 'objects of sin'.

In October that same year, another delegation – this time of twenty women from three European countries, aged between twenty-four and seventy-five – was held under guard for four hours by the *carabinieri*, who had been given orders from the Vatican to detain them. They were told demonstrations were forbidden, even though they weren't demonstrating but were holding a forty-seven-hour public fast. In the ensuing struggle, one woman had her nose broken. After this visit, the association received letters from women and priests as far away as the USA, Canada and Africa.

In April 1994, they tried to table a question to the conference of Catholic bishops in Paris, which refused to even recognise the question. Members were received by the spokesman and secretary of the conference, who treated them courteously but without making any promises.

In June 1994, six women went to Rome for the third time. Again, they were met by civil police, who followed them to the Vatican. This time, however, both they and the Swiss Guard treated the women politely. They were interviewed on French and Italian television. A third open letter to the Pope told him of their intention to come again and again until they obtained recognition.

The group's aim now is to establish a tripartite discussion between the Church, the priests and the women to investigate the question of clerical celibacy. They are also pressing for a special commission to be set up. So they have no plans to abandon the fight, despite criticism and intimidation from some quarters of the Church. 'We want to right the injustices of generations of priests and women,' says Noelle.

In the last five years, they have come across a wide range of stories, many of which feature in Odette's book *Rivales de Dieu*, which she wrote to increase public awareness. Among them is that of Janine, a young, attractive woman abandoned by her priest lover when she became ill and lost her looks. Desperately unhappy, she still hopes he will come back to her, yet he hasn't ever visited her – despite his parochial responsibilities to the sick and infirm.

Then there is Madeleine, whose lover of thirty-eight years was suddenly taken seriously ill. Unable to accompany him to hospital, or to confide in her family, who had turned their backs on her, she was in despair. Through Claire-Voie, she found the strength to go to his bedside. During his last hours, she recited the canticles he loved, and he died in her arms, 'having finally realised that was where he belonged'. She watched over his coffin, along with his fellow priests and his family, who welcomed her to her rightful place.

Simone is a fifty-year-old social worker in the south of France. Through her work with handicapped children, she got to know the head of a large seminary. From being friends, they fell in love. He would invite her over for a weekend as his 'friend'. After four years, she found she wasn't his only girlfriend. While preaching celibacy to young would-be priests, he had been enjoying a series of affairs. Once found out, he disappeared into thin air, leaving behind a typed letter breaking off their relationship. She was told he had gone abroad. Two years later, she is still waiting for him to come back.

In Claudine's case, the priest was a friend of the family. One day, he kissed her and she 'knew immediately that it was love'. She had a child by him, who is now twenty. The priest was and still is adamant that the child should never know who his father is. Two years later, she had another baby. He refused to see it. A third baby was born in hospital. Surrounded by other women with their partners, Claudine realised how alone she was. She rebelled and said he would have to choose between her and his children and the Church. He chose the Church.

Some years later, they met again by chance. They are now together, though he is still a priest. Before talking to Odette Desfonds in 1990, she had never, in twenty-one years, confided in anyone. Her story finally convinced Odette of the need for an association. Claudine now sees a kind of progress in her own story: 'Before, he used to talk about them as "your children". Now he talks about them as "our" children.' They still don't know who their father is, though. What does she tell them? That their father is absent, lives abroad, is dead?

Claire fell in love with a priest thirty years ago. Her family were so worried that they pushed her into marriage which ended in disaster. She never forgot the priest. When she was fifty, had brought up her family and was widowed, she met him accidentally. They still felt the same way about each other, so she moved in as his housekeeper. They lived together until he died of a heart attack five years later.

All these stories appear in Odette's book. According to Claire-Voie, a not untypical relationship is one where the woman and priest see each other after Mass on Sunday; eat together; she washes his clothes; they occasionally spend a day together, sometimes go away together for a few days; he discusses his family and his problems with her; he wants her to be there all the time for him and disapproves of her spending time with other friends; she wants a child but he doesn't; she is basically a slave.

'These men of the Church,' says Noelle Colle, 'think they are superior, but they don't even manage to behave like normal human beings.'

What of Noelle herself? Forty years ago she was at a turning-point in her life and sought advice from a priest. 'We had a long talk, then, as I was leaving, we looked at each other. In that one look, everything we hadn't said was expressed. If anyone had told us we had fallen in love, we would have been scandalised. Yet that was exactly what had happened. A great, wondrous love which would guide us all our lives had been born between us. A love which had been destined to be since the beginning of time and which would last till eternity.'

At first, they were just friends. When the day came that they acknowledged they loved each other, it was, she says, 'a wonderful discovery'. But, instead of being able to proclaim their happiness, they had to enter the world of clandestine meetings. 'It's impossible to describe the suffering caused by this secret life. We couldn't confide in family or friends and felt completely isolated.'

Then Noelle had a child. She and her priest decided to make the break, and left the Church. 'It was one of the hardest things we'd ever done. We had no money, no jobs; we were objects of criticism, of insults. It wasn't easy, but the overriding feeling was one of joy that we were at last free.'

They moved away from France and joined a Protestant church, determined to bring up their children – four in all – in the full knowledge of what had happened.

'Often, we thought with sadness of all those who hadn't been able to leave the clandestine world of secret love, and had led a life of great suffering. This problem has existed for a long, long time. And it's time the Catholic hierarchy recognised it honestly.'

Noelle's husband is now dead – of an illness which she believes was connected with his years of moral suffering. She finds it hard not to hate the Church but, she says, 'He was so good, so generous, that he wouldn't have wanted me to have such feelings. That's why I joined Claire-Voie, to help others as much as I possibly can.'

From its beginnings in Lyons just five years ago, Claire-Voie is now expanding into Belgium, Canada, Germany and Switzerland. Members like Noelle are now writing their own stories, which are to be published under the title *Livre Blanc*.

GERMANY

Thanks to women, the issue of clerical celibacy has received wide coverage in Germany over the past decade. Now, every time a priest leaves the priesthood, it's news, not least because half the parishes in the country will soon have no priest.

As a result of this shortage, some congregations keep quiet about their priest having a relationship. Others demonstrate outside churches.

In 1992, the bi-annual conference of Catholics heard repeated demands for the abolition of mandatory celibacy. In February of last year, 65,000 Catholics wrote a letter to the Pope on the issue. They are still waiting for a response.

In the meantime, it is estimated that over half the priests in Munich are now married and therefore no longer active. Many of the rest have secret partners. Other priests, including leading theologians, have been admitted to other churches, notably the Lutheran and Old Catholic, where they can combine Christian ministry with a wife and a family. Others, who have been granted dispensation, still work in the Roman Catholic Church as lay employees in social organisations. In southern Germany, a small community of Christians and people from other faiths have applied to the Vatican for recognition as a Catholic order of married men and women. The German Association of Catholic Priests and their Women (Vereinigung Katholischen Priester und ihrer Frauen) has 600 members.

In 1990, the diocese of Mainz suspended a hospital chaplain, Wolfgang Eifler, after he went on television to condemn celibacy as 'collective schizophrenia', and to admit that he was living with his then girlfriend – they subsequently married. Since then, Rita Waschbüsch, president of the Central Committee of German Catholics, has stated publicly that celibacy is not a dogma, but a changeable rule. Criticism, then, is growing, even from within the heart of the Church.

And the public debate all started with women: journalists Karin Jäckel and Ursula Goldmann-Posch, and priests' wives Anne Lueg and Gisela Forster.

In 1983, Karin Jäckel put an advertisement in the national press in Germany, asking for women who had become pregnant by priests to contact her. She heard from 200, mainly from West Germany, but also from East Germany, Switzerland and Austria. Their ages range from eighteen to sixty, mostly in the twenty-five to forty-five age group. Between them, they had borne 143 children, nineteen of whom had fathers who were still active priests. Some of the women had had abortions. Among them were the wives and widows of priests, priests' 'housekeepers', women married to other men, women in secret relationships, and women who had finished their relationships. The priests themselves came from all levels of the Church

241

hierarchy, including monks and seminarists.

The result was *Sag Keinem, Wer Dein Vater Ist!* (Don't Tell Anyone Who Your Father Is!), bravely published in Catholic Bavaria. The chapter headings give some indication of the problems faced by children in this situation: 'A child of Sin'; 'Dad, When I Grow Up, I'll Become a Priest For You'; 'I'm afraid to Betray My Father'; 'Why Do I Have to Lie?'

After three years' research, Karin Jäckel concluded that many clergy children, especially those of secret relationships, do suffer psychologically. She has come across children who hurt themselves with knives, those with suicidal tendencies, and one child who literally went dumb when he found out his father was the priest he had always called Uncle. Psychotherapists discovered that his mutism had occurred because he had totally lost his inner and external security, and no longer knew what was real. 'These are children the Church doesn't want, children that mustn't be born because, in the eyes of the Church, they bear witness to sin.'

In official Church language, a priest's children are called *sacrilegus* – temple burglar – as if they have robbed the Church of its priests. For the mothers, there is often frequent intervention as priests come home every few months and say, 'I've a right to this child, and it's not being brought up properly.' As Karin says, 'He doesn't get thrown out, because the woman is emotionally tied to him.'

As long as the father's identity remains secret, she cannot ask the Church for maintenance. If his identity becomes known, he will either lose his job and be unable to pay maintenance, or keep his job and lose the relationship. In such instances, there are so-called black cash boxes, and many women have received money, but the decision remains an individual diocesan one.

In 1985, eight years before the publication of Karin Jäckel's book, Ursula Goldmann-Posch wrote *Unheilige Ehen: Gespräche mit Priesterfrauen* (Unholy Alliances: Conversations with Priests' Wives), about women's experiences of clerical celibacy.

In that same year came the publication of the first book by the Initiativgrüppe der vom Zölibat betroffenen Frauen (Movement for Women Affected by Celibacy), the group founded two years earlier by Anne Lueg.

Anne has been with Heiner Lueg, now a prominent member of the German Christian Democratic Party, since 1979. In 1983, when she decided to found a support group for priests' wives, friends, 'de facto' wives, lovers, and the mothers of priests' children, fifteen women replied to her advert in a Christian magazine. Now the group has over 350 members throughout Germany, who meet nationally twice a year, and regionally much more often. Their newsletter, *Zölibat* (Celibacy), is published twice a year.

According to Anne, the women fall into three categories: those who are married to a Catholic priest, with or without dispensation; the majority, who are in a relationship with an actively working priest, and a small group who have left the relationship and are still mourning their loss.

All, though, are affected by the same thing: a rule of celibacy which she believes is hostile to women, and damaging to the Church. Her group aims to publicise the 'misogynistic' attitude of the Church, to help women out of anonymity through sisterly solidarity, to allow personal experiences to reflect the political reality. 'It is important to us,' she says, 'that women gain some insight into their own situation by talking to others.'

Women like Rosa, who had a child alone in hospital while all around her were women with their partners and their families. When the midwife asked her the name of the father, she didn't know what to say. She wept as red roses were delivered to the other women.

Women like Caroline who saw an advert for the self-help group a couple of years ago, when she was seventy. For the first time, she could talk about her relationship, which consisted of sexual encounters followed by coffee and cognac. She saw herself as simply the sex object of an immature man, whose biggest compliment to her was that she reminded him of his mother. The group gave her the strength to end the relationship. Sadly, however, she could not cope with the ensuing loneliness, and took her own life.

Women like Inge, who lied for years to protect her priest, the father of her sons: 'Today, I tell the truth, because only the truth will liberate me.'

Like Agatha, now seventy and suffering from cancer, who has had a forty-year relationship, during which time her partner became Provincial of his order three times. She only recently discovered that he has also been having a relationship with another woman who has given him money and bought him expensive presents, and even took him on all-expenses-paid holidays when Agatha thought he was on official Church trips.

In the group there are fifty children of priests who are still in office, and a dozen women who have had abortions. One woman went to the clinic with the priest. When the doctor asked if he was the father, he denied it. While she was having her operation, he officiated at Church. Other men have threatened suicide if their lovers do not agree to an abortion.

As with Claire-Voie, the German group have found that, while bishops and even cardinals are available to speak to women individually, they are not prepared to enter into formal discussions. Yet, as Anne Lueg says, with so many parishes priestless, the Church will have to address the issue formally sooner or later.

If celibacy were optional, she believes the Church would not only have more priests, but also mentally and physically healthier priests, as well as priests who are *convincingly* celibate. Until it does, the Church is fostering psychological damage, not least among those priests and women forced to inhabit two worlds, one open and one hidden. As a result, they can lose touch with reality, and the hidden world can engulf them, often before they realise what is happening, because their Catholic upbringing has blinded them to the possibility of falling in love if the object of that love is a priest.

In 1985, the group wrote a book called *Ein Sprung in der Kette* (A Break in the Chain) about mandatory celibacy and its effects. But Anne insists that what is happening, in Germany as elsewhere, is not just individual cases but a phenomenon. To back up this claim, last year she published a second book, *Wenn Frauen Priester Lieben* (When Women Love Priests), which received enormous publicity and 90 per cent public support.

As the group has progressed, so its ideas have changed and become more radical. Anne herself has become angrier, talking of 'Ten years of stagnation in official Church policies; ten years of making the problem seem less serious than it is; ten years of silencing something out of existence.' And every new secret relationship supports that silence.

Clora Chriss is a former board member of the German Association of Catholic Priests and their Women: 'Many people feel guilty about "taking" priests away from their profession,' she says. 'I count myself among them. I had not insisted on his leaving, for I pitied his not being able to get a job as a theologian. But now I think differently. He should never have continued to work as a priest as long as women are excluded from the office – what if only white men could be admitted? Blacks would expect him to step down for the sake of the principle of human rights.'

Like other wives of priests, she is all too aware that the problems do not end on marriage. 'It's not purely a problem of celibacy, but of a priest understanding that his position makes him different from everyone else. So a partnership in marriage is terribly difficult, because there's still that separateness. They can't deal with their special position, and the expectations of that position make some of them ill. And some women have married ill men from compassion, so the tragedy gets bigger. So many of us women could identify immediately with the stories and analysis that Eugen Drewermann, the priest psychoanalyst, put in his gigantic book – 900 pages! – called *Kleriker: Psychogram eines Ideales* [Clerics: Psychogramme of an Ideal]. It's all about the illnesses that come about because of the priest losing his basic character and personality.'

Gisela Forster is a long-time member of the German group. Her relationship, with the Benedictine head of art at the monastery grammar school at Schäftlahren, near Munich, resulted in three children. 'For me,' she says, 'priests were men who dealt with the transcendental. They were closer to God. Today, I'd say I tried to gain access to God via priests.'

She got to know her husband through taking a job as art teacher at the same school. 'I liked him from the first phone call. His voice was very melodic and warm. When I saw him for the first time, I immediately felt we were on the same wavelength. We had the same ideas about teaching and it was very enjoyable to work as art teacher under his guidance. He was never authoritarian, but always full of understanding. He was everything to me: a colleague, a man I admired, someone to idolise. Each hour with him was wonderful.'

At the time, she was twenty-six and he was thirty-seven. 'The

245

longing for greater closeness and sexuality existed, but at the same time there was fear, especially in him. I couldn't understand it. To me, if spiritual closeness is there, physical closeness is normal.'

Intimacy crept up on them almost before they knew it: 'You slide into it. First, you notice you like him; then you get frightened, because you know the Church doesn't want you to love each other, but at the same time there isn't a lot you can do against love. I just somehow thought, "I love him and I will give birth to the children I carry – why shouldn't I have children just because he's a priest?" I followed my feelings, my conscience and nature.'

Two years after they met, the relationship became intimate. 'It was marvellous for both of us, and he immediately had a strong urge for a child. So did I, though I saw the difficulties that could arise. We both felt extremely happy when I became pregnant. The fears about Church and society I ignored. Man and child were the most important for me, even though there was no marriage or family. When he never mentioned marriage, I thought, "That's his decision." I always tried not to expect anything of him. Then I wouldn't be disappointed.'

Gisela had their first child and brought him up on her own. She refused to divulge the name of the father, though, as she says, 'there are always rumours'. As a result, she became isolated. When his family found out, they turned against her, seeing her as the seductress. 'I still find that unbearably painful. They still don't talk to me, after twenty-two years.' Then she had a daughter. In between, there were times of crisis when she felt alone and unable to carry the responsibility any more. But she had to. 'I never felt guilty. The Church's proscriptions never meant anything to me. For me, God was important.'

Nonetheless, having children without a visible father is not easy. 'They cried sometimes because they hadn't got a father. When they asked, I didn't know what to say. Then I talked my way out. I cried a lot during the night then, because the children didn't have a father they could name.

'It was easiest when the children were little,' she says. 'But at three or four, they notice that other children have a father. I just put together a story. I thought, "It's really the Pope's fault that they haven't got a father." So I told them he was imprisoned in Italy. "He lives in Rome, and he can't live with us." I always visualised the Pope holding him in chains. Then the children would ask for a photo, and I had to say I hadn't got one. Then they started saying, "Are we going to Rome to see him? A father wouldn't abandon his children." It got harder and harder.'

In the end, when her son was nine, she told him. But she had to swear him to silence at the same time. 'Imagine, a nine-year-old, sentenced to silence.' Nonetheless, he covered up for his parents.

Because they were so afraid of being found out, the family never went out in public together. The children's father and Gisela met at work, but had little private time together. Everything was secret. 'Somehow, we lost contact with the real world and with a normal life.'

She was afraid of losing her job and not being able to provide for her children. He was afraid of God. 'We weren't afraid of each other, or of our sexuality. We were like children, simply close to each other. We tried not to turn sex into a problem area. There was this primeval longing in us for closeness and warmth, and we wanted to remain in this warmth, especially since the outside world offered us no home.'

After seventeen years, she found out about the self-help group and he met another priest who had left the active ministry. He could bear the secrecy no longer and told his Abbot. Both he and Gisela were dismissed from their jobs.

'I had been at the school for seventeen years,' she says. 'I had never had any complaints, I was a successful teacher, yet, simply because the father of my children is a priest, I was sacked. From one day to the other, I and my three young children literally had no food. We lived off the odd 100-mark note from people we knew. Imagine this: they venerate Mother Mary, but at the same time desert us mothers who become needy!'

She took the monastery to court for backdated maintenance. 'I see it this way: the children have a 100,000-mark share of the monastery assets, because the monastery was his employer, but all his money went into Church coffers. When he admitted to being the father, the state put a compulsory court order against the monastery for 90,000 marks – the maintenance he owed. Otherwise, he couldn't have his paternity recognised.'

Despite a long fight, the German courts threw out her claim, maintaining that the Church is self-regulating, and that canonic law takes precedence over state law. She then took her claim to the European Court of Human Justice, who ruled that there was no law available to help her. She and her husband are now separated.

'The situation now is that the past still makes us suffer tremendously. Even though we got married, many friends didn't want to know us any longer. We have lost so much: our jobs, our material basis – we had to start from scratch, aged forty-three and fifty-four, when we got married. The pressures were huge, and we didn't really manage them.'

Although her faith in God continues, she no longer has faith in the Church that views them and their children as 'outlaws'. 'It is very lonely outside the Church. I am very lonely in my faith. My husband doesn't talk to me about God. I don't know whether he suffers, whether he is in despair. I don't even know whether he believes in God. I often think he has lost God through the punishment and power of the Church. I daren't talk to him about this.

'I wish the Church would let people love. The law of celibacy destroys men and women and leaves wrecks behind. Good as my life has been in many respects, I feel I have come to the end of my strength, destroyed by this Church and its morality. I am still searching for the Church of love and of human beings.'

Until very recently, Uschi Haertlé's story has been, despite many early hardships, a happier one. She met her husband, Wolfgang, at her local church, when applying for the job of kindergarten leader: 'I always say it began in the vestry and ended at the altar!' She was twenty-two at the time – this was in the late sixties – and he was the chaplain in charge, so he was always available to advise and support her.

When her mother visited the kindergarten, she said, 'It can't go well. You two understand each other too well.' Uschi protested, 'But he's the chaplain. That's really taboo for me.'

Nonetheless, over the months, they realised how much they liked each other. Wolfgang, who had never had a relationship with a woman before, was experiencing disappointment in the wake of the Second Vatican Council, as well as loneliness, which meant he was more open to the relationship which developed.

'In the early years,' says Uschi, 'I had terrible guilt feelings, and I worked through them by undergoing psychoanalysis. We both did. Today, I wouldn't have those feelings. But at the time, I felt very lonely. I looked on myself as a seductress – which is how my relatives and acquaintances condemned me, although that wasn't the case. I felt guilty because I saw that my husband was very well liked as chaplain, that the young liked him as much as the old, and I was the last straw which contributed to him no longer being able to continue in his work. That caused me a lot of tears, I have to say.'

Uschi and Wolfgang owned up to their relationship in the early 1970s. 'Except for a few, who reacted positively,' recalls Uschi, 'the greatest part of the community has given me the Guilty verdict – not my husband, but me. I am the snake that has coiled around him. My relations said it was me who dared interfere with a priest – it didn't seem to matter that it takes two. People simply weren't aware that we might have thought a lot about it. No, the woman is the seductress of the man.'

In fact, 'An intimate relationship was out of the question for me, for both of us, while my husband remained a priest. We only became intimate after he had been to the Bishop, had said that he wanted to leave and why. I couldn't have tolerated intimacy with my husband back in the pulpit the next day; I couldn't have coped.'

Once he had left the priesthood, they moved to a different diocese and Wolfgang studied social work. 'We did feel badly done to by the Church authorities at that point,' remembers Uschi. 'I was dismissed without notice, even though I told the priest that the dispensation was in progress, that the papers were in Rome. In that diocese, they were really obstructive wherever possible. I was at my wits' end. Feelings of hatred began building up inside me, because we were treated so badly, and later on over the whole way of dealing with priests' wives and children. Those feelings have abated, now that I've gained some distance from the Church.'

The Haertlés have now been married twenty-three years and have two children. She is back in charge of a kindergarten, while he works for the Catholic student community in Münich and for the counselling service for secret clergy couples.

'Today,' she says, 'these fears are over with and I feel well within myself, with the children, who are sweet and little devils at times, and with my husband, because we continue to be on the same wavelength. I believe it was meant to be.'

In 1993, a survey reported to the German bishops' conference showed that nearly three quarters of Catholic women in Germany disagree with the law of celibacy. For a third of those, the point is so serious that it is affecting their relationship with the Church. They believe it's another way of the Church keeping women on the outside.

Another poll, conducted in the archdiocese of Cologne in the late 1980s, showed that three quarters of the 1,500 priests questioned believed many priests would cohabit with a woman, regardless of the consequences. Other statistics show that between 10 and 30 per cent of the 24,000 priests and monks in Germany have some sort of secret relationship. The effect of celibacy on young men wishing to be priests, here as in other European countries, is disastrous, with numbers falling from nearly 900 seminarists at the beginning of the 1980s to fewer than 400 in 1992.

Yet, despite the statistics, despite the growing disquiet, time and again Church leaders reiterate the binding nature of the law of celibacy and the impossibility of its abolition. No matter how explicit society becomes, or how much pressure there is for equality.

Where children are concerned, Bishop Lehmann, the chairman of the bishops' conference, is adamant that the Church tries to make a priest feel responsible towards the children he has in a secret relationship. As for maintenance matters, he insists: 'It's the responsibility of the individual.' And for that reason among others, the Bishop maintains, the Church is compassionate towards priests who leave. Seventy per cent of dispensations sought are granted, 'And we can help priests to find new work by offering them the opportunity to study something else or retraining them.'

That Rome is on principle disinclined to rescind the celibacy law was recently demonstrated by the conservative Cardinal Ratzinger. At a meeting in Austria, he was asked whether it wouldn't be sufficient if monks lived in celibacy but secular priests could marry. He replied, 'On this point, the Holy Father and the Church tradition in its entirety have pronounced again and again, with intensity, that it is essential for the Church to link priesthood with celibacy. Therefore, a limitation to monks would not be appropriate to the importance of this decision for the Church or, looking at it more pragmatically, it would not be a solution.'

As long as the clerics in authority see the debate only in terms of whether a man's job is to be linked with a man's celibacy, all their well-chosen words will ring hollow. It's really their fear of women that has to be brought out into the open – even when a priest has left and is safely married. Up until the end of summer 1994, Wolfgang and Uschi Haertlé were relatively at peace. But they are once more being haunted by the past, all because Uschi took over at the helm of the group Women Affected by Celibacy. Wolfgang is being put under pressure: either his wife resigns, or his life at work as student pastor will be made so miserable that he will want to quit before being sacked.

'Centuries ago they would have burned us at the stake,' he observes. 'Today they lord it over us with psychic terror.' He recalls the warning he got ten years ago in a conversation with Church leaders about future dialogue between the Church hierarchy and the Association of Catholic Priests and their Women: 'We were strictly instructed not to have anything to do with Anne Lueg's women's group.'

On this issue, at least, women are obviously regarded as being stronger and more powerful than men.

THE NETHERLANDS
According to the Dutch Cardinal Simonis, in an interview in 1989, 'Of 3,500 priests in the Netherlands, some dozens, maybe a hundred, have had problems [with celibacy], but these figures are no more than a guess.' According to Netwerk Philothea, the women's support group, one out of two priests in the Netherlands, a country traditionally confrontational to Rome, leaves the active ministry in order to get married.

Nearly twenty-five years ago, the Dutch Pastoral Council, expecting change in the wake of Vatican II, petitioned for optional celibacy. Their request was rejected, although Pope Paul VI let it be known, via Cardinal Bernardus Alfrink, that the abolition of compulsory celibacy was inevitable sooner or later. Not long afterwards, however, an eminent churchman asked the University of Utrecht to sack seven professors who were married priests. In the event, three resigned of their own accord.

Another famous case was that of Fr Willem Berger and Henriëtte Röttgering. He was a priest in the diocese of Haarlem, and professor of the psychology of religion at Nijmegen University. She was always presented as his housekeeper and secretary. But in 1981, they went public about their twenty-five-year relationship, and later married. The catalyst was the news that the special Synod of Dutch bishops had given up trying to persuade the Pope to change his mind.

Nonetheless, opposition to the established Church view continues to grow. When Tineke Ferwerda put an advert in the national press in January 1987, she received 150 replies, half from women still involved with priests. The result, her book *Sister Philothea*, covers a wide range of experiences, from child abuse, through homosexuality, to adult heterosexual abuse, and close, loving relationships.

Among them is Eve, a religious since 1965, who talks frankly about her sexual repression, the lesbian advances she fended off in the convent, and her decision to leave the order in 1978. She then made friends with a priest, fell in love with him, discovered he was bisexual, and experienced much suffering until he finally decided to share his life with her. They signed an affidavit that they would stay together, even if it meant him leaving his priesthood.

Another woman, unnamed, was left a widow at forty, with two children, one of whom has Down's Syndrome. For a radio broadcast, she talked to her local priest, Father Paul, about living alone. Afterwards, he kissed her passionately. They started an affair. Two years later, in casual conversation with someone else, she discovered that he 'lodged' with another woman two nights a week and had been on holiday with her. He was also having other relationships.

Mara was married with six children when her priest brother-in-law asked her to undress in front of him because he had never seen a naked woman. From then on, she was 'wife' both to him and to her husband, who agreed to the triangular relationship. Eventually, tired of her husband's drinking and abuse, she left him. On her own, she saw more of her brother-in-law until she began to love him too much, at which point he left her. Now, she is totally alone.

Greeje is a spinster in her forties who nursed both her parents through their final illnesses. The chaplain who visited began to make sexual advances towards her. Passively, she let him. Passively, she agreed to everything he asked, including masturbation. Eventually, she confided in his superior and the priest was moved to another parish. She hears that he is still playing around. She, meanwhile, is trying to come to terms with the abuse and the loneliness.

Tineke Ferwerda concludes that most of these women work in the 'soft sector' – social work, nursing, teaching. Their average age is forty-three, that of the men fifty-five. The average duration of the relationship is ten years, and most began after 1980. Half the partners belong to a religious order.

'I continue to remember,' wrote one woman, 'especially from the initial period, that it was something special to be chosen by a priest. I went to Communion with head held high. I never felt bad in this relationship, though people wanted to give me that feeling. I felt above their gaze.'

SOUTH AFRICA

At the end of the Southern African bishops' visit to Rome in May 1992, Bishop Wilfrid Napier raised the subject of celibacy in his address to the Pope. In at least four dioceses in the region, he said, one priest had to minister to 5,000 people. Many older people living in rural areas were effectively disenfranchised from the institution of the Church, deprived of the sacraments because of the celibacy rule. 'Unless there is a clear sign from the "official Church" that relief is on the way,' he said, 'many will lose heart and fall by the wayside.'

Twenty years ago, a meeting of the Council of Priests was shown that, if the ratio of one priest to 500 people was to be maintained until the year 2000, at least seventy-five new priests needed to be ordained each year. In fact, ordinations average only a third of that. The current 250 seminarians, presupposing they are all ordained, will hardly fill the priestless parishes. So a number of parishes have no one to say Sunday Mass.

As yet, there is no official support group for women in South Africa. But that isn't to say relationships between women and priests do not exist.

Anna, a teacher, contacted me after reading an appeal in *The Tablet* journal. She's been married twenty-five years, has two grown-up sons, and is about to become a grandmother. Fifteen years ago, she went to a priest for counselling and gradually fell in love with him. A year later, the relationship began, though it didn't become fully sexual until she had a hysterectomy five years later.

'Life would be much less complicated without Pieter,' she wrote, 'but it would also be much emptier. I don't love my husband any more, but I can't leave him. He's not well, and we have been through a lot together. But it's Pieter who feeds me emotionally, spiritually and sexually.'

At first, her husband suspected nothing, even though her visits to the priest grew more frequent. One day, he discovered a letter from her to Pieter on the hall table and read it. 'There was a big row and he was very upset, but I said I couldn't live without seeing Pieter. He said he couldn't live without me, which I think is true. So he's had to accept the situation, though I don't know how happy he is with it. We don't talk about it.'

AMERICA

When Annie Murphy wrote her book, *Forbidden Fruit*, about her relationship with the Bishop of Galway, media coverage concentrated on the situation in America, as though such relationships were peculiar to that country. 'What else can you expect?' seemed the common view. The same was said when, five years ago, the Archbishop of Atlanta resigned after being accused of having a two-year relationship with a woman in his diocese.

Even Rome seems to share that opinion. According to Cathy Grenier, founder of the Good Tidings support group for women and priests, writing to the Seven-Eleven group in England, in 1993, 'The Roman Curia would have it that sexual activity among Roman Catholic priests, either in the form of ignoring celibacy in intimate loving relationships with women, abusive relationships with adult women or children, or homosexual relationships, is primarily an American problem.

'As an American,' she wrote, 'I wonder if Rome judges Americans in general as more sexually promiscuous and irresponsible, or whether it is merely American Catholic priests who are perceived as rebelling or ignoring Roman authority in their sex lives. Are we all more sexually "immoral" than Europeans, or is it just our priesthood that is judged and condemned?

'Or is what disturbs Rome and prompts rash judgements merely the fact that here, in America, we don't tolerate as much cover-up of the truth regarding those who say they are "serving" us as celibate priests? If we were sneakier or more reticent about our intolerance of mandatory celibacy in the priesthood, or about our decision to ignore Roman "celibate" authoritarianism and interference in the sex lives of faithful average Catholics, would we be perceived by Rome and the world as more faithful and obedient or just as better liars?

'Or is this American-bashing by Rome just a papal temper-tantrum over the fact that Rome cannot subjugate American customs and laws to Roman customs and canon law? It seems the Roman approach is to kill the messenger (the media and the reformers) rather than listen to the message. Blame us for speaking a heretofore hidden truth, a sick secret, rather than admit celibacy is not working and never has worked.'

It's fifteen years since Cathy, a former nun, and her French Canadian priest husband Joseph took over Good Tidings from Maggie Olsen, who founded the group after a woman friend took her own life when abandoned by her priest lover. They themselves had met at a prayer group in New York and fallen in love. During the next two years, Joe, a priest for twenty-two years, had a 'crisis of vocation', which ended in the decision to leave the priesthood – with $500 in his pocket – and marry.

As the Greniers found, if a priest has an affair and keeps it quiet, the Church will turn a blind eye. If, however, he leaves and marries, it's a scandal, because the Church then loses face.

In a television interview five years ago, Cathy said, 'If you define scandal in simply sexual terms – as a priest having an affair, what a scandal – that has some truth in it. But the greatest scandal is the evil that is institutionalised, the punishment of priests and women who are in love. "Transfer him or get rid of her" – that's a greater scandal, to treat the woman as though she were not worthy of love and good treatment.'

In the past fifteen years, she and her husband have been in contact with 1,500 people and have 700 women on their books. Three of them have relationships with bishops, twenty have had children and taken out paternity suits.

Now, the group is expanding into the rapidly growing Hispanic community and the French Canadian community in Quebec and New England with two new groups, Buenas Nuevas and Bonnes Nouvelles: 'The patriarchal society they face,' says Cathy, 'is even greater than the English-speaking Church here.'

Ten years ago, they also set up Holy Innocents, to unite women who have conceived, borne or aborted the children of priests, and who have been abandoned. Writing in the Good Tidings bulletin, Cathy talks of priests who, 'Like Herod . . . panic at the thought that their position of respect and authority could be challenged by the birth of an innocent child. The unborn child's right to life, love and the pursuit of happiness is sacrificed to protect the father's hypocritical status of moral leadership within the community and the Church.' And she writes scornfully of abortions carried out 'in the name of God', and of men who 'disappear' to another diocese, to avoid having paternity papers served on them.

Among the women who have contacted Good Tidings is Marie, who conceived Fr Bob's child when she was twenty-one and he came to minister to her dying father. His superior told him he had no responsibility to Marie or to the child because he did not choose fatherhood. Fr Bob was moved to another diocese, where he started another relationship. Counselling revealed he was a sex addict and he was dismissed from the priesthood.

Meanwhile, Marie was receiving threatening phone calls from Catholics looking to stone her and her baby if she pursued a paternity suit. Years later, having sorted himself out psychologically, Bob tracked Marie down. By this time, she had married someone else, who had adopted her child.

Another phone call to the Greniers was from Terri, who had a baby by Fr Pat in 1988. Although he had agreed to the pregnancy going ahead, when the child was born, he told Terri he was in love with another woman, who had loved him enough to put their child up for adoption. Terri now brings up her child alone, enduring the taunts of her Catholic neighbours.

'These children,' says Cathy, 'are too frequently dealt with as commodities by Church authorities, and either cash settlements or monthly pay cheques replace, rather than supplement, fatherhood in the children's lives. Spiritual or psychological intimidation, secret moral or legal agreements, and pressure to keep silent prevent mothers from speaking out publicly on an individual basis.'

The Greniers, who have a young daughter, run the non-profit-making organisations from their home in Canadensis, Pennsylvania. They invested $10,000 into it in the first eight years, and still have to cope with huge phone and postage bills. Although Joe has a PhD in theology, he took a job in real estate, which ended when the market collapsed at the end of the 1980s. They then took foster children full-time to make ends meet. Nonetheless, they have managed to establish a nationwide network of counsellors, therapists and lawyers to help women in distress. Yet at no time during those years has the Church offered a public forum for discussion. And Cathy in particular gets very angry about the Vatican's intransigence and the abuses that spread like disease in a hothouse.

'We are not brave,' she says, 'we are angry, filled with righteous indignation that the double standards are permitted and encouraged.

'To be taken seriously,' she adds, 'we must be more than a loosely knit group of women and priests. We have found that the spiritual and human suffering involved must be healed but, in addition, the cause – mandatory celibacy – must be brought to light in a powerful way.'

To Cathy and Joe, Good Tidings is a healing ministry for women and priests wounded by the conflicts between love and laws, conscience and compulsory celibacy. As such, it is also draining, as they have to deal with people's confusion, anguish and grief on a daily basis, try to sustain their Christian faith, and are often the only people the women and the priests can turn to. But they both see it as a vocation: 'Where God wants us to be.'

Even in up-front America, finding women to speak out is fraught with difficulty. But, as Cathy – currently writing her own book on the subject, along with Californian Pamela Sweeney – knows all too well, 'This problem will never be solved if they don't find the courage deep in their core to demand respect from the priests and the institution and from the people in the pews. It will go on just as it has for the last 800 years.'

That is, as 'the secret everyone knows about', or 'the facade of celibacy'. Because, as Peter Isely, who runs an American group for people abused as children by priests, says: 'Secrecy is an excellent climate in which abuse can take place.'

Still, progress has been made over the last fifteen years. A committee of bishops has been established by America's National Conference of Catholic Bishops to examine the problem of sexual abuse by priests, particularly in relation to children. And, in addition to Good Tidings, there are various other support groups across the US. Promises was established in Alexandria, Virginia, in 1991; the controversially titled Men of God and the Women Who Love Them has recently been formed in Branford, Connecticut.

There's also a pressure group, Priests and the Faithful for a Married Priesthood, numbering 1,250 members, both priests and laity, among them six bishops. And LAMP (Laity Acting for a Married Priesthood), which points out that forty-eight married Anglican and Lutheran ministers who have converted to Catholicism serve in the US as married Catholic priests; that half of American priests under sixty have married; and that 70 per cent of the laity, 60 per cent of the clergy and 25 per cent of bishops would favour a married priesthood.

Most influential of all is CORPUS (Corps of Reserve Priests United for Service), founded twenty-five years ago by four priests after a bishop declared that priests who resigned and married could have no further interest in the Church. There were 10,000 priests already in that position. Today, there are 18,000, compared to 34,000 active diocesan priests. Today, CORPUS is a powerful voice in the US Catholic Church, with over 4,000 members, a mailing list double that, and unofficial financial support from some bishops.

Yet still there are 3,000 parishes within the US without a resident priest, and over 200 seminaries have closed as ordinations have declined by almost a half over the last thirty years to just under 10,000. Yet the Catholic population continues to rise, disenfranchising thousands who never or rarely see a priest.

To help out, Louise Hagget set up an organisation called 'Rent-a-Priest,' which has a register of married priests willing to minister in cases of necessity. (There are now similar organisations in Austria and Germany). According to the terms of a dispensation, a man can only function again as a priest in an emergency. The priests who register with Louise's group have a wide understanding of emergency, to include those in nursing homes, far-flung parishes and hospitals without access to a Catholic priest.

As Louise Hagget has said, 'There are many areas where people have just taken it upon themselves to utilise married priests. For instance, if it becomes a question of having Mass or not having one, or not having a priest available for baptism or giving a loved one the Last Rites, Catholics are realising that a married priest is as much a priest as a celibate, and can legally administer the sacraments. Even divorced Catholics who don't want to go through the emotional trauma and financial burden of the annulment process in order to remarry in the good graces of the Church prefer married priests to a justice of the peace for a remarriage ceremony.'

What of those priests who choose not to marry but to stay within the priesthood? And what of their women? Early on in my research, I heard from Laura, whose relationship with Fr John was never sexual but was a close, loving relationship which lasted for four years. During that time, he rang her nearly every day and they met three or four times a week. He hated it when she went away for a weekend and once, when she booked a fortnight's holiday, he threatened to kill himself. So she cancelled her trip.

Gradually, she became as dependent on the relationship as he was. 'When we met, I could never let him go without arranging our next meeting. I needed to know when we'd meet again, and where. He was the centre of my life.'

He was also immature and a manipulator, spoiling intimate moments by saying he had done the same thing with someone else, and possessively demanding she cancel arrangements at a moment's notice if he was free. On one occasion, when a big group of them were away for a long weekend, he took another woman dancing while Laura sat waiting in the bar for him. 'The feeling that I had no right to be with him was intensified on that occasion,' she recalls, 'and I had to listen to the gossip and comments of other members of the group as to where they had gone.'

Six months later, she discovered he was having another relationship, this time a sexual one, with a married woman. 'He said he was prepared to have the two of us in his life; that he felt much closer to me, but he went to her for the sex I wouldn't give him. But he'd never actually asked me to have intercourse with him! When I challenged him about that, he said it was my fault, because he'd got frustrated and she was available. It was almost as though he wanted me as the virgin in his life, and her as the whore.'

Shattered by this disclosure, Laura ended the relationship. She later heard he had collapsed from exhaustion, been sent for a 'rest cure', and moved to another parish. It took her two years to recover from what she saw as a bereavement. She is now engaged to another man, who is not a Catholic.

Celia contacted me twice before sending a short tape of her story. Each time, she said how scared she was to go public, even under a pseudonym, and how she could only do so because England seemed a long way away. Although she knew of Good Tidings, she had never contacted them for fear of being found out – because she is a minister in another faith.

She met her priest at an ecumenical conference eight years ago. Having read books about non-possessive friendships 'in the Lord', she was open to a platonic relationship with a man with whom she seemed to have a lot in common, spiritually and socially. Both enjoyed sport and, having discovered they lived in neighbouring towns, they were soon meeting up a couple of times a month to play tennis.

Afterwards, they would go for a drink and talk about their respective parishes. They swapped books and ideas, and gradually she realised that she was also attracted to him. At that point, she tried to get out, but it was too late. 'I started saying I wasn't available for tennis, that I had such a lot of pastoral work to catch up on. He sounded hurt, but I kept insisting I was busy. One day, he turned up at my house. That's when it came out that he felt the same way. And we weren't strong enough to end it.'

Although they have never 'gone all the way', the relationship is an intimate one. And now it's the most important one in Celia's life. 'I realised that, while he was around, I wasn't likely to want to marry anyone else,' she says. 'I see myself as good as married to him.'

The dilemma now is that she is being moved to another part of the country. 'I just don't know what to do,' she says. 'Every time I think about it, I burst into tears. I know I've got a vocation to ministry, but I desperately want to be with him. I can't bear the thought of being so far away. God knows what will happen now.'

The irony, of course, is that she is free to marry but can't while she still loves him. And he is not free to marry – though he has assured her she would be the one he would marry if he was. So it's an impasse. 'I want total commitment, but that's what I can't have. What I can have is him at the end of a phone helping me. And he does help. He's the person I turn to whenever I have a problem, emotionally, spiritually, practically. He's my spiritual director, in a way. He's the person I trust most and who has had most effect on me. The person I can talk to. So why can't we sort this out?'

Barbara was a thirty-four-year-old single woman with a good career in publishing when Fr Lawrence arrived as the new curate. He swept her off her feet and, just a year later, they were married. Only then did she discover that not only did he have a drink problem, but he had fathered a child in his previous diocese, hence the move. The marriage lasted under two years, during which time he was unemployed, drifted round the house and became violent towards her. 'Really, it was just a sexual relationship,' she says now. 'He couldn't cope with life outside the priesthood – he couldn't cope with life, period.'

Eventually, she told him to leave. It was as though that was what he was waiting for. He left that night and she has not seen or heard from him since. A mutual friend, however, tells her he is back in the priesthood.

Alicia met Brother Dan when she sought counselling over her empty marriage to a non-Catholic. When they first met, he was the listener and she was the speaker. 'He reflected myself back at me. Then I became aware that the balance was shifting, that I was listening and he was talking. And I was attracted by that; by the fact that he was vulnerable and human. I felt flattered.'

One day, they kissed. When she next visited, six weeks later, they made love. That was ten years ago, and they still see each other every couple of months. 'It's given me the strength to carry on with my marriage, and to try to improve it. I know we can't ever marry, but we do sometimes talk about what will happen when my husband dies, and how he will give up his order and come and live with me. But I couldn't leave my husband now. He's done nothing to deserve that. I couldn't hurt him. He depends on me too much. On the other hand, if anything did happen to him, I'd feel like making up for lost years.'

A few years ago, she started having panic attacks. Her doctor put them down to the menopause, but Alicia feels they have more to do with her relationship and the strain of leading two lives. 'It gets easier. I still have to suppress my feelings when I'm at home, which is hard, especially when I want just to cry, for joy or for pain. But I've had longer to practise now, so I've got it all down to a fine art. Our phone conversations are limited to certain times. We don't write – not since my husband found a note I'd written Dan. I told him it was just a passing thing and I'd get over it, and after a while he stopped asking. I think, deep down, he suspects. But he doesn't want the marriage to end. He says he couldn't live without me. So we just carry on as though everything were normal. I know he'd rather I didn't go and see him, but he only ever says, "You'll go anyway, so what's the point in me objecting?"'

Once, she didn't see Dan for six months. 'It was awful. I had to tell my husband I couldn't carry on like that. I had to get in touch with him again. I've got no idea how it will all end. I just go from day to day.'

Debby is also married. She's known her priest for six years, but the sexual relationship started only eighteen months ago. To date, she's managed to hide it from her husband. But her phone bills are enormous: 'The last one was for over $600. I can't get away with that, especially as it's all itemised. I just had to go and pay it and tell my husband it was for $300.'

Another time, she went on holiday and sent a card, in an envelope, to her priest. It was delivered to the nearby convent by mistake. 'All it said was "Missing you" – no name or anything. But, of course, the sisters opened it and then left it for him, marked "Opened in error – this is obviously yours". He nearly died. To me, it's like spying.'

Because her job takes her all over the state, she has endless excuses for being away from home, and usually makes sure she spends time with the priest while she's 'away'. Nonetheless, the strain of lying, of snatched meetings and inquisitive acquaintances, has put her on tranquillisers. But she can't end the relationship. 'I was swept off my feet when I realised he was as attracted to me as I was to him. I thought

I wasn't good enough, so his attention made me feel quite something. He seemed so superior. So my self-esteem has increased enormously through knowing him.'

Sometimes, she does wonder if she is being exploited: he makes no promises to her, no commitments, never consults her about decisions he makes, even those involving his social life. 'But then I think, "What if I am being exploited?" I'm so involved and so in love with him that the feelings are too strong to be rational. So if I am being exploited, well, I'm a consenting adult. And I don't care.'

Maybe one day her husband will find out. She has mixed feelings about that: 'On the one hand, I dread him finding out. There'd be such fall-out, it would be just terrible. But on the other hand, what the hell? At least then, I'd be able to see more of Eddie. I just don't know *what* I want.'

Nancy's husband did leave her when he found out what was going on. By that time, she and Fr Padraig had been intimate for four years. Despite the pain of separation, the shocked response of family and friends, and the tears of her children, she thought it would all work out well, because Padraig had always promised he would stand by her if anything awful happened.

At first, he did – as long as no one knew that he was involved. Then rumours started to spread which came to the notice of the Bishop. Padraig confessed and promised not to see Nancy again. He was immediately moved to another parish, but he did keep in touch, though less often.

Nancy takes up the story: 'When I heard they were moving him, I just sobbed and sobbed. He told me not to be silly, that we'd still be able to meet. It was just before Thanksgiving, and after a while, he said, "I don't know why you're getting so upset. I don't want to go, either, especially not just before Thanksgiving. At least you'll have some of your family here. I'm going to be in a new place where I don't know anyone. Think about me for a change." I just couldn't believe what I was hearing. I'd gone through hell and back, lost my husband, who was threatening to take the house and the kids away from me, yet he was still a priest, no one in the new parish knew anything about us, and he was telling me not to be so selfish!'

After that, Nancy woke up to the truth of the situation and started seeing less of him. Now, she is divorced, has moved to a new home with her children and has started seeing another man. 'But I'd never get involved with a priest again. Never!'

Conclusion

'By your own free choice you seek to enter the order of deacons. You shall exercise this ministry in the celibate state, for celibacy is both a sign and a motive of pastoral charity, and a special source of spiritual fruitfulness in the world. By living in this state with total dedication, moved by a sincere love for Christ the Lord, you are consecrated to him in a new and special way. By this consecration you will adhere more easily to Christ with an undivided heart; you will be more freely at the service of God and mankind, and you will be more untrammelled in the ministry of Christian conversion and rebirth. By your life and character you will give witness to your brothers and sisters in faith that God must be loved above all else, and that it is he whom you serve in others.

'Therefore, I ask you: in the presence of God and the Church, are you resolved, as a sign of your interior dedication to Christ, to remain celibate for the sake of the kingdom and in lifelong service to God and mankind?'

The candidate answers: 'I am.'

The Bishop adds: 'May the Lord help you to persevere in this commitment.'

That promise is made by every Roman Catholic priest at ordination. In a society infused with images of sex and sexuality, he promises to remain unmarried and abstain from sexual activity. He deliberately goes against the culture of the time.

Why? At the tail end of the twentieth century, why adhere to a law made 800 years ago? Especially a law that is creating such a crisis in the Church? No one disputes that celibacy, freely chosen, can be a

265

positive option. But how positive is it when enforced on an increasingly reluctant secular clergy?

The idea that clerical celibacy is a success is, as German theologian Ute Ranke-Heinemann says, 'a fiction, a dying patient whom no amount of artificial respiration by the Vatican will succeed in saving'. The number of men entering the priesthood has been declining ever since the Second Vatican Council of the 1960s. Vocations are down from 48,000 seminarians in 1965 to just over 10,000 today. Scores of priests leave the active ministry every year, for a host of different reasons, one of which is celibacy. They, like many who remain in the priesthood, see it as quite a separate calling to priesthood, with some people better psychologically suited to it. American research has revealed that nearly half – 42 per cent – of priests in the United States leave within twenty-five years of ordination, 90 per cent because of the celibacy mandate. An alarming number of mainly older priests, who take with them years of experience in matters both theological and pastoral.

Can the Roman Catholic Church afford to lose them? Already, over two fifths of the parishes in the world have no resident priests. By the turn of the century – just five years from now – it's expected to be half. Brazil, the largest Catholic nation in the world, is suffering from a desperate shortage of priests – just one for every 10,000 faithful. No wonder David Rice, in his book *Shattered Vows*, estimates that Brazil also has one of the largest number of non-celibate priests in the world – nearly 60 per cent. If the law of celibacy is contributing to the shortage of ordained ministers, who can blame bishops for turning a blind eye to the sexual activities of some of their priests?

But the celibacy crisis is not just a Third World issue, as I hope this book has helped demonstrate. Survey after survey shows that many priests worldwide are not celibate. Psychiatrist Richard Sipe, quoted in the introduction, estimates that 40 per cent of American priests are not celibate at any one time. A survey carried out among South African clergy in 1987 emerged with strikingly similar figures: just over 40 per cent of priests had, at some time in the previous two years, engaged in 'casual sexual encounters', while 43 per cent were involved in 'a love relationship', and nearly 38 per cent had recently 'ended love relationships' (researcher Fr Victor Kotze's quotes).

So much for the 'charism' of celibacy. As many of my respondents have pointed out, celibacy may be a gift from God, but how can you enforce a gift? Yet, for the last eight centuries, celibacy has been forced upon those who wish to be priests.

The roots of this law lie in the Bible, specifically in two quotations from the New Testament. In Matthew 19:12, Jesus says 'For there are some eunuchs which were so born from their mother's womb: and there are some eunuchs, which were made eunuchs of men: and there are eunuchs who have made themselves eunuchs for the sake of the kingdom of Heaven. He who is able to receive this, let him receive it.'

This is seen by supporters of compulsory celibacy as a definition of celibacy as a prerequisite of the 'official' apostles. Yet Christ's disciples, including Peter, were all married. So the opposing school of thought asks, is it not more likely that Jesus was proposing celibacy as a free act of obedience to a special vocation?

The second quote is from St Paul's first letter to the Corinthians (7:7), in which, talking of marriage, he says, 'I wish that all were as I myself am. But each has his own special gift from God, one of one kind and one of another.'

While regarding celibacy as superior to marriage, Paul, therefore, left it as a free choice. Later, in his first letter to Timothy (3:2-5), he demonstrates that those who presided over the first Christian communities were as likely to be married as unmarried men: 'A bishop then must be blameless, the husband of one wife . . . One that ruleth well his own house, having his children in subjection with all gravity.' (Echoed in Titus 1:5-7.)

Are these rules, expectations or demands, or, to quote Richard Sipe, 'a granting of permission to practise [celibacy]'? The debate continues to rage.

The fathers of the early Church appear to have accepted that a priest could not be compelled into virginity. Even the great sexual ascetic St Jerome wrote that 'if this virginal life is forced, it is *contra naturam*' (against nature). Family life coexisted in the early Church with the celibate lifestyle, with neither being seen as superior. After all, while some of the early Popes were celibate, others fathered their own successors, and some were the children of lesser clergy.

So why did celibacy become enshrined in canon law? One theory is that it springs from a suspicion of the body, of sexuality, and of the power of women. Intertwined with this deeply rooted suspicion, however, are other factors, chiefly those of power and separation.

The idea that celibacy should be associated with leadership in the Church gradually developed over the third, fourth and fifth centuries, as a combination of pagan ideas of ritual purity, Christian unease with the tainting influence of sexuality on the sacred mysteries and the prevailing philosophies of stoicism – which held up passionlessness as an ideal – and gnosticism, with its distaste for sex.

Stoicism, or sexual asceticism, was deeply misogynistic. According to this Greek philosophy, the true man was virile, detached and self-sufficient. So anything that spoke of softness and effeminacy or of losing essential powers – which, clearly, from a male perspective, meant sexual relations – was going to undermine that.

In the fourth century, St Ambrose linked this stoical idea from secular philosophy to the Christian virtue of integrity. To Ambrose, this was essentially a male virtue, to do with both maintaining powers behind a barrier and keeping yourself untarnished from any kind of intrusion from outside. So integrity meant separation, and virginity was the best symbol of that, as well as the best protection. It kept entire not only the body, but also the soul, because the man was not dissipating his energies into emotional relationships.

Allied to this, therefore, was a sexual distrust of women. If a priest was to be untouched, he had to be shielded from the harmful influence of sexuality and, therefore, of women who might defile that sanctity. And this ideology was firmly entrenched in the Church by the sexual hostility of Jerome's contemporary, St Augustine, who saw women as essentially physical, men as spiritual.

During his lifetime, a law came into being that forbade a married priest from having sexual intercourse the night before celebrating the Eucharist, the belief being that Old Testament instructions concerning ritual purity needed to be followed before celebrating the sacred mysteries – which, of course, only men had the power to perform. Initially, with the Eucharist celebrated just once a week, this meant only weekly abstinence. But when the Church began to celebrate the Eucharist daily, this abstinence became a permanent condition for married priests.

As Dutch theologian Edward Schillebeeckx, in his book *The Church with a Human Face*, says of this cultic purity idea, 'At the origin of the law of abstinence, and later the law of celibacy, we find an antiquated anthropology and an ancient view of sexuality.' Or, as St Jerome put it, 'All sexual intercourse is impure.'

As a result, married priests and their wives were officially required to live as brother and sister – as, bizarrely, married men who are ordained in Latin America are still required to live. To date, this has not been applied to Anglican ministers ordained as Roman Catholic priests in Britain.

Irrevocably, this ruling led to a move from married couples leading chaste lives within marriage to the notion that it was better that priests didn't marry at all: from married men allowed to be priests to men forbidden to marry after ordination and thence to permanently unmarried men.

Various Church councils of this era stressed the idea of continence and purity, and charismatic celibacy – the belief that it was a gift from God – began to spread from the monastic communities where it already existed to the whole clergy.

It didn't do so without opposition, however. Or without suffering. There are many horrendous tales from this period about priests' children and, eventually, their wives, being enslaved. While some killed themselves, others physically attacked the bishops who separated them from their husbands.

However, with the fall of the Roman Empire, priests once again married or took 'concubines', while others were sexually dissolute. But the ideal of priestly perfection revived during the eleventh century, and the Second Lateran Council of 1139 enshrined celibacy as a requirement for a priest. No longer would they be allowed to marry. And male elitism was ensured.

This belief in celibacy as the greatest spiritual ideal increased the priest's power as a higher being. Nonetheless, four centuries later, priests were still living in sin, marrying, and fathering children – who, together with their mothers, were still often abused, right up to Reformation times. The sixteenth-century Council of Trent solemnly sanctioned universal celibacy for clerics, so married men were precluded from becoming priests. Almost 400 years later, in 1917, this was

269

enshrined in the Code of Canon Law that still pertains today.

Alongside a theology of sexuality which many today would see as outdated is a move towards a priesthood separated not just from its own lay people, but also from the priesthoods of other Churches: a priesthood which, from the tenth century, became more distant and ceremonial, in which the laity participated much less, and which enhanced the status of the ordained minister who alone went into the sanctuary and carried out the sacred mysteries.

Two centuries later, that sacred and social enhancement reinforced a more political separation of the priesthood, this time from the state. By building up the status of the priest, the Church's own status was improved, as was its independence from secular control. At the same time, it reinforced the separation of the priesthood from the ordinary members of the Church – and rescued Church property, land, economics and inheritance. Up to then, if a priest married and had several male children, the inheritance was dispersed. By making priests' children illegitimate, the Church secured its economic interests.

So what started as a symptom of disgust with the sexual act is actually as much to do with power, separation and control (social, sexual and moral) as with sex. Celibacy, clericalism and male power in the Church are so closely associated that it's difficult, socially and spiritually, to disentangle it. Hence the reluctance of the Church to do so. As David Rice says, 'compulsory celibacy is . . . the ultimate management technique, giving total control and total mobility of personnel, and rendering priests independent of this-worldly interests and free of lay control.'

That is how the situation remained up to the Second Vatican Council of 1962-65. Prior to that, priests were very much 'icons of strength, virility, honesty and dedicated service', as Richard Sipe calls them. Institutionalised bachelors, authority figures right down to the clothes they wore – the black suit, the clerical collar – which separated them from the rest of the world. They were priests first and foremost. But, as Pope John XXIII's 'wind of change' swept through the Church, it swept away much of that myth of authority. And there were many priests, as well as lay people, who realised they could no longer sanction the inbred clericalism of the priesthood; who, now standing facing the congregation, rather than with their backs to it, realised that the altar still served as a barrier, that too much power was invested in them, that inequality was institutionalised.

Some stayed and found great difficulty adjusting to a redefined priesthood where service, rather than superiority, was stressed. Others responded enthusiastically to the new challenge. Yet others, when the expected coexistence of married clergy and celibate failed to materialise, left – and many, for whom celibacy was not a disease but a symptom, married.

The liberalism espoused by Pope John XXIII found expression not just in an updated liturgy and in the development of a liberation theology which blended religion with radical politics, but also in a more relaxed relationship between priest and parishioners: potentially a strength, but in some ways also a weakness in the Church's armour. As one priest who deals with priests' psychological problems said, 'In the past, there wasn't all this talk about relationships. The priest wasn't there to relate to people. He was there to administer the sacraments.'

The change of emphasis meant that priests didn't always have to be on their guard, that they could start looking and acting more like other people, which meant they could start moving from the stereotypical lonely, forbidding figure enclosed in the presbytery to become more sociable, more involved in ordinary parish activities, more human.

As a result, the lines between priest and parishioner became blurred and celibacy became confused. Up to thirty years ago, priests were warned during their seminary formation about 'particular friendships', both with other men and with women, for fear of sexual stirrings and emotional possessiveness. As a Catholic counsellor told me, 'Training before was one word – Don't.' Now, with the growth in psychology, psychiatry and sociology has come an understanding that friendships, ordinary human relationships, are important, especially for men whose workload is enormous – who are on call twenty-four hours a day, six days a week – and whose circumstances are often isolated: they may be cut off in a large, draughty presbytery, perhaps on their own or with a fellow priest to whom they can't relate.

So now seminarians are positively encouraged to have close, chaste friendships with both sexes: 'closeness in distance'. The issue of 'appropriate' friendships was addressed by the Synod of bishops in

1990, and the Church's commitment to obligatory celibacy was strongly reaffirmed at the same time. But such friendships don't always work, as we have seen. They don't always remain chaste. Even where they do, there is little general acceptance that they will remain so; little genuine encouragement. Always at the back of the hierarchy's mind is the deeply rooted belief that, sooner or later, one party – usually the female – will want to cross the boundary of friendship into something more intimate. So, despite all the fine words, friendships are still treated as a potential minefield of repressed sexual passions. And, sooner or later, it seems, one or other party gets hurt.

Yet, despite the 100,000 priests who have left the active ministry over the last thirty years, despite the general and quite genuine unhappiness over compulsory celibacy, there are no official plans for change. Why not? Because those in favour of mandatory celibacy talk of its prophetic side, its sign to society that there is more to life than the temporal, its value as a gift by which some 'see the invisible' and therefore 'can do the impossible'.

No one I have spoken to denies the value and power of freely chosen celibacy. But they point to the shaky foundations of clerical celibacy: fear, hatred of women, a desire for a privileged and discriminating status, and lack of appreciation of the wonder of sexuality. And they ask whether such foundations can support an institutionalised state. They also point out that love and sexuality are themselves precious gifts – though not always regarded as such by a Church which still has to develop a credible theology of sexuality.

Opponents of change also claim that marriage can distract priests from their service to the world; that there are places in the world where the pastoral situation demands such effort and dedication that there would be no room for a healthy, committed, full relationship. There is also the mobility argument – the need for some priests to maintain the freedom to move beyond their own countries and cultures to respond to pastoral needs elsewhere.

Admittedly, if priests were allowed to marry, there would have to be many major changes to the structures of the Church. There would also be radical changes in the way priests relate to and are viewed by the community. A married priesthood could be seen as a huge financial burden on the parishioners. But that's dependent on seeing the present parish structure as the only possible one, instead of as one option. Another option might offer a quite different attitude to the hierarchical structure: a community structure, where ministry is the right of all the baptised and where parishes are smaller, as during the time of the early Church.

But when priests in Brazil, Ecuador or the Philippines are allowed to live with women, even to marry; when married Anglican priests are beginning to be ordained into the Roman Catholic Church without any requirement to be celibate; when priests who leave to marry are allowed back into the priesthood if they change their mind, questions about the continuing validity of compulsory celibacy are, not surprisingly, being asked by those already ordained, whose ordination debars them from marriage.

Reports show that the numbers of ordinands would double, even quadruple, if priests were allowed to marry, and that celibacy is 'the most significant element in not choosing an ordained or religious vocation'. And statistic after statistic shows that significant numbers of practising Catholics would like a rethink on this issue. As long ago as 1971, one half of bishops questioned at the Synod wanted a married priesthood. Four years later, the National Federation of Priests' Councils presented a resolution calling for the full utilisation of married priests. Similar calls have come at regular intervals since, from around the world.

As recently as 1990, a report stated that 58 per cent of American Catholics were in favour of optional celibacy. A similar report that same year by the *Catholic Herald*, which questioned delegates at the National Conference of Priests, showed that three quarters wanted a review of the situation. But the Church is not a democracy. Papal instructions on the value of celibacy have been given by every Pope from Pope Pius X to the present Pope who, since 1978, has made celibacy the subject of twenty-eight important pronouncements and seventeen speeches on visits abroad. So the Church continues to lose a great deal by ignoring married priests and their wives, congregations continue to be effectively disenfranchised, individuals excommunicated or endangered through secrecy. And the Church itself remains seriously challenged.

A change in the law would take a lot of pressure off priests to be celibate or to be married. It could conceive a credible theology of sexuality.

Some priests may view celibacy as an escape from a sexuality they do not wish to confront. Others remain celibate quite happily, accepting it willingly as part of the package. Others, the reluctant celibates, accept the sacrifice of their sexuality, despite the difficulties, and remain faithful to it. Some become sexually frustrated, which can translate into deviant behaviour. What starts as grace can become an intolerable burden to men who find their personal freedom and growth sacrificed so that the Church may be centrally and hierarchically controlled.

Of those who enter into relationships with women, some play around, wanting sex without commitment, even regarding their celibacy as an opportunity to be promiscuous, despite the risks. One woman discovered her priest had had an AIDS test some years before they met. What does that say about the 'charism' of celibacy?

The 'lucky' ones have a stable, mutually affirming relationship which either keeps them in the priesthood or forces them to leave. If they stay and seek advice from their Bishop, they will quite possibly be pressurised into staying in the Church. As one priest said, 'It's good that a woman should love a priest, but not in a way that compromises his celibacy. If a man becomes involved with a woman, he needs to find advice, and he needs to disentangle himself pretty quickly.' The talk is all of compromise, disentanglement, temptation, falls from grace, distance, unravelling, as though love is a threat, something to fight against, something to sacrifice to the greater good.

Some men would say, if the relationship makes them better priests, more understanding of the complexities of human emotions, more sympathetic to confusion and suffering, they're not prepared to give it up. It sounds compassionate to talk of men 'rediscovering their vocations' after having an affair. What thanks do the women receive for helping their partners to a renewal which can only benefit the entire Church? What sympathy, when the man deserts them? He may return strengthened by his vows, his training, his sense of vocation. She, by definition, has none of this.

Emotional conflicts abound. Some priests deal with them by ignoring them, by compartmentalising their priesthood and their sexual behaviour.

Yet others can detach celibacy from the priesthood, can convince themselves that their faithfulness to the act of ordained ministry is not compromised by failing to observe a law which they no longer regard as necessary, nor personally life-giving. It may look like slack morality, but possibly it's more a mature realisation that theory can be quite different from practice. That life is emotionally, spiritually and morally complicated. That one's own conscience is as good a guide as any other. And that celibacy is a historical law of the Church and, as such, could be changed.

Whatever the reason, for many priests and their women, a sexual relationship presents a very real and genuine dilemma. How is it to be resolved? Most of the women I've talked to not surprisingly would like to see optional celibacy, to see it removed from its current position as the essence of priesthood. Others want their priest to leave the ordained ministry. Others want a different model of priesthood that echoes the early house churches, a further redefinition of ministry to suit the contemporary scene. But if they're waiting for the Vatican to change its mind, they're in for a long wait.

If and when changes occur, the process is likely to be piecemeal. The shortage of clergy in Third World countries may persuade Rome to ordain married men in those countries or to allow back to the ministry men who have been laicised. That may then spread. Already, there are married priests, a number of whom are married officially and who have come from other Churches. The largest number of these are in the Eastern Churches which are in communion with the Roman Catholic Church, like the Greek or Russian Orthodox. Their normal parish clergy are usually married, though their bishops are unmarried and drawn from monastic communities.

Unofficially, there are parts of the Western world where a substantial number of parochial clergy are married, or in faithful, sustained, lifelong relationships, though they are not officially recognised as such. And there is often a large measure of social acceptance, even preference, for these relationships.

Yet there is no guarantee that marriage is the solution to the problems inherent in either celibacy or ministry. Nor will there be until the Church learns to emphasise the positive, rather than the negative, elements of sexuality.

275

Yet the secrecy that surrounds the celibacy issue within the Church has very detrimental effects on those concerned, particularly the women. The men have a rescue structure built into their vocation. The women do not. Is it Christian to offer support to him – counselling, therapy, financial support – and not to her? No wonder she feels isolated and betrayed. No wonder some of these women lose their faith. Members of Seven-Eleven have had a meeting with the Bishop appointed to oversee women's issues. They were less than impressed by the attitude and commitment shown.

Until it is tackled adequately, men and women – often those who most sustain the Church – continue to suffer in silence. So long as they do that, nothing will change. The Church will carry on saying it isn't a problem. But it *is* a problem, especially for the women. Why, after all, should their partner speak out and risk losing everything? Why should he challenge a system which accords him privilege and status? Why should he acknowledge publicly a love which is actually a threat to his public identity, his economic and emotional security, his ministry?

As long as compulsory celibacy remains, there will be a power imbalance. One way of dealing with this is for women to retrieve power: either by speaking out about their relationships with priests like the prophetesses of earlier times, in the belief that change has to come from the grass-roots membership rather than from the hierarchy; by questioning, as more and more women – and men – are doing, the structures and beliefs surrounding the mystique of the priesthood; or by being allowed more positions of responsibility within the Church. To show they are more than 'domestic collaborators of the priesthood', as Pope John Paul has called priests' housekeepers. Were that to happen, they would be less dependent on the men to provide them with an identity, even this very secret one of a hidden woman. With more power, there might be fewer instances of power being sought through relationships.

At the very least, the Church should make clear, oft-repeated statements about the unethical nature of sexual relationships with clergy. At the moment, some American states are in the process of enacting stronger civil and criminal laws against sexual abuse by therapists and pastoral counsellors. In time, these may be extended to include clergy.

At the most, until the law on celibacy is changed, the Church could set up a working party akin to the one on child abuse, chaired by a bishop and members of involved agencies within the Church, to carry out formal investigations; to draw up similar guidelines; to call on each of the country's twenty-two dioceses to appoint a special representative; to conduct special inquiries into individual cases; and to impose forcible laicisation on priests who are seen to have abused their positions.

Guidelines issued by the working party looking into cases of child abuse state, 'Misguided loyalty or fear of public disclosure can create a conspiracy of silence which, in turn, can breed more evil. Fear of public scandal is no reason for silence.' This statement is just as valid when those involved are adult men and women.

ADDRESSES
Catholic Marriage Advisory Council, Blythe Mews, Blythe Road, London W14 (0171-371 1341).
Advent Group, c/o 24 Bann Close, South Ockenden, Essex RM15 5QT.
Seven-Eleven, c/o Anne Edwards, ISCS, Oxford House, Derbyshire Street, London E2 6HG.
Catholic Women's Network, 4 Windmill Drive, London SW4 9DE.
Bethany Revisited, c/o Fr Pat Buckley, 6 Princes Gardens, Larne, Co. Antrim, Northern Ireland.
Association Claire-Voie, BP 6, 69131 Ecully, Cedex, France.

SELECT BIBLIOGRAPHY

Peter Brown, *The Body and Society: Men, Women and Sexual Renunciation in Early Christianity* (Faber and Faber 1989).
James F. Colaianni (ed.), *Married Priests and Married Nuns* (Michael Joseph, 1969).
Odette Desfonds, *Rivales de Dieu: Les Femmes de Prêtre* (God's Rivals: The Women of Priests) (Albin Michel, 1993).
Anne Dördelmann-Lueg: *Wenn Frauen Priester Lieben* (When Women Love Priests) (Kösel-Verlag, Munich, 1994).
Tineke Ferwerda, (tr. John Bowden), *Sister Philothea* (SCM Press, 1993).
Ursula Goldmann-Posch, *Unheilige Ehen: Gesprache mit Priesterfrauen* (Unholy Marriages: Conversations with Priests' Wives) (Kindler-Verlag, Munich, 1985).
Donna Tiernan Mahoney, *Touching the Face of God* (Mercier Press, 1992).
Annie Murphy and Peter de Rosa, *Forbidden Fruit: The True Story of My Secret Love for the Bishop of Galway* (Little, Brown, 1993).
Ute Ranke-Heinemann, (tr. John Brownjohn), *Eunuchs for Heaven* (Andre Deutsch, 1990).
David Rice, *Shattered Vows* (Michael Joseph, 1990).
Peter Rutter, *Sex in the Forbidden Zone* (Mandala/Harper Collins, 1990).
Kate Saunders and Peter Stanford, *Catholics and Sex* (Heinemann, 1992).
Edward Schillebeeckx, *The Church with a Human Face* (SCM Press, 1985).

A.W. Richard Sipe, *A Secret World: Sexuality and the Struggle for Celibacy* (Brunner/Mazel, 1990).
Heinz-Jürgen Vogels, *Celibacy* (Kösel-Verlag, Munich, 1978).
The Way Supplement 1993: Celibacy.